MR. GEORGE EDWARDES.

THEATRE

...ning at 8, a New Musical Play

...RCHID

...ANNER.
...sic by IVAN CARYLL and LIONEL MONCKTON.
...UL A. RUBENS.

...cultural College) ... Miss GERTIE MILLAR
...turn) ... ... Miss CONNIE EDISS
...ss) ... ... Miss GAYNOR ROWLANDS
...Chesterton) ... Miss GABRIELLE RAY
...er) ... ... Miss PHYLLIS BLAIR

...ultural College) Miss MARIE STUDHOLME
...ephew) ... Mr. CHARLES BROWN
...ioner) ... Mr. LIONEL MACKINDER
...merce)... ... Mr. HARRY GRATTAN
...say) ... ... Mr. ROBERT NAINBY
...Hunter) ... Mr BERT SINDEN
...ignat's ... ... Mr. W. SPRAY
... Mr. HARRY TAYLOR
... ... Mr. ARTHUR HATHERTON
... ... Mr. J W. BIRTLEY
...State) ... ... Mr. H. LEWIS

...al College) .. Mr. EDMUND PAYNE
...LIVE MAY, MINNIE BAKER, GERTRUDE GLYNN,
... ROSSMORE.
...FRED LABARTE, DORIS DEWAR, LYDIA WEST.

... ... Mr. SYDNEY ELLISON,
...Mr. IVAN CARYLL.

...Barwick's Horticultural College
... ... Place Massena, Nice
... ... Promenade des Anglais
...rior of the Opera House at Nice

...Drop by Mr. JOSEPH HARKER.

...supervised by Mr. WILHELM
...ur PATRICK, JAYS (Ltd.), LIBERTY & Co., Mrs. NETTLESHIP,
...VESTORY & Co. Hats by "ADELAIDE," 28, Wigmore Street, W.
...ral Decorations by A. GATTI & Co. Properties by H. ELLIOTT.
Machinist, J. SHELDON.

...ting Manager ... Mr. E. MARSHALL

...N DAILY, 10 till 6, and 8 till 10.

...he Management, and all articles sold are specially
...of the finest quality.

...e Lord Chamberlain.
...printed on every play bill
...t and entrance doors, which must open outwards.
...owered at least once during every performance to ensure its being

...ny other obstructions whether permanent or temporary

Spread a Little Happiness

With 134 illustrations, 15 in color

SHERIDAN MORLEY

Spread a Little Happiness

THE FIRST HUNDRED YEARS
OF THE BRITISH MUSICAL

THAMES AND HUDSON

For Graham Payn

Frontispiece. Violet Loraine, leading lady in *The Bing Boys* (1918) at the Alhambra, was one of the first English stars of stage musicals to suggest that she might have a mind of her own, as well as a voice and ever-dancing feet.

Picture researcher: Catherine Haill

© 1987 Sheridan Morley

First published in the United States in 1987 by Thames and Hudson Inc., 500 Fifth Avenue, New York, New York 10110

Library of Congress Catalog Card Number 86-71620

Printed and bound in Spain by Artes Gráficas Toledo, S.A. D.L. TO: 1664-86

Contents

Acknowledgments

THE AUTHOR wishes to thank Catherine Haill, without whose dedicated research and efforts in obtaining the illustrations this book would not have been possible. Thanks are also due to the owners of the Dress Circle record store in London, who located invaluable source material in the form of soundtracks, the existence of which had been almost forgotten, even by them.

Permission to reprint extracts of lyrics from various shows is gratefully acknowledged as follows:

pp. 65, 73, 103, 210: lyrics by Noël Coward from *Tonight at 8.30* (1936), *Cavalcade* (1931), *Pacific 1860* (1946) and *Operette* (1938) by courtesy of Graham Payn and the Noël Coward Estate.

p. 7 from *Salad Days* © 1954 Francis Day and Hunter Ltd; used by permission of EMI Music Publishing Ltd.

p. 15: from *The Maid of the Mountains* © 1917 Aschenberg, Hopwood and Crew Ltd; used by permission of Redwood Music Ltd.

p. 41: from *Mr Cinders* © 1928 (Renewed) Warner Bros., Inc. All Rights Reserved; used by permission of Warner Bros. Music and Chappell Music Ltd.

p. 52: from *Oh Kay!* © 1926 (Renewed) WB Music Corp. All Rights Reserved; used by permission of Warner Bros. Music and Chappell Music Ltd.

p. 68: from *Ever Green* © 1930 (Renewed) Warner Bros., Inc. All Rights Reserved; used by permission of Warner Bros. Music and Chappell Music Ltd.

p. 71: from *Tantivy Towers* © 1931 J. B. Cramer & Co. Ltd.

p. 76: from *Derby Day* (1932), by courtesy of Elkin and Co. Ltd.

p. 90: from *The Dancing Years* © 1939 Chappell & Co. Ltd. Copyright renewed. Published in the U.S.A. by Chappell & Co., Inc. International Copyright Secured. All Rights Reserved; used by permission.

p. 123: from *The Boy Friend* © 1954 Chappell & Co. Ltd. Copyright renewed. Published in the U.S.A. by Chappell & Co., Inc. International Copyright Secured. All Rights Reserved; used by permission.

p. 128: from *Gay's the Word* © 1951 Chappell & Co. Ltd. Copyright renewed. Published in the U.S.A. by Chappell & Co., Inc.

International Copyright Secured. All Rights Reserved; used by permission.

p. 153: from *Oliver!* © 1960 and 1968 Lakeview Music Co. Ltd. TRO-Hollis Music, Inc. controls all rights for the U.S.A. and Canada. Used by permission.

pp. 173 and 191: from *Evita* © 1976 Evita Music Ltd.

p. 181: from *Jesus Christ Superstar* © 1969 MCA Music Ltd.

p. 182: from *Joseph and the Amazing Technicolor Dreamcoat* © 1969 Novello & Co. Ltd.

p. 192: from *Songbook* (1979), reprinted by permission of ATV Music.

p. 199: from *Cats* (1981), lyric of 'Memory' by Trevor Nunn after T. S. Eliot (incorporating lines from 'Rhapsody on a Windy Night'), reprinted by permission of Faber and Faber Ltd and Harcourt Brace Jovanovich, Inc.

Sources of illustrations

With the exception of the subjects listed by source below, all the illustrations were specially photographed by Graham Brandon from items in the collection of the Theatre Museum (Victoria and Albert Museum), London. The task of supplementing the Theatre Museum material was made easier thanks to the help of Catherine Ashmore, Paula Chesterman, John Cowell, Jonathan Crump, Fiona Duff, Joanna Holmburg, Tee Heskith, Ron Moody, Helen Nicholson, Peter Thompson Associates, Andrew Treague Associates and Veronica Wald. The following subjects (identified by page numbers) were kindly supplied by: BBC Hulton Picture Library 40, 57, 102, 109, 117 (above), 118 (above), 122, 148 (below), 150 (below); Nobby Clarke 221; Donald Cooper 195 (above and below), 196–7, 198, 208 (above), 209 (above), 214–15, 216 (above and below); De Wynters Ltd 190 (left and right), 204; Zoë Dominic 149, 168–9 (above), 169, 170 (below), 171, 172, 178–9, 180, 194; John Haynes 193, 209 (below); Angus McBean Photos (Harvard Theatre Collection) 93 (below), 129, 167, 168 (below), 170 (above); Cameron Mackintosh Ltd (photo by Michael Le Poer Trench) 207; Gerald Murray 208 (below); *Punch* 51, 159, 205; Rafael 152; Victoria and Albert Museum (Department of Prints and Drawings) 28.

Another Opening, Another Show

So if I let nostalgia blind me,
And my resolution is slack,
I'll remind you to remind me
We said we wouldn't look back.

Julian Slade and Dorothy Reynolds, *Salad Days*, 1954

IN CELEBRATING, as this book does, the first century of the British stage musical, we would do well to remember the complaint of one of its greatest and most successful exponents, Noël Coward, who in a moment of uncharacteristic despair commented that 'the only trouble with the British is that they have never taken light music seriously enough'. To a lyricist and composer of his generation – he was born ten days before the last Christmas of the last century into a world of Gilbert and Sullivan – it was a source of regular amazement and regret that his fellow-countrymen seemed to be getting progressively less interested and/or confident in the whole notion of the West End score as an indigenous art form, so that by the end of his long working career Coward, that most quintessentially English of writers and men, was actually premiering his musicals on Broadway.

Since his death in 1973, the pendulum has happily swung back to the point where hit shows like *Evita* and *Cats* now open in London and only later transfer to Broadway. But before accepting the convenient contemporary theory that the British musical only really found its international dancing feet with *Cats*, we would do well to recall that two English librettists, P. G. Wodehouse and Guy Bolton, were enjoying considerable Broadway musical success as early as 1917, and that ever since the traffic across the Atlantic has always been two-way. Long decades before Tim Rice and Andrew Lloyd Webber, not only Wodehouse and Bolton and Coward, but Sandy Wilson and Lionel Bart and Anthony Newley had all achieved hits in New York to rival many of those achieved by American composers in London.

Admittedly, the British stage musical has never achieved on its home territory the dominance that its American counterpart has had on Broadway: the musical is without any doubt America's greatest achievement in the live theatre in this century, whereas in Britain there lingers a faint unwillingness to accord classic status to song-and-dance shows, hence the general critical reluctance to acknowledge the greatness of a musical like *Les Misérables* even when it comes from the subsidized stage of the Royal Shakespeare Company.

But what has changed in British musicals can be measured in economic terms: early in January 1986, when Andrew Lloyd Webber announced that his Really Useful production company was to be floated on the Stock Exchange, that company was immediately valued at over £35 million largely on the basis of his own *Cats* and *Starlight Express*, since the earlier shows, written with Tim Rice, were the property of other managements. Clearly the valuation was also a declaration of faith in Lloyd Webber's future success, but it signals a drastic change in British musical fortunes: if you added up all the lifetime earnings of all other British stage composers in this century, the total would be unlikely to reach even 50 per cent of what Andrew Lloyd Webber is now thought to be worth.

What has also changed, of course, is the international record market: Lloyd Webber was, with Rice, the first to present such shows as *Jesus Christ Superstar* and *Evita* on disc rather than on stage initially, and in that way theatrical composers were at last able to share in the worldwide goldmine that had been opened up by such British pop composers of the 1960s as John Lennon and Paul McCartney. That goldmine was never open to Coward or Novello, nor to any of the other British musical writers whose work predated the 1960s.

Even so, there has always been something subtly different about the British musical at its most native: something that becomes immediately apparent if one starts to consider what are commercially and internationally three of the most successful musicals having a British setting. All three, as it happens, are the work of a German composer and an American lyricist who was sent to school in England at the age of thirteen by a millionaire shopkeeper father who believed that no American ever spoke properly. One of those three hits of theirs is set in Scotland, one in London and one at the court of King Arthur. All are based on quintessentially British material, carefully researched and reasonably faithful to their sources, their periods and their conventions. And yet there is no way that *Brigadoon*, *My Fair Lady* or *Camelot* could be considered British musicals, despite the fact that the last two at any rate opened initially on Broadway with all-British names above the title. Something in their scale, in their approach to the original subject-matter, in the big-band sound of their orchestration, in the tone of their dialogue, brands them as unmistakably American musicals.

But if *My Fair Lady*, based by Alan Jay Lerner and Frederick Loewe on Bernard Shaw's *Pygmalion*, designed by Cecil Beaton and starring Rex Harrison and Julie Andrews and Stanley Holloway and Robert Coote, was still not a British musical, what is? To answer that question, and to explain why an often underfinanced, critically derided, small-scale and fundamentally nostalgic art form should have exploded into the multi-

W. S. Gilbert and Sir Arthur Sullivan, whose Savoy Operas were effectively the precursors of the stage musical, depicted in cartoons by Arthur Bryant published in 1878. A century after the staging of their comic opera *The Pirates of Penzance*, that work was to receive the full Broadway treatment and return to the London stage, this time at Drury Lane.

ONE OF THE PARENTS OF THE PIRATES.

national musical hits of Rice and Lloyd Webber in the 1980s, we have to begin at the very beginning.

The identity of the first-ever British stage musical will be explored at some length in the next chapter, but there can be no doubt that it was Gilbert and Sullivan who had made it possible. By the turn of the century 'Take A Pair of Sparkling Eyes', 'Tit Willow', 'We're Very Wide Awake, The Moon and I' and 'I Have A Song To Sing-O' had been fairly inculcated into the bloodstream not only of the Coward family in south London but into that of theatregoers across the country. In writing the first modern hit songs, and in writing them exclusively and specifically for the theatre, Gilbert and Sullivan had opened up the way to an Edwardian era that was to be saturated with operettas and musical comedies. In the years up to the outbreak of World War I, starting out from the Royal Strand Theatre (where now stands the Aldwych Underground station) at which in 1887 Fannie Leslie had introduced a 'musical comedy drama' called *Jack in the Box*, London was to celebrate one of its richest orchestral periods. Not only were there the foreign imports of Franz Lehár, Leo Fall and André Messager, all bringing across the English Channel echoes of a European café and cabaret world to an audience, very few of whom had yet acquired the wealth or the means of transport to find it for themselves abroad, but on home territory Lionel Monckton, Paul Rubens and Leslie Stuart were all at the height of their success: *The Quaker Girl*, *Our Miss Gibbs*, *Miss Hook of Holland*, *Floradora*, *The Arcadians* and *A Country Girl* all served within a very short time to establish the notion of the musical comedy as a regular feature of the London theatrical scene.

But critics were still deeply uncertain about the new theatrical form: 'one of the most curious examples of composite dramatic architecture that we have for some time seen,' wrote one reviewer of *A Gaiety Girl* (the 1893 show which was first described in its own advertising as a 'musical comedy'). 'It is sometimes sentimental drama, sometimes comedy, sometimes almost light opera and sometimes downright variety show, though it is always light, bright and enjoyable,' the reviewer concluded.

A Gaiety Girl (which toured America in its original London production as early as 1894) was rapidly followed by *A Runaway Girl, A Country Girl, The Shop Girl, The Casino Girl, The Pearl Girl, The Quaker Girl, The Girl Behind the Counter, The Cherry Girl, The Girl Friend, The Girl from Kay's, The Girl From Utah, The Girl in the Taxi, The Girl on the Film* and *The Girls of Gottenberg.* Then there were the various *Belles* (*Belle of Mayfair, Belle of Brittany, Belle of New York*) and the occasional *Maids* (mainly of the *Mountains*) and *Princesses* (*Charming, Caprice* and the *Dollar* variety). Titles were not allowed to vary much, and gradually an all-purpose plot began to establish itself. This usually had to do with either royalty or millionaires in disguise, misunderstood romantic entanglements, apparent betrayal or sudden loss at the end of Act I followed by restoration and/or reconciliation at the end of Act III.

The arrival of the American musical in London ('they prance, they bubble, they make rings of joy like a dog let loose in a field, they go with a swing and a scamper', wrote Herbert Farjeon later) changed forever the West End idea of what a night out with an orchestra was supposed to look and sound and feel like, and when half a century later *Oklahoma!* arrived, 'smelling', as the poet Carl Sandburg noted, 'of hay mown up over barn dance floors, stepping around like an apple-faced farmhand and rolling along like a good wagon slicked up with new axlegrease', it was to make all English musicals seem overnight about thirty years out of date in terms of choreography, orchestrations, lighting, sets, costumes and action. British producers and composers alike went into a state of prolonged and understandable shock, from which they only really began to emerge in the 1970s with the advent of Rice and Lloyd Webber.

But at precisely that moment, when on Broadway Stephen Sondheim had renounced the showbiz of both *Gypsy* and *A Funny Thing Happened on the Way to the Forum* for the more obscure and courageous barrier-breakers that were *Pacific Overtures* and *Sweeney Todd* and *Follies,* the feeling in Britain was that international success could be achieved, on disc as on stage, only with extremely simple and familiar material. Just because English musicals had been so deeply unsuccessful in the world market unless, like *Oliver!,* they dealt with Dickensian familiarity or, like *The Boy Friend,* they offered perfect period-piece nostalgia, Rice and Lloyd Webber fell back on such ready-made sources as the Bible (for *Joseph and the Amazing Technicolor Dreamcoat* and *Jesus Christ Superstar*) or the life of Eva Peron (for *Evita*).

It is not to belittle or attack those shows that I would suggest that they were not actually about anything or anyone we did not already know: and it was precisely that quality of pre-sold familiarity which made them acceptable abroad and to the many American tourists in theatre

Lady Clients at Garrod's Stores

Photo Foulsham & Banfield

The opening chorus of *Our Miss Gibbs*, by Ivan Caryll and Lionel Monckton,
staged at the Gaiety Theatre in 1909.

audiences who account for a high percentage of London box-office
takings. The selling of *Evita* did not start with the concept album: the
selling of *Evita* started when Eva Peron herself made the rainbow tour of
Europe back in the 1950s. Significantly, a musical like Willy Russell's
Blood Brothers (1983), which cannot be considered in its score or its book
or indeed its original production to be the inferior of any of the Rice or
Lloyd Webber shows, has never triumphed internationally or even
commercially at home just because it cannot be readily described or
defined or sold to someone who has not already seen it.

Similarly, the big musical hits of the current British theatre are not in
fact about anything very much: *Cats* is certainly a superlative
celebration of the poems of T. S. Eliot and *Starlight Express* a hugely
commercial roller disco, but neither has a plot which would occupy more
than the back of a matchbook. That is why they work so well: they ask
nothing of their audience beyond attendance at a certain theatre on a

certain night. No language problems for foreign tourists, no demands of a shared heritage or education, no cultural barriers to be stormed. And that, I fear, is the way ahead: if a musical is to earn back the initial investment, it now needs to be an event rather than a plot with songs, and therefore the less a show is actually about, the better its chances of crossing the Atlantic in either direction. It is not purely an English problem: as the scores of Sondheim have become more and more specialized, less and less of them have gone from Broadway to the West End. What we now send each other are the easy spectaculars: New York gets *Starlight Express* and London gets *42nd Street*. The fact that we could learn vastly more about America from *Merrily We Roll Along* or *Follies* or even *Dreamgirls* and they could learn vastly more about us from *Blood Brothers* or *The Hired Man* is, alas, irrelevant to the men who do the financial estimates.

Moreover, as the stage musical becomes increasingly oriented towards cinematic special effects in the manner of Steven Spielberg, with *Cats* ascending to the Heaviside Layer by way of a space-lift that appeared to be on loan from *Star Wars*, it is the sets that have become the real stars – a danger foreseen by the late Kenneth Tynan in his 1962 review of an otherwise unmemorable Lionel Bart show called *Blitz!*: 'It does, however, have Sean Kenny's scenery, and there are distinct signs that sets are now taking over. They swoop down on the actors and snatch them aloft; four motor-driven towers prowl the stage, converging menacingly on any performer who threatens to hog the limelight; and whenever the human element looks like gaining control, they collapse on it in a mass of flaming timber. In short they let the cast know who's boss. They are magnificent and they are war.'

Twenty-five years later, it is clear that the war has been won, and not by the actors; Tynan's nightmare vision of a show 'in which the curtain will rise to reveal sets which advance in a phalanx on the audience and expel it from the theatre' is not so far from what has happened in *Starlight Express* or *Time*. All we need now is a set which can write songs and applaud itself and the cycle will be complete.

But what we have lost along the way is precisely Tynan's 'human element', and that in essence is what this book is going to be about: the days when musicals were still about somebody and something, even if not very much. A couple of lyrical lines from Sandy Wilson's *The Boy Friend* will tell you all you need to know about being English and in love in the South of France in the 1920s: find me a couple of lines from *Starlight Express* that tell you anything about trains that is not already a resounding cliché.

Happily there has been, in the mid-1980s, a return to the Elgar choral tradition in *The Hired Man*, a musical which like *Blood Brothers* has had no theatrical life at all outside Britain and a not hugely profitable one within, but which nevertheless has done more to restore one's faith in the possibility of the specifically British musical than anything ever written by Rice or Lloyd Webber. In all fairness, it should at once be noted, however, that the staging in London of this cavalcade of working-class life in the Lake District around the turn of the century was in fact largely financed by Lloyd Webber from his current profits earned elsewhere. Even I could just about stomach another *Starlight Express* if it were to lead to the staging of another *Hired Man*.

The other crucial development of recent times has been the spread of the Songbook show: it was London, not Broadway, that invented *Side by Side by Sondheim* (1976) and since then have come similar small-cast shows devoted to the work of Tom Lehrer, Noël Coward and Jerome Kern, often set and performed in semi-workshop conditions. 'When the English try to perform Broadway material, forget it,' wrote Frank Rich in a January 1986 issue of the *New York Times*, having presumably never seen what the English made of Sondheim's *A Little Night Music* or Kander and Ebb's *Cabaret*, both of which came up looking vastly better in London than in their original New York staging, as did *Cage Aux Folles*.

These are admittedly exceptions to the usual rules, but there are still, I believe, certain causes for celebration even as the musical stage gets polarized into tiny local cabarets or huge mid-Atlantic conglomerates. A post-*Starlight Express* belief that musicals have to challenge Hollywood visual trickery to justify soaring seat prices has happily coincided with a new awareness among young British composers of their own musical heritage, and alongside that there has been the marvellous realization that both the National Theatre and the Royal Shakespeare Company are also in the business of putting on musicals. The National admittedly had a catastrophic time with a remarkably ill-conceived musical about Jean Seberg, but their *Guys and Dolls* was, until it went into a tawdry West End tailspin, a production to rival any that that show has ever had on its native Manhattan territory, while it was after his Shakespearean semi-musicals that Trevor Nunn of the RSC turned first to *Cats* and then to *Les Misérables*, thereby proving that great stage musicals can now be a preserve of the classical as well as of the commercial theatre in Britain. And that surely is a sign of progress over the past century. By the summer of 1986, Nunn also had *Chess* and a triumphant Glyndebourne *Porgy and Bess* to his credit, while on Broadway the only musical hit to rival his *Cats* was the revival of Noël Gay's *Me and My Girl*, starring Robert Lindsay. The British had triumphantly stormed the barricades of a hitherto American stage empire.

DALY'S THEATRE

LEICESTER SQUARE

DALY'S THEATRE

SOLE LESSEE & MANAGER — — Mr AUGUSTIN DALY

THE GEISHA

Mr GEORGE EDWARDES' COMPANY

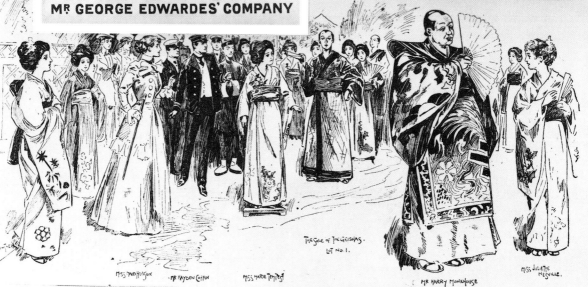

THE SALE OF THE GEISHAS.
LOT No. I.

MISS LETTY LIND · Mr HAYDEN COFFIN · MISS MARIE TEMPEST · Mr HARRY MONKHOUSE · MISS JULIETTE NESVILLE

'A Gaiety Girl' to 'Chu-Chin-Chow'

If faithful to my trust I stay,
No fate can fill me with dismay.
Love holds the key to set me free
And love will find a way

Harry Graham and Harold Fraser-Simson, *Maid of the Mountains*, 1917

THE PRECISE ORIGINS of the modern musical are still open to some debate: Alan Jay Lerner, one of the most distinguished historians of his own field, considered that they could be traced back to street celebrations at the time of the French Revolution, while there have always been those who reckon that it began with Milton's masque *Comus* back in 1634 or else with John Gay's *The Beggar's Opera* of 1727. What seems open to less argument is that a fire on 14th Street in New York during the late summer of 1866 led to the largely accidental staging of *The Black Crook*, which is now generally accepted as the first indoor non-operatic stage show to integrate plot, song and dance. Not that it was ever meant to, and for those of us who have always regarded the development of the modern musical as a remarkably haphazard kind of miracle there is something deeply reassuring in discovering that this was also the way it began.

Two American theatre managers, Jarret and Palmer, had booked in a French ballet company to open their autumn season at the theatre on 14th Street when, with the dancers already embarked on their journey across the Atlantic, the building was burned to the ground. Having nowhere else of their own to place the troupe for their season, Jarret and Palmer turned to the owner of Niblo's Garden, a rival auditorium where a melodrama entitled *The Black Crook* was already in rehearsal. Its chances were not thought to be especially promising, despite a complex plot involving an alchemist bound to deliver one soul to hell each year in order to extend his own life on earth, and the management at Niblo's were duly persuaded to take on the French dancers plus such of their scenery as had survived the fire and the Atlantic crossing.

Only then did Niblo's producer William Wheatley realize that there was no way of integrating thirty French ballet dancers into a Faustian

Opposite. Daly's Theatre in Leicester Square was the first London home of the musical. George Edwardes had one of his greatest successes there with *The Geisha*, which ran from 1896 to 1898. A contemporary poster featuring the English girl disguised as a Geisha and a cartoon showing members of the cast (*below*) convey the exotic appearance of the Japanese costumes.

melodrama unless some songs could also be found to explain how the dancers had finished up in the arms of the alchemist. Giuseppe Operti was therefore commissioned to write 'The March of the Amazons' and 'You Naughty, Naughty Men', which thus became the first pop songs ever to emerge from a musical. On its first night, *The Black Crook* ran from 7.45 until just after 1.00 a.m., but by the time the last-act curtain had fallen on the alchemist and his amazing dancing girls, the first modern hit musical had been safely born.

It took six years, however, for *The Black Crook* to cross the Atlantic, and when it did finally open at the Alhambra in London on 23 December 1872, it was more cautiously billed as 'opéra-bouffe'. Audiences seemed largely unimpressed (even in New York the production had led to no immediate sequels), and it was not until twelve years later that another American management, that of the actress Minnie Palmer, introduced to the West End at the Royal Strand Theatre a show called *My Sweetheart* which, billed as a 'musical comedy drama', had been enjoying a two-year run on Broadway. This fared considerably better than *The Black Crook* (reviews noted 'costumes and players of considerable delight'), but seems to have left critics and audiences alike largely unaware that something new was being attempted. A mix of song and dance and plot was, after all, now the staple ingredient of the Gilbert and Sullivan operettas; the only difference in the American musical was that it seemed to have become slightly more up to date and to be sung or spoken in language rather less arch or high-flown than that of W. S. Gilbert.

By 1887 George R. Sims and Clement Scott, two of the most prolific and experimental dramatists of the time, had come up with the first-ever wholly British musical, *Jack in the Box*: it starred a burlesque queen, Fannie Leslie, was variously billed on its own posters as 'a musical drama' and 'a musical comedy', presumably in the interests of appealing to as wide an audience as possible, and again managed to run respectably but not spectacularly for a few months.

No other British dramatist or composer seems to have thought the genre worth exploring further, and it was left to another American, Charles Arnold (who had starred in *My Sweetheart*), to open 1891 with yet one more try: *Hans the Boatman* promised theatregoers 'home ballads, songs and dances' as well as a plot, in itself the work of about half a dozen different writers. By now it was clear that in some form or other the American musical had arrived in London: the British musical might, however, never have arrived there at all, had it not been for yet another accident a year later.

During the 1880s, under its impresario and 'Guv'nor', George Edwardes, the Gaiety Theatre had become established as a home of burlesque: though not precisely identical to what was meant in the United States by burlesque, this was a vaguely similar mix of topical songs and sketches played in lavish costumes and owing very little to coherent plot or sustained characterization. Burlesque thrived through the 1880s precisely because it provided a downmarket alternative to the comic operas of Gilbert and Sullivan or still more highbrow musical imports from the Continent. For those who did not want to stoop as far as the music hall, burlesque offered an alternative; for a while it even achieved a kind of respectability (one manager solemnly saw himself sustaining 'the sacred lamp of burlesque', while another more plausibly described himself as 'a licensed dealer in legs, short skirts, French adaptations and music') and like the later revues, it had of course the huge advantage to Victorian diners of no particularly important beginning or end. Burlesques could be visited and abandoned at almost any point during the evening, depending on what other pleasures – either culinary or sexual – were on offer to its largely male clientele.

The historical accident which changed all that in 1892 was the sudden death and serious illness of the two leading burlesque stars of the Gaiety: deprived almost overnight of Fred Leslie and Nellie Farren, Edwardes was forced to think of an alternative not just to them, but to the kind of shows they did. Over the past few seasons, enthusiasm for burlesque had become enthusiasm for Leslie and Farren. Without them, the form seemed suddenly dated and aimless, and all that Edwardes could find to replace it was the still somewhat shapeless notion of the English musical comedy.

Edwardes had, however, one remaining and tangible asset: a contract with a singing and dancing comic actor by the name of Arthur Roberts. Though totally forgotten now, preserved if at all only in photographs, mostly in early theatre magazines, Arthur Roberts was the first great star of the British musical. A contemporary critical account of his presence suggests a talent somewhere halfway from Ray Bolger to Bert Lahr: 'It is impossible to pin that amazing man down to any category of particular stage entertainment. He pervades them all, bestriding them like a Colossus. He is the comic genius of his age, the master gagster.'

Another critic later noted: 'Roberts has absolutely no counterpart today. He was in himself the embodiment of Puck, the merry wanderer of the night. But he did not wander through Athenian woods, he wandered through the West End, in and out of theatres, music halls, bars, pubs, restaurants and clubs, leaving a trail of laughter behind. He was a man who could bluff anybody and play the most remarkable jokes. He invented the word for this activity – he called it Spoof. It is a part of the language now, but there was never a master of that art to compare with its inventor. He was a law unto himself. When you engaged Arthur Roberts for a part, you did not trouble to give him a script. You just told him the story and explained the situation and he did the rest. Yet despite his almost completely extempore performances each night, he never let anyone go without the right cue, he never ruined an entrance or an exit for a fellow player, and he never tried to steal the limelight. There was no need for that. He was Arthur Roberts.'

The son of a penniless Suffolk family, Roberts had got his first laughs on the Music Halls with a bad limp that was the legacy of a childhood illness: a small man with a curious waddle-walk and highly expressive hands, he had become the foremost eccentric comedian in the country and he owed Edwardes a show. Though not always as popular among his fellow actors as contemporary reports would suggest ('Ah, Roberts,' said Arthur Bourchier to him once at a midnight party, 'time all good actors were in bed.' 'All good actors already are,' replied Roberts icily) his value to a script was inestimable, particularly if that script had yet to be put together.

What Edwardes now planned was a show to be built around Roberts, but not in the conventions of Burlesque: instead this would be what the *Sunday Times* was to describe in October 1892 as 'a curious medley of song, dance and nonsense, with occasional didactic glimmers, sentimental intrusions and the very vaguest attempts at satirising the modern "masher" about town.'

The writers of *In Town* were Adrian Ross, James Leader and Osmund Carr, all of whom can perhaps claim (as Edwardes always himself did) to be among the founding fathers of the modern musical. But there was no critical or public doubt that without Arthur Roberts they would all have been in deep trouble. The plot, such as it was, concerned 'a gay Lothario' (gay, be it understood, in its pre-1960s connotation) who divided his time between a West End hotel bedroom and the chorus dressing-rooms of the 'Ambiguity Theatre' in his tireless search for a skirt. Intriguingly, Roberts' success as Captain Coddington meant that his ties, hats, boots and shirts were being imitated and worn all over London, while his own special walking stick was also widely copied and carried. It would take another half-century for theatre managements to think of going into the souvenir business for themselves.

In Town ran (initially at the Prince of Wales and then at the Gaiety) for almost three hundred performances, and one critic began to see it as 'a reflex of London life, illustrating the doings there and the spirit that actuates English life all over the country, embodying the very essence of the times in which we live'. As the principal plot merely concerned Coddington having invited all the chorus girls of the Ambiguity to lunch and then finding that he couldn't afford to pay for it, historians might take the view that London life of the period must have been remarkably uneventful. But what mattered about *In Town* was that it became an immense and immediate popular hit: Roberts suddenly began to set a fashion in tailoring as in diction, and the musical had established itself as a social and theatrical force.

Roberts had moreover pioneered a line in apparently carefree and throwaway elegance that was to stretch down the years through George Grossmith and Seymour Hicks to Jack Buchanan and the young London Astaires: Edwardes had realized that the leading man of a musical was an altogether different stage animal to the leading man of a comic opera or burlesque. In that sense, Roberts was the first of the modern song-and-dance men to leave his footprints on the sands of time.

When the box-office takings for *In Town* began to waver, Roberts remained undaunted: reverting to one of his old music-hall routines, he closed the first half with 'Daddy Wouldn't Buy Me A Bow-Wow' and achieved another few months at the Gaiety with audiences drawn from his vaudeville fans, tempting them often for the first time towards a show with some semblance of dramatic narrative. The only problem with this immense personal success was that it made it difficult for Edwardes to estimate whether the musical in general was a good idea, or only the musical that starred Arthur Roberts. Accordingly he decided to play safe at the Gaiety by reverting next to a season of comic operas and burlesques, while at his other theatre (the Prince of Wales) continuing the experiment with musicals.

It was therefore at the Prince of Wales, on 14 October 1893, that *A Gaiety Girl*, by Owen Hall and Sidney Jones, had its first night. In the finest traditions of musical-comedy plotting, Owen Hall was in fact someone else entirely: a respectable solicitor called James Davis who had once met Edwardes on a train and told him he could write a better musical than *In Town* with one hand tied behind his back. Edwardes encouraged him to try, and the result was in the view of the *Era*'s critic, 'one of the most curious examples of composite dramatic architecture that we have seen for some time . . . but it is always light, bright and enjoyable.'

Light, bright and enjoyable: for the next half-century they were to be the principal requirements and achievements of the British stage musical, and to that extent *A Gaiety Girl* set the tone. Unlike *In Town*, it was not a star show, though several of the original cast (notably Hayden Coffin and Marie Studholme) were to remain in the nucleus of players who kept the British musical alive through World War I, and unlike *In Town* it actually had a plot which appeared to have been written down rather than assembled in rehearsal.

Essentially, it concerned chorus girls breaking into high society, a regular preoccupation of the time since a number had in real life done just that, but the plot needs to be recalled in some detail since it would serve as a model for so many others. As the curtain rises on a garden party given by officers of the Life Guards 'near Windsor Castle', some well-born young ladies are appalled to find themselves at the same social function as a group of actresses from the Gaiety Theatre. After the latter

19

have provided a kind of alfresco musical diversion to occupy the rest of Act I, the plot duly thickens: one of the actresses refuses to marry one of the officers on the grounds that such a marriage would ruin his career, but meanwhile one of her well-born rivals for his affections has her maid slip a diamond comb into the actress's pocket. Duly accused of having stolen the comb, she then has another act and half (partially set on the French Riviera, where the party has moved for the summer) in which to establish her innocence in the matter, before finally falling into the arms of her Guards officer.

The plot of *A Gaiety Girl* was loose enough still to allow Hayden Coffin a solo number of stunning irrelevance but lasting popularity ('Tommy Atkins', with its Kiplingesque salute to the ordinary foot soldier) and yet it contained virtually all the elements that were to characterize the stage musical for the twenty years preceding World War I – social class divisions, robbery, mistaken identity, transfer to a French beach-resort setting in Act II, all followed by a dénouement in which, at often breathtaking speed, villains were unmasked, missing parents located, impostors shown up, lovers reunited and the best songs sung again as curtain calls. When, sixty years after the opening of *A Gaiety Girl*, Sandy Wilson wrote the brilliantly mocking tribute to 1920s musicals which he called *The Boy Friend*, he was in fact parodying a genre which had started with *A Gaiety Girl*.

But in the immediate future, all it led to were a great many more *Girls*: fourteen more musicals with *Girl* somewhere in the title were staged in London over the next two decades, and most featured plots and even scores of quite remarkable similarity. It was as though, having discovered the musical as a potential theatrical form for the coming century, theatre managers and writers alike had only in fact discovered one serviceable storyline. But *A Gaiety Girl* did something else, of course: it established in the public mind immediately and irrevocably the notion of a mobile team of singer-dancers attached to one theatre and one management. From 1894 to 1914, Gaiety Girls were to London precisely what the Ziegfeld Girls of a later generation would be to Broadway – the 'Beautiful Girls' recalled in the Sondheim song of that title from *Follies*.

A Gaiety Girl gave way at the Gaiety to *The Shop Girl* (girl serving behind counter falls in love with aristocrat), *My Girl* (girl gets caught up in Stock Exchange share dealings, but all ends happily), *The Circus Girl* (girl on high wire falls in love) and eventually *The Runaway Girl*; this last work achieved a kind of immortality of fiction-into-fact when one of its leading Gaiety Girls, Rosie Boote, ran away from the theatre to become the Marchioness of Headfort – though not before she had taken part in a rousing chorus of 'O, Listen to the Band.'

Few English musicals of this period survived without Gaiety Girls, and as early as September 1894 Edwardes was already exporting them to

The Quaker Girl (1910) was yet another successful production for George Edwardes: a contact sheet of photographs shows the cast on stage at the Adelphi.

America: that year, the Broadway season opened with *A Gaiety Girl* at Daly's, and the company then went on tour to Boston, Philadelphia and Milwaukee before travelling on to Australia and returning home via India.

At home, through what remained of the last decade of the last century, Edwardes consolidated his position at the Gaiety while also using Daly's in London as a home for shows like *An Artist's Model*, which was billed as 'a comedy with music', as distinct from a musical comedy; this distinction did not, however, make much sense to critics or to an unruly first-night audience appalled to find that their newly discovered musical was being pushed back up the intellectual ladder towards something altogether more thoughtful. After its rough opening-night reception, Edwardes rebuilt the show, simplifying its storyline and so guaranteeing it a run of just over four hundred performances, after which Daly's was occupied for a further seven hundred by *The Geisha*, it having been reckoned by the management that *The Mikado* had not quite exhausted a London passion of the time for all things oriental.

'In the whole province of theatrical criticism,' audibly groaned *The Times* in April 1896, 'there is no task more distracting than that of setting forth the plot of an average modern comic opera. Hence it is the initial duty of a grateful critic to state that *The Geisha* so far deviates from familiar usage as to give us a genuine and coherent story, not very convincing or plausible perhaps, but at any rate tolerably continuous and logical in its development.' The fact that the plot concerned an aristocratic English girl disguised as a Geisha, a wily French fortune-hunter and a Japanese Marquis, and that it appeared to have been cobbled together by a team of writers who believed that the only thing more commercial than *The Mikado* or *A Gaiety Girl* would be a merger of the two storylines, did no harm of any kind at the box-office of what was to become the most commercially successful musical of the 1890s. Any thoughts that Richard d'Oyly Carte, not to mention Gilbert and Sullivan, may have had about it are alas unrecorded.

And from Japan, on to China: *San Toy*, which opened at Daly's in October 1899 in the midst of a thick fog and the Boer War, went on to become the hit of the turn of the century, outlasting *The Geisha* by eight performances, and thereby setting up a new record run for a musical, 768 performances in just under two years. By now, Edwardes had learnt certain lessons of the musical business, the first of which was that his audiences liked to see where their ticket money was being spent. Running costs of a show at Daly's in 1900 were in the region of £2,500 a week, vastly more than was being spent by any other management of the period, but these shows were built to last and Edwardes knew that, heavily recast, they could be toured around the regions for several seasons after the initial London run, thereby guaranteeing him an eventual profit of tens and sometimes hundreds of thousands of pounds over the ten-year life of one of his productions.

He also had a sharp eye for female talent: his companies at the Gaiety and Daly's around the turn of the century included not only the usual high-stepping chorus girls but such actresses as Marie Tempest, Constance Collier, Zena and Phyllis Dare, Gladys Cooper, Ellaline Terriss and Ada Reeve, many of whom were later to carve out careers in the legitimate theatre and one of whom (Zena Dare) was to play on across half a century through most of the Novello musicals, right up to the London premiere of *My Fair Lady*, in which she was the original Mrs Higgins.

The twentieth century thus did not start with any great change in the state of the London musical: *San Toy* ran on at Daly's, the Shaftesbury had a rare Broadway import (*The Belle of New York*, which – almost fifty years before *Guys and Dolls* – concerned a Salvation Army girl 'singing a fast song in some public gardens where a fancy ball is being held') and at the Gaiety three months into the new year *The Runaway Girl* gave way to *The Messenger Boy*, a musical by Lionel Monckton and five other composer-librettists which was quick to celebrate the sudden arrival in London of small uniformed boys bearing hand-delivered correspondence across the West End.

Yet behind the scenes there were signs of change: a road-widening

ST. ERMIN'S HOTEL
WESTMINSTER.

St. Ermin's Handsomely Furnished Suites or Single Chambers

St. Ermin's Luxury and Home Comforts.

St. Ermin's Unexcelled Cuisine.

INCLUSIVE TERMS:
9s. & 10/6 per day.

Telephone 181 or 278 Westminster.
Telegraphic Address:
"Unparalleled," London.

SUPPORT HOME INDUSTRIES.
BRYANT & MAY'S MATCHES
Are used in the Bars of this Theatre.

DALY'S THEATRE,

SOLE PROPRIETOR ... ... Mr. GEORGE EDWARDES.

To-Night, and Every Evening, Matinee every Saturday at 2.30, Mr. GEORGE EDWARDES' New Production.
An entirely New and Original Musical Play, in Two Acts, entitled

SAN TOY,

Or, THE EMPEROR'S OWN.

Book by EDWARD MORTON. Lyrics by HARRY GREENBANK & ADRIAN ROSS. Music by SIDNEY JONES.

Yen How	(a Mandarin)	Mr. RUTLAND BARRINGTON
Sir Bingo Preston	(British Consul at Pynka Pong)	Mr. FRED KAYE
Sing Hi	(President of the Board of Ceremonies)	Mr. COLIN COOP
Lieut. Harvey Tucker		Mr. LIONEL MACKINDER
Fo Hop	(a Chinese Student)	Mr. SCOTT RUSSELL
Fang	(a Boatman)	Mr. J. McLEAN
Hu Pi	(Jewellers of Pynka Pong)	Mr. S. ARRIGONI
Wai Ho		Mr. J. MURPHY
Li Hi	(Tartar Guards)	Mr. T. H. DAVID
Li Lo		Mr. F. VIGAY
Old Mandarin	(at Court of Pekin)	Mr. AKERMAN MAY
AND		
Li		Mr. HUNTLEY WRIGHT
Poppy	(Daughter of Sir Bingo)	Miss HILDA MOODY
Dudley	(her Maid)	Miss GRACIE LEIGH
Chu	(a Widow)	Miss MAY BUCKLEY
Wun Lung	(Perpetual Corporal of the Emperor's Own)	Miss GLADYS HOMFREY
Ko Fan	(of the Emperor's Own)	Miss MAIDIE HOPE
Trixie	(with Pas Suel in Act II.)	Miss TOPSY SINDEN
Yung Shi	(Six Little Wives of Yen How)	Miss FLORENCE COLLINGBOURNE
Me Koui		Miss MARIE FAWCETT
Siou		Miss MARGUERITE ROCHE
Shuey Pin Sing		Miss F. ALLEN
Li Kiang		Miss ETHEL HOPE
Hu You		Miss MARY COLLETTE
Miss Harley Streeter		Miss ALICE DAVIS
Hon Mrs. Hay Stackporle		Miss K. FRANCIS
Miss Mary Lambkin		Miss ADA CARTER
Lady Pickleton		Miss HILDA CORAL
Captain Bobby Preston	(Son of Sir Bingo Preston)	Mr. HAYDEN COFFIN
AND		
San Toy	(Daughter of Yen How)	Miss MARIE TEMPEST

Act I. ... A STREET IN PYNKA PONG. *Hawes Craven*
Act II. ... HALL IN EMPEROR'S IMPERIAL PALACE AT PEKIN. *Joseph Harker*

The elaborate Setting of the Second Scene will necessitate an interval of 20 minutes between the Acts on the first nights.
Produced under the Stage Direction of Mr. RICHARD BARKER (by kind permission of Mr R. D'OYLY CARTE).

Additional Musical Numbers by Mr. LIONEL MONCKTON.
The Words of the Song in the Second Act, "The One in the World," are by Mr. HARRY HAMILTON.

Chinese Ladies' Costumes by Miss FISHER. Gentlemen's by B. J. SIMMONS & Co. English Ladies' Costumes by Mrs. NETTLESHIP. Hats by Misses F. J. & L. WILSON. Gentlemen's Costumes by COOLING & LAWRENCE. Properties by SKELLY. Electrical Engineer, G. A. POYNTON. Machinist, H. SHELDON. Limes by KERR. Wigs by CLARKSON. Floral Decorations by A. GATTI & Co.

Chinese Costumes designed by Mr. PERCY ANDERSON. The Dances arranged by Mr. WILLIE WARDE.

Musical Director .. Mr. BARTER JOHNS. Stage Manager ... Mr. E. T. STEYNE.

Box Office open 10 till 10. Telephone (3995 Gerrard). Private Boxes, £2 12s 6d. to £5 5s. Orchestra Stalls, 10s. 6d. Balcony Stalls, 7s. Upper Circle (Front Row), 5s. Other Rows, 4s. Pit, 2s. 6d. Gallery, 1s.

Acting Manager ... Mr. G. E. MINOR.

E. CHIVERS,
FLORIST,
GOLD MEDALLIST, R.B.S.
Wreaths, Crosses, Bouquets, &c.
Sole Decorators to THE EDWARDES MENU Co., Ltd., and to the following Theatres:— Shaftesbury, Lyceum, Prince of Wales, Terrys, Vaudeville, Comedy, Globe, Strand, Avenue, St. James's Hall and Gaiety Buffet.
Telegraphic Address:—Chivers, Covent Garden.
Only Address:—124, CENTRE AVENUE, COVENT GARDEN, W.C.

Mouilla
LIQUID SOAP
FOR THE
COMPLEXION.

FREE SAMPLE BOTTLE
Sent on application, mentioning this Programme.

DR. DUNCAN' MOUILLA Liquid Soap. After one day's use the hands and Complexion will be vastly improved.

THE *Proprietors:*
Mouilla Liquid Soap Co.,
8, CECIL COURT,
CHARING CROSS ROAD, W.C.

The Berlitz School of Languages.
231-233, OXFORD ST.
REGENT CIRCUS.
CONVERSATIONAL METHOD.
TRIAL LESSON FREE.

Hotel Victoria
Northumberland Avenue.
Orchestra plays during
Table d'Hôte
Luncheon & Dinner.
Open to Non-Residents.
Gordon Hotels, Ltd.

Another early musical with a plot inspired by the Orient was *San Toy* (1899), staged by George Edwardes at Daly's; here, the leading role of the Chinese girl was played by the resolutely English Marie Tempest (see p. 38).

scheme in the Strand meant that the old Gaiety would have to be pulled down by 1903, and with it ended the first era of the West End song-and-dance show. Moreover the London success of *Belle of New York*, which survived nearly seven hundred performances at the Shaftesbury, after having been turned down by Edwardes and nearly every other West End management, alerted impresarios and audiences alike that Broadway shows were no longer only to be glimpsed on brief European tours. They were in London to stay, and it was the critic of the *Sunday Times* who noted: '*The Belle of New York* certainly meets the ever-present want for novelty but is best described as bizarre. It is like nothing we have ever seen here, and it is composed of the oddest incongruities of plot. Characters include sailors and professional pugilists, not to mention twin Portuguese brothers, the lunatic Karl von Pumpernick and Mr Frank

Lawton whose talent as a whistler sends the audience into raptures by his clear, sweet, long-sustained trillings. Doubtless the actors here represent types of theatrical people who exist in the United States, though we have nothing like them on this side of the Atlantic . . . the chorus, who must have to do some hard work behind the scenes in changing costume, still have plenty of spirit left for their business on stage, and do it most vigorously and smartly. The music is decidedly above average, indeed over-elaborate; the scenery is effective and the dresses bright and cheery. *The Belle of New York* is destined to be very popular, for it is the brightest, smartest and cleverest entertainment of its kind that has been seen in London for a long time.'

The success of *The Belle of New York* gave London a new leading lady in Edna May, who was to make much of the rest of her career in West End exile from her native America: it also led directly to two further imports in 1900, *An American Beauty* and *The Casino Girl*, both of which also came across the Atlantic as complete productions from Broadway.

Edwardes fought back with *The Toreador*, but there was now the distinct feeling that his position as 'The Guv'nor' was being challenged on all sides: Seymour Hicks and his wife Ellaline Terriss had left the Gaiety to set up their own management with the American Charles Frohman, while another rival producer, George Curzon, achieved in 1901 the longest-ever run of a London musical of the period with *A Chinese Honeymoon* (1,075 performances). With Leslie Stuart's *Floradora* at the Lyric from the end of 1899, Edwardes started the new century having to build a new Gaiety in a West End suddenly full of precisely the kind of lavish musicals which had once been his own exclusive territory.

Yet there was still a certain critical uneasiness about the genre and its audiences: 'It seems difficult,' wrote the critic of the *Illustrated Sporting and Dramatic News* in November 1899, 'in any one musical comedy to get away from the musical comedies which have preceded it. The personages always seem to be doing much the same sort of thing in much the same sort of way. I am not sure whether the special class of playgoer for whom musical comedy is written would appreciate a genuine new departure. I should not like to say even that they would understand one.'

Opposite. The sheet-music cover for 'The Black Crook Valse' arranged by Charles Coote from the original composition by Georges Jacobi for *The Black Crook*, the show which reached the London stage in December 1872, at the Alhambra, having already established itself – albeit accidentally – as the first American musical to integrate plot, song and dance.

Overleaf. A poster for *A Gaiety Girl*, first produced in October 1893, and a page from a souvenir of the show, both designed by Dudley Hardy. For some of the chorus girls, the idea of their marrying into high society was one to be pursued and turned as soon as possible into a reality.

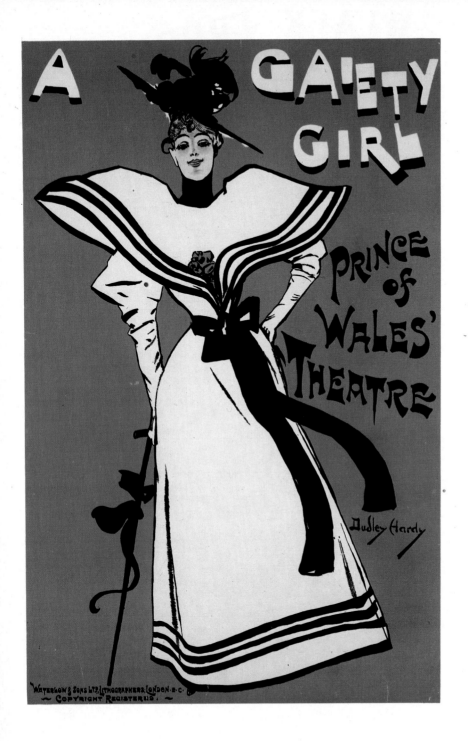
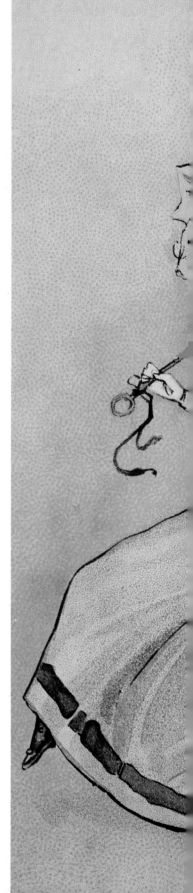

CHU·CHIN·CHOW

HIS·MAJESTYS·THEATRE·

All of which makes it the more surprising that by 1903, the year the new Gaiety opened with a new musical, *The Orchid*, and a new King, Edward VII, sitting in the royal box, there should also have been playing in London the first-ever black Broadway hit: 'Negro entertainments,' wrote the drama critic of the *Era* in some amazement, 'have in this country been associated almost invariably with coon songs, cakewalks and plantation walk-rounds. It is therefore a really fresh and novel experiment to introduce to the jaded Londoner *In Dahomey*, an American musical comedy that is not only played throughout by real coloured people, but written and composed by clever and able representatives of the Negro race with lyrics from the pen of a member of the same interesting nationality . . . the remarkable thing about the whole entertainment is the immense enthusiasm of the cast. Every member of the company, principals and chorus, sang and danced with a sense of thorough enjoyment of their work, and that enjoyment was speedily communicated to a large and enthusiastic audience. *In Dahomey* with its wonderful vitality, its quaint comedians, its catchy music and its unique environment should be one of the dramatic sensations of the London season.'

Behind that review's remarkably patronizing tone lies a realization which was to haunt English reviewers of Broadway musicals right through to the 1960s: the shows that came to us from New York for the first half of this century were much more energetic, more enthusiastic than the shows born here, and that did not just start from *Oklahoma!* As early as the turn of the century, home-grown musicals had settled into a tasteful kind of calm from which they had to be regularly jolted by occasional glimpses of how these things were done on the other side of the Atlantic. Naked showbiz enthusiasm for the show at hand was already regarded as somehow vaguely un-British by and for those directly involved in the staging. Ironically, however, it was only to be in these very early years of the century that original-cast productions were to cross the Atlantic in both directions with no union difficulties: such freedom of theatrical travel became restricted once British and American Actors' Equity organizations began demanding reciprocity of employment, and from the 1920s onwards shows were invariably recast from country to country.

But as the fascination with the Orient and America gave way to an Edwardian rustic revival (*Country Girl*, *Cherry Girl*, *The Orchid*, *Bluebell in Fairyland*), so the Atlantic seemed once again to grow wider: Jerome Kern, living in London as early as 1904, was in fact working there not on

Opposite. A 1916 poster for *Chu-Chin-Chow*, the show which became the first smash hit of the British musical theatre, helped by an advertising campaign on an unprecedented scale.

29

scores for the West End but simply interpolating American numbers in 'Edwardesian' shows that Broadway managers like Frohman found too tame for New York.

By now Edwardes himself was running three musical theatres (the rebuilt Gaiety, Daly's and the Prince of Wales), with a range from light opera to low comedy; Seymour Hicks and his company were at the Vaudeville and Robert Courtneidge at the Shaftesbury. All had their own house styles, but the musicals were essentially similar in plot and character. Locations might range from Arcadia to Ruritania by way of Europe and the Far East, but they were still peopled by winsome English maidens in distress, jovial character men, dashing heroes in disguise. Most of the plots could have been neatly inscribed within the margins of the cast-lists, and some shows appeared not to have been written at all, merely assembled from stretches of old dialogue interrupted by songs that could be whistled and forgotten while leaving the stalls.

Apart from *The Catch of the Season* (1904), which introduced London to the Gibson Girls, and *The Belle of Mayfair* (1906), which was essentially *The Belle of New York* relocated, the outstanding musical success of the Edwardian years was *The Merry Widow*, in which Lily Elsie played the title role for a deeply uneasy George Edwardes in 1907. Overtaken on his own home-grown musical territory by other managements, desperately short of the money required to keep three big theatres running, unable to find enough native products, he had turned reluctantly to the Vienna Woods. Though Franz Lehár had already enjoyed a considerable success with the operetta in his native country, Edwardes was in no doubt that it would have to be drastically reshaped for London: accordingly he put in a new last act set in Maxim's, brought in an American light comedian with no musical track record of note (Joe Coyne), added several English stock comedians to the already shaky plot and achieved a run of eight hundred performances.

A year later, as if in chauvinist reaction to the European invasion of London orchestra pits, Robert Courtneidge launched *The Arcadians*, a rustic English fable with minimal plot which yet achieved a comparable run. Audience choice was now plain: West End theatregoers could have either the urban sophistication of *The Merry Widow* or the rural simplicity of *The Arcadians*. Elsewhere, not a lot: the American invasion continued with *The Dollar Princess* (1909), Europe fought back with *The Count of Luxembourg* (1911), and the most interesting import of the immediate pre-war years (an American jazz musical comedy called *Little Miss Ragtime*) did no better than a short regional tour in 1913.

So as war was declared, with George Edwardes currently convalescing in a German spa town and having to be rapidly repatriated, an era had evidently come to a close. Edwardes himself was broken in health, spirit and bank balance; Robert Courtneidge was also coming to the end of his years in management, and as always at the start of a war, all bets were off until the effect of hostilities could be accurately assessed at the box-office.

As all Germanic and mid-European shows were swept hastily off the London stage in 1914, no matter that most had already been so drastically adapted as to be unrecognizable to their original creators, there was a rapid return to such all-English concoctions as *Betty* and *A Happy Day* and *The Bing Boys Are Here*, this last in fact derived from the French, but described as 'a picture of London life in seven panels' and so successful that it led to two sequels, *The Bing Boys Are There* and *The Bing Boys on Broadway*, as well as a Jewish variant entitled *The Other Bing Boys*. These *Bing* shows provided three of the great army marching-song hits of World War I: 'Let the Great Big World Keep Turning', 'First Love, Lost Love, Best Love' and most famously 'If You Were the Only Girl in the World'.

But the two biggest musical hits of World War I, both of which set up longevity records that were to remain unbeaten for twenty years afterwards, were still set abroad, though nowhere as dangerously close and inimical as Europe. Nor were they set in America: the United States, though undoubtedly friend rather than foe, and indeed ally after 1917, was still not regarded by London producers as a suitable setting for their musicals. You might borrow a star or a song from there, you might even borrow an entire show and its score, but if you were setting up a musical yourself then you went somewhere more exotic. Like the house of Kasim Baba, an Arabian merchant prince who was preparing to receive a still richer Arabian merchant prince by the name of Chu-Chin-Chow.

Loosely based on one of the Arabian Nights tales, *Chu-Chin-Chow* was the first modern smash hit of the British musical theatre. It ran longer than World War I (a total of 2,238 performances) and showed an eventual profit of more than £300,000 on an original investment of just over £5,000. Its author was the Australian-born actor-manager Oscar Asche, who had worked with Ibsen in Norway before joining Benson's touring Shakespeare company in England at the turn of the century. Bored with the Bard, he took to managing large London theatres and playing Haaj the Beggar in *Kismet*, from where it was not a very great step to *Chu-Chin-Chow*. But the success of that show meant something else: it meant the beginning of the modern mass-merchandised musical. *Chu-Chin-Chow* was given a poster-advertising campaign on buses and hoardings, the like of which had never been seen in London, and its long run suggested that there was, during and after World War I, a new kind of audience for the stage musical: an audience hooked on spectacle and easily singable songs, but an audience eager to get away from old Vienna, rustic England or New York, which had until now been the principal locations of all song shows.

31

The real importance of *Chu-Chin-Chow*, however, lay in its spectacle: Asche had been unable to raise the necessary capital without first producing a working model of the set, yet once that was achieved, investors came forward and both they and audiences had the novel experience of coming out of a theatre impressed first and foremost by the scenery. Up till then, musical comedies had always depended for their success largely on the costumes, glamorous leading ladies and a star comedian: with *Chu-Chin-Chow*, the show itself became the star. A breakdown of its pre-first night costs shows that an unprecedented £1,400 went into scenery, while rehearsal salaries had cost the management only £150, and the orchestra came in at £235. Somewhere halfway between pantomime and operetta, *Chu-Chin-Chow* had a generally undistinguished score and no discernible finale, though 'The Robbers' Chorus' became a popular hit and Courtice Pounds had a success with 'Anytime's Kissing Time'.

Against the background of World War I, *Chu-Chin-Chow* became for those in uniform the show to see on one's last leave night – as *Me and My Girl* would be in the early years of World War II – and as such it acquired sentimental and even patriotic qualities that were far more to do with the nature of the audience than with the actual score. Like many of the West End's greatest musical hits over the years, however, *Chu-Chin-Chow* proved largely unexportable: a year after the London premiere, Tyrone Power Senior opened it on Broadway, accompanied by a huge advertising campaign promising 'all the romance, splendour and inscrutable mystery of the East', but it failed to achieve a run even one-tenth as long as that of the London original. Subsequent revivals in Britain have also tended to suggest that *Chu-Chin-Chow* was as unrepeatable as World War I itself.

Beerbohm Tree may have sniffed that *Chu-Chin-Chow* was 'more navel than millinery' on account of the amount of gauze used in its costumes, but of the musicals that immediately followed it, only *The Maid of the Mountains* achieved a remotely comparable success. The musical had been cobbled together from an old stage plot by Frederick Lonsdale which had already been rejected by most of the managements in town. It was the new manager of Daly's, Robert Evett, desperately trying to restore that theatre's fortunes after the death of George Edwardes, who happened upon the script and billed it as 'a play told to a musical setting' which seemed to give it an altogether new critical stature. Jose Collins was the Maid taken hostage by a band of brigands and eventually falling into the arms of their leader, a fate she repeated nightly for over thirteen hundred performances, thereby enabling the management to show a profit of over £200,000. No musical in the twenty years that separated *Chu-Chin-Chow* from *Me and My Girl* did better at the box-office or had as long a run.

The Count of Luxembourg, with a score by Franz Lehár, opened at Daly's in May 1911 and ran for 340 performances. Its star, Lily Elsie, is seen here (featured in *The Sketch* on 21 June 1911) wearing various costumes created for her in the role of Angèle.

Some early stars

Nellie Farren, who came from the world of burlesque (*above*), was neither a dancer nor a singer, but became known – on the strength of her talent for broad caricature – as the 'Queen of the Gaiety'. Though somewhat less celebrated, Fannie Leslie and Madge Vincent each achieved at least one major West End success, Miss Leslie – portrayed (*above, right*) in an 1887 Strand Theatre advertising handout – in *Jack in the Box*, and Miss Vincent (*right*) in *The Toreador* at the Gaiety in June 1901.

The light comedian
Arthur Roberts, seen
(*right*) as Captain
Coddington in *In
Town* at the Prince of
Wales' Theatre in
1892, pioneered the
casual, often
impromptu style of
musical-comedy
playing which was to
live on in the
performances of such
later stars as Sonnie
Hale and Jack
Buchanan; photo by
Alfred Ellis from *The
Album Supplement*, 18
March 1895.

The first invasion of the American musical occurred around the turn of the century. Camille Clifford, seen (*opposite*) in a page from a contemporary magazine, brought the Gibson Girl to London in Seymour Hicks' *The Catch of the Season* (based on the drawings of Charles Dana Gibson) at the Vaudeville Theatre (1904); earlier, *The Belle of New York* – of which the chorus was shown on stage (*above*) in *The Sketch* in April 1898 – had achieved a run of over 700 performances at the Shaftesbury. By the time *The Belle of Mayfair* arrived at the Vaudeville in 1906, with Edna May in the title role (*below*), the London musical had gathered considerable pace to match that of the Broadway imports.

Oriental inspirations

Long before Courtice Pounds appeared in 1916 in *Chu-Chin-Chow* (*top left*), two unmistakeably English stars had performed leading roles as Chinese ladies: Marie Tempest (*left*) in *San Toy* at Daly's (1899); and (*below*) Lily Elsie in *A Chinese Honeymoon* at the Strand Theatre (1901).

Rustic pursuits

For several Christmas seasons from 1901 onwards, *Bluebell in Fairyland* – the story of a little London flower girl transported to the kingdom of the fairies – was a triumph for Ellaline Terriss and her husband Seymour Hicks at the Vaudeville (*left*), while Lionel Monckton's *A Country Girl* (1902), concerned with the love of a farmgirl for a naval lieutenant (poster, *top left*), ran for over 700 performances. Monckton's *The Arcadians* (1909) was even more successful, with over 800 performances at the Shaftesbury Theatre; Florence Smithson as Sombra, the principal Arcadian nymph, is seen (*above*) in the love duet with the comic Simplicitas, played by Dan Roylat.

The Twenties

SOMETHING about the frenzy of the 1920s, the pace of its flapper life, militated against the development of many coherent British musical comedies: revue was the invention of the age, a lightning, quick-change medium in which songs and sketches could be flashed on and off the stage for the entertainment of West End audiences whose attention-span was at an all-time low. In this context it needs to be recalled that Coward did not write his first 'book' musical (*Bitter Sweet*) until 1929 and that Novello did not achieve his first great hit (*Glamorous Night*) until 1935. Both men had of course been writing songs since the later years of World War I, but they were invariably individual numbers for cabaret or revue. The end of that war saw both *Chu-Chin-Chow* and *The Maid of the Mountains* settled into record-breaking runs that were clearly not about to be interrupted by any armistice, but by then there could be no doubt that if new musical comedies were to come from anywhere, then they would be coming across the Atlantic from Broadway.

A war with Europe, a war in Europe, had cut Britain off from her great Victorian links to Germany and Austria, and American composers were quick to step into that breach. Some, in Europe for the first time as soldiers after the United States joined the war in 1917, simply stayed on in Paris or London to write music for the Jazz Age: others returned home to Broadway but continued to write with at least one eye still on the West End, where much of the acting and singing talent was still centred.

Early in 1919, backstage at the Kingsway Theatre, a remarkable meeting took place between three men who in their individual ways were to epitomise the history of the stage musical across three generations. The manager George Grossmith, himself the son of the great

Opposite. Binnie Hale playing the parlourmaid who is really a millionaire's daughter in *Mr Cinders* (1929), which ran for over 500 performances when first produced at the Adelphi, and was revived with similar success in 1983.

Gilbert and Sullivan star and an actor who had worked his way through the Gaiety musicals before co-writing the successful series of *Bing Boy* shows in World War I, was then auditioning young West End actors for a production he was staging of a Broadway hit called originally *Oh Boy!* and now retitled for local audiences *Oh Joy!* With him was the show's composer, Jerome Kern, and the actor they were auditioning was the young Noël Coward. In the event he failed to get cast, but *Oh Joy!* (with a book by P. G. Wodehouse and Guy Bolton) went on to considerable success and made a star of Beatrice Lillie, first of the Charlot revue players to cross over into a 'legit' musical (soon to be followed by such others as Gertruce Lawrence, Jack Buchanan and eventually Coward himself). *Oh Joy!* was carefully billed for 1919 as 'a new musical peace piece' and seems to have survived on a plot shamelessly lifted from *Charley's Aunt*: 'little more than old material skilfully rearranged,' thought the drama critic of *The Tatler*, 'and not at all ambitious either musically or dramatically . . . there is one haunting melody ['Till the Clouds Roll By'] which crops up at every available opportunity and tum-te-tums itself into your head until it would be quite impossible to forget . . . but the real joy of the evening is Miss Beatrice Lillie who breaks away from the authors and indulges in quips and antics and little asides which have nothing to do with the plot or character but yet add greatly to the enjoyment and unexpected laughter of the evening.'

Bea was evidently starting as she meant to go on across another half-century, as the greatest eccentric of the musical stage; but this production of *Oh Joy!* laid down certain guidelines (larger-than-life star, flexible plot, repetitive scoring, careful plugging of the 'big number') which were not to change until the coming of another World War.

In the meantime, Bolton and Wodehouse and Kern were the musical men of the new age: *Oh Boy/Joy!* was in fact their third collaboration after *Miss Springtime* (1916) and *Have A Heart* (1917), and already Broadway was in no doubt of their importance:

> *This is the trio of musical fame*
> *Bolton and Wodehouse and Kern,*
> *Better than anyone else you can name,*
> *Bolton and Wodehouse and Kern.*
> *Nobody knows what on earth they've been bitten by;*
> *All I can say is I mean to get lit an' buy*
> *Orchestra seats for the next one that's written by*
> *Bolton and Wodehouse and Kern.*

They were in some ways a curious team: two Englishmen and an American from widely different backgrounds but all essentially 'fixers' who could work over a song, a thread of foreign plot, a synopsis even, until they got it right for New York: they would take whole shows apart and put them back together again for London, deleting and adding characters, as well as entire scenes and production numbers as they judged right for local needs. Thus, between 1916 and 1924, Kern and Wodehouse and Bolton wrote a dozen musicals, almost all of which crossed the Atlantic from New York, though of those perhaps only *Leave It to Jane* (1917) and *Sally* (1920) and *The Beauty Prize* (1923) can claim lasting fame. But, as Dorothy Parker once said, 'I like the way they go about a musical comedy. I like the way the action slides casually into the songs. I like the deft rhyming of the song that is always sung in the last act by two comedians and one comedienne.' And considering that Wodehouse was essentially a comic novelist who could not read a note of music, his contribution to the genre was, as Richard Rodgers once noted, quite remarkable: 'Before Larry Hart, only Wodehouse had ever made any assault on the intelligence of the song-listening public.'

Of all the Kern/Wodehouse/Bolton shows, it was perhaps *Sally* that could claim to be the first great Twenties musical: originally commissioned by Florenz Ziegfeld as a vehicle for Marilyn Miller, it concerned a Greenwich Village foundling, who, while dreaming of becoming a world-famous dancer, actually works in a boarding house washing dishes. That plot had never hurt *Cinderella*, and in a ritual transformation scene Sally became if not a princess then at least the star of that year's *Follies*. But what really made *Sally*'s fortune, on Broadway as in London (where it cleared over £40,000, a record profit for the period), was a score which featured not only a notable title song and 'You Can't Keep A Good Girl Down', but also and most memorably 'Look for the Silver Lining'.

Sally did not reach the Winter Garden until September 1921, with Dorothy Dickson in the title role and a remarkable supporting cast (George Grossmith, Leslie Henson and Heather Thatcher), all of whom were to prove stalwarts of the London stage musical across the next decade. And one of the other reasons why this great Kern hit from Broadway was welcomed so fervently by London critics was the current lack of anything else around the London musical theatre of even vaguely comparable stature. The cheering that marked the end of World War I had faded away into an eery kind of silence: *Chu-Chin-Chow* and *The Maid of the Mountains* had become part of the landscape of the West End, but between them and *Sally* the only shows of note were either pale imitations (*Shanghai* and *The Rebel Maid*) or else one like *Kissing Time* (this also the work of Wodehouse and Bolton, though with Ivan Caryll rather than Kern), which attempted to persuade its audiences, with some success for it ran for more than four hundred performances, that World War I was by now just something else to sing about.

The other great musical hit of the early 1920s was of course the Nigel Playfair staging of *The Beggar's Opera* at the Lyric Hammersmith: not within our scope here, certainly, but a potent reminder of a light-operatic tradition which was to live on alongside the sharper and slicker Broadway imports of the same period. The year 1920 itself could also boast Edith Day as a waif singing of her Alice Blue Gown in *Irene* (this suggested a plot not unlike that of *Sally*), and Jose Collins back at Daly's as yet another *Southern Maid*; however, there was not a lot else, and though 1921 brought *Sally* to London, the year was otherwise mainly notable for such catastrophes as *The Golden Moth* (Wodehouse and Novello on unusually uncommercial form) and *Cairo*, with which Oscar Asche managed to lose most of the money he had made on *Chu-Chin-Chow*, despite its remarkably similar plot and staging.

By 1922 it had become clear that London managements in search of material for a musical hit had two options: the Old World and the New. With the Great War almost five years over, audiences could once again be tempted back to Viennese operetta, or at least to Kalman's *Gypsy Princess* and another tale of the Vienna Woods, *Lilac Time*, which, being the story of Franz Schubert's unrequited love set to his own music, achieved such a flowery grip on London theatres that after its initial 1922 staging at the Lyric (for six hundred performances) it achieved West End revivals in 1925, 1927, 1928, 1930, 1932, 1933, 1936 and 1949. A similar musical biography was tried for Tchaikovsky a year later (*Catherine*, 1923), while Chopin was celebrated in *The Damask Rose* (1929), though with considerably less success. The other option, that of the New World, was taken up swiftly by George Grossmith: on an Atlantic crossing he pinned P. G. Wodehouse down to a rapid five-day collaboration on the book and lyrics for *The Cabaret Girl*, which they duly took to Kern for scoring. Yet another musical title to capture the public interest of the moment, it ran happily into 1923, by which time – despite Evelyn Laye as a musical *Madame de Pompadour* and Jose Collins as an all-singing *Catherine* (the Great) – there was no doubt that the Americans were effectively ousting the old Europeans from the orchestra pits of the West End.

Or at least two Americans were: in that year Fred and Adele Astaire made their London debuts on 30 May at the Shaftesbury in an unremarkable musical farce by Fred Jackson called *Stop Flirting*: unremarkable save in one detail, for the programme acknowledged in very small print 'additional numbers by George Gershwin', and one of those just happened to be 'The Whichness of the Whatness'. The rest of

Opposite. Programme cover for Jerome Kern's *Sunny* (1926), in which the stars were Jack Buchanan and Elsie Randolph.

Overleaf. Poster for *Lilac Time* at the Lyric Theatre (1922); and (*right*) cartoon by Nerman in *The Tatler*, August 1924, showing Fred and Adele Astaire in *Stop Flirting* at the Shaftesbury (1923).

7 Oct 1926

SUNNY

Programme

LONDON
HIPPODROME

CHESNEY

C. BUCHEL

LILAC TIME

ADELPHI THEATRE

Mr CINDERS

course is a kind of history: the Astaires would return to London in two other Gershwin scores during this decade (*Lady Be Good* in 1926 and *Funny Face* in 1928) and almost alone they transformed the London musical stage. Not only had audiences simply never seen singing and dancing of such speed and dexterity: people actually working in the London musical theatre had never seen the like of it either. Within weeks of his first arrival in London, Astaire was already teaching Coward and Jack Buchanan the essentials of American tap-dancing, and it was Fred's uniquely casual, understated elegance of foot and voice that was to be the hallmark of the musical in this decade. From Coward and Buchanan to Sonnie Hale and Bobby Howes, they all wanted to dance and sing and star like Astaire: in that sense he was the first modern showman, the first to come on stage with no lingering traces of vaudeville or light opera in his manner. The kind of show that we now think of as a musical first came to London with the Astaires in *Stop Flirting*.

That year, 1923, also brought Heather Thatcher and Leslie Henson doing their famous three-legged dance on the deck of a luxury liner for *The Beauty Prize*, but as if frozen by the technical brilliance of Gershwin and the Astaires, London seemed to be waiting for the next show to come off the boat at Southampton rather than able to create any musical style of its own. The next year found Jose Collins in a red wig trying to be a musical *Nell Gwynne* (a task that would fall thirty years later to a no less implausible Anna Neagle) while in *Toni* Jack Buchanan and June established a dancing partnership which was, if not quite the Astaires, at least four feet in the right direction.

Other home-grown musical comedies were still largely the work of Harold Fraser-Simson, composer of *The Maid of the Mountains* and represented several years later by two West End scores: *The Street Singer*, which also had a book by Lonsdale and was respectfully considered by *The Times* to be 'a tuneful yet somewhat reminiscent account of a French painter in love with an English girl'; and *Head Over Heels*, which starred W. H. Berry as a circus tumbler masquerading as the heir to a dukedom. As Mr Fraser-Simson had also written (with Ivor Novello) the *Nell Gwynne* score a few months earlier, he could charitably perhaps have been considered over-extended at the keyboard in 1925. Yet a list of the other home-grown West End musicals for that year (*Bamboula*, *Betty in Mayfair*, *Love's Prisoner*, *Entente Cordiale*, *Nicolette* and *The Good Old Days*, not one of which seems to have yielded a hit song, let alone a subsequent revival) makes deeply chilling reading when set beside a list of the four shows that opened on Broadway that year within the month of September: first *No No Nanette*, then the *Dearest Enemy* that marked

Opposite. Programme cover for *Mr Cinders* (1929), featuring the stars of the show, Bobby Howes and Binnie Hale.

Rodgers' first encounter with Hart, then Friml's *Vagabond King*, and finally Jerome Kern's *Sunny* (marking his first collaboration with Hammerstein).

Sooner or later, all were naturally to make their way to London (indeed *No No Nanette* had already played there earlier in the year) but the West End was still limping badly: one hit song or one hit show could make it a good year, whereas on Broadway the strike rate was now up to about one a month. All the same, 1925 did have its charms: 'I Want To Be Happy' and 'Tea for Two' (both from *No No Nanette*) were the songs people were whistling in the streets around Shaftesbury Avenue, while Cochran and Coward revues entitled *On With the Dance* and *Still Dancing* suggested that the Astaires had not crossed the Atlantic in vain. Then there was *Rose Marie*, which opened at Drury Lane a week after the first night of *No No Nanette* and, after a shaky critical and box-office start, settled down to a run of 850 performances.

Nor was the traffic across the Atlantic totally easterly. Gertrude Lawrence left her training-ground in the London revues of Charlot and Cochran to take on her first-ever 'book' show: by appearing on Broadway to premiere the Gershwins' *Oh Kay!*, she became the first English star to create a leading role there in an American musical. Meanwhile, it was only by adding at a dress rehearsal the 'I Want To Be Happy' singalong that Vincent Youmans and Otto Harbach ever got *No No Nanette* right for the West End production.

Next year the Astaires returned to London for *Lady, Be Good* (Guy Bolton now working with George and Ira Gershwin instead of Kern and Wodehouse): this was the first of the Gershwin brothers' Broadway collaborations, their first for the Astaires, and the one that offered such memorable numbers as the title song, 'Little Jazz Bird' and 'Fascinating Rhythm' in a score so rich that they could afford to drop 'The Man I Love' on a pre-New York tour. The plot, carefully crafted for Fred and Adele, concerned a brother-sister dance team fallen on hard times and forced to masquerade as Spanish grandees, but then again it was not the plot that mattered here.

Nor was every critic totally won over by the Astaires: 'It is high time,' thundered the *Daily Telegraph*, 'that musical comedy returned from the hysterical to the historical.' And, as if in answer to that plea, several other hits of the year were set in locations as far from New York as possible. *The Student Prince* came from Heidelberg, *Princess Charming* was set in deepest Ruritania and *Lido Lady* was not surprisingly located on the Lido in Venice. All those scores survived six or more months and none lost money: equally, none of them managed, as had the Astaires and the Gershwins, to set the stage musical bubbling on a hob of inventive choreography and orchestration. To go from *Lady Be Good* to *Princess Charming* at a neighbouring theatre was in fact to take a journey back in time, one of several decades. The only surprise was that both styles managed to co-exist in the West End for so long, each apparently finding its own audience of devotees either ancient or modern.

With the notable exception of Noël Coward, virtually all the most promising singing and dancing players of the period had by now started to work for the Americans: Binnie Hale, Irene Browne, Jessie Matthews, Evelyn Laye, Beatrice Lillie and Jack Buchanan all began turning up in works by Kern and the Gershwins or their immediate Broadway contemporaries, though there was still discernible among some London theatre critics a distinctly anti-Broadway bias. In the case of *Sunny*, a 1926 reviewer could write in *The Tatler*: 'I know these American shows, I shall come home with one tune in my head, recovering slowly from a heavy bombardment by the orchestra and the whole company leaning over the footlights to tell me that they love me a little more at the close than they did at 8.15. Very nice of them, I'm sure, but if it happens again I shall stand up and sing back at them. It won't be the least difficult. It's sure to be the one tune in the show. Wouldn't it be fun if the entire audience suddenly rose en masse and, pointing back at the stage, sang at the top of their voices that one dreadful tune which has been rammed into their ears all evening?' Among *Sunny*'s 'dreadful tunes' were 'Who?' and 'Two Little Bluebirds', both of which were to remain in Jack Buchanan's cabaret repertoire for the next thirty years.

The following year brought Buchanan's old dancing partner from the Charlot revues, Gertrude Lawrence, back to London in *Oh Kay!* An entry in Guy Bolton's journals explains how she came to be involved in the American premiere of that show: 'I had seen her performing in the Charlot revues and had written her a note saying that I was willing to provide her with a straight comedy, a musical comedy or a revue, whichever she preferred. I slipped in a reference to my collaborator Pelham Grenville Wodehouse. I thought that might fetch her. It did. She replied by telegram – twelve sheets of it, saying that as soon as she was free she would put herself in my hands . . . The musical we wrote for her was a saga of those romantic days of the Prohibition era. It was laid at Montauk at the tip of Long Island with the Rum Fleet anchored twelve miles away, the hero's beach house boarded up for the winter, its cellars loaded with bootleg liquor and Gertie, coming ashore from her brother's liquor-laden yacht, intent on finding the man she had met for one magical evening and fallen in love with.'

Meanwhile, the Wodehouse diary records that apart from having to change shirts three times a day on account of the heat, PG had spent a happy American summer working on the new show with Bolton, secure in the knowledge that as George Gershwin was doing the score, his brother Ira would be doing the lyrics and therefore Wodehouse was only required to help out with the plotting.

That score was to include 'Clap Yo' Hands' and 'Do-Do-Do' and 'Maybe', but its show-stopping moment came when Gertie, alone on stage in a spotlight, sang a wistful number to a strange rag doll that George Gershwin himself had once bought her in a Philadelphia toy shop:

Won't you tell him, please, to put on some speed
Follow my lead?
Oh, how I need
Someone to watch over me . . .

As a summary of Gertie's own offstage needs throughout a remarkably disorganized private life, and as an echo of the desire for some sort of security that lay beneath the more insistent rhythms of the Jazz Age, that seems to me quintessentially the song of the era and one of the very few that can still grab you by the throat half a century later:

There's a somebody I'm longing to see
I hope that he
Turns out to be
Someone to watch over me.

But 1927 was also the year of *Hit the Deck* and *Lady Luck* and *The Blue Train* bringing the Merry Widow herself, Lily Elsie, back to the West End after a decade away. It was also the year of strong conservative rearguard action from *The Vagabond King* and *The Desert Song* ('The Riffs are Abroad', to which a jaded voice from the audience called back 'Oh yes? And where have they gone this year then?') for those who preferred their musicals more lustily sung. Then too there was *The Girl Friend*, a musical by R. P. Weston and Bert Lee which perhaps more than any other lent itself to the loving parody treatment that was – almost thirty years later – Sandy Wilson's *The Boy Friend*, though there was also a Rodgers and Hart *Girl Friend* which never made it over from Broadway, and Mr Wilson was in any case always careful to point out that he was parodying and celebrating a whole genre of flapper romances rather than any single period score.

In 1928 the Astaires were back in London together for the last time; in *Funny Face* they danced the 'Oompah Trot' and sang their way through that greatest of Gershwin scores, the one with 'S'Wonderful' and 'He Loves and She Loves' and 'My One and Only', not to mention 'High Hat' and the title song itself and 'Babbitt and the Bromide', among half a dozen others. But this was also the year that brought the collegiate *Good News* to the Carlton (where the orchestra tactfully dressed in American football sweaters) and above all else, towering above not just the season but the decade, Jerome Kern's *Show Boat* with Paul Robeson on stage to sing 'Old Man River'.

Gertrude Lawrence in the 1927 Gershwin musical *Oh Kay!*, in which she starred first on Broadway and then in London at His Majesty's; cartoon by Haselden.

In the face of such breathtaking competition, what else could the British musical look in 1928 but insipid? A show called *Lumber Love* all too aptly recalls its wooden score, while *Lady Mary* and *Virginia* were every note as pallid as their titles suggested. If the decade was not to end in total eclipse for the British, new composers had to be found or established ones borrowed from the world of revue: happily both proved possible in 1929. In a final and, some might think, unpredictable rally, the Twenties ended with two classic English musicals which could hardly have been more different in period or style.

The first of these was an enchanting small-scale reversal of the Cinderella legend: *Mr Cinders* brought Bobby Howes and Binnie Hale together for a lyrical romance between an impoverished young bounder and the millionaire's daughter he mistakes for a parlourmaid. As a plot, that was about as far as it went, but as a score it was magic, and as the one-man girl looking for a one-girl man Miss Hale gave what many believe to have been the greatest performance of her career. Few shows can ever have spread so much happiness from such a simple role-reversal, and when *Mr Cinders* reopened over half a century later, in the West End of the early 1980s, it was to find a whole new and delighted audience.

The other great hit of 1929 was at the other end of the economic and historical scale, born one weekend in the summer of 1928 when Noël Coward went to spend a weekend in the country with the family solicitor of his old friend and stage designer Gladys Calthrop. At the end of a long line of revues of which he had been author and star, from *London Calling* through *On With the Dance* to *This Year of Grace*, Noël found himself thinking about how and why romantic operettas had now virtually disappeared from the London stage to be replaced by the slick, fast, funny but somehow more heartless American musicals of the period.

53

Paradoxically, Coward had been one of the first of his 1920s generation to recognize the virtues of the Broadway stage, its pace and its urgency and its attack, but he was also the first to detect now around the West End a kind of nostalgia for the more sentimental escapism of the old Gaiety and Daly's musicals, and out of that the idea for an operetta began to take shape in his mind.

But it was only on the Monday morning after that weekend with Gladys Calthrop's solicitor, when they began to play a new recording of *Die Fledermaus*, that Noël found his setting. Alfred Lunt suggested the title *Bitter Sweet*, and the rest of the music progressed smoothly once the main tune, 'I'll See You Again', had established itself firmly in Noël's mind during a traffic jam on the way home from the theatre. His first idea about his heroine Sari (the character who starts the operetta as a dowager Marchioness in London and then, in a flashback to the Vienna of 1880, becomes the young tragic romantic heroine of fifty years before who loses her lover in a duel) had been that Gertrude Lawrence should play the part. But both he and she came reluctantly to realize that her voice simply wasn't strong enough for a score as long and elaborate as the one Noël was now embarked upon, so he promised her a play instead. As the play turned out to be *Private Lives*, Gertie never felt the loss of *Bitter Sweet* too keenly.

Coward then approached Evelyn Laye, the only other obvious choice for the role; she, however, was at the time less than delighted with the Cochran management who were to present *Bitter Sweet*, since it was Cochran who had brought her husband Sonnie Hale together with Jessie Matthews in a revue, a pairing that was to lead to the break-up of their marriage. *Bitter Sweet* was therefore still without a leading lady when, in New York, Coward ran into the American actress Peggy Wood in the lobby of the Algonquin. His old friend Alexander Woollcott suggested she might be right for Sari, and after a rapid audition she had signed the contract to open in London, though Cochran was to have severe doubts about the choice on account of her faint American accent.

Bitter Sweet then went into rehearsal on the stage of the Scala Theatre at the end of May 1929. It was, wrote Noël later, 'a musical that gave me more complete satisfaction than anything else I had yet written. Not especially on account of its dialogue, or its lyrics, or its music, or its production but as a whole. In the first place, it achieved and sustained the original mood of its conception more satisfactorily than a great deal of my other work. And in the second place, that particular mood of semi-nostalgic sentiment, when well done, invariably affects me very pleasantly. In *Bitter Sweet* it did seem to me very well done, and I felt accordingly very happy about it.'

Noël's first and most successful venture into the world of the nostalgic musical was in fact a lavish return, in three acts and six scenes, to the

The sheet-music cover, designed by Gladys Calthrop, of a pianoforte selection of
tunes from Noël Coward's triumphant venture into the Vienna Woods,
Bitter Sweet (1929).

Viennese past, and it represents Coward at his closest to Ivor Novello
with lilting, unashamedly sentimental numbers like 'Zigeuner' and 'If
Love Were All', as well as the classic 'I'll See You Again' which over the
years proved to be one of the greatest of all his song hits. Not
surprisingly, that number retained a very special place in his musical
affections: 'Brass bands have blared it, string orchestras have swooned it,

Palm Court quartettes have murdered it, barrel organs have ground it out in London squares and swing bands have tortured it beyond recognition . . . and I am still very fond of it and very proud of it.'

In the gloom of the Depression, Coward had realized that the time was more than ripe for a little romantic escapism, and *Bitter Sweet* was just that. It is true that in numbers like 'Ladies of the Town' and the jaunty 'Green Carnation' there were signs of a wittier, more pointed and less schmalzy musical, but by and large Noël and his audiences seemed happy enough to surrender themselves to the charm and the emotions that had filled the Gaiety and Daly's so successfully for so many years; if *Bitter Sweet* was not one of the original tales from the Vienna Woods, then it was certainly a very passable imitation.

With Peggy Wood engaged and arrived from New York, the rest of the characters proved easier to cast: Ivy St Helier was playing the lovelorn diseuse Manon, a part written specially by Coward for his tiny friend ('Miss St Helier has broken her leg in two places,' a distraught stage manager told him during the run; 'You mean it has two places?' queried Noël), and George Metaxa (who had only recently abandoned a promising career in the Romanian Ministry of Agriculture for the comparative insecurity of the stage) was cast as the music teacher Carl Linden. The young Robert Newton played Sari's priggish fiancé, and Alan Napier (like Newton a subsequent member of the Hollywood English Raj) turned up as the Marquis she ultimately marries back in London. Cochran left Coward totally in charge of the production after an initial squabble had been resolved over who should design the all-important sets; Noël had wanted his usual designer Gladys Calthrop to do them all, but Cochran insisted reasonably enough that if the second act, which was to take place in the Vienna café, was to stand apart from the London scenes of the first and last acts, it should be designed by a different artist. Accordingly, he brought in Ernst Stern, who had done the sets for Reinhardt's production of *The Miracle*, to design the second act. Expert help was also sought from Tilly Losch, who came in to choreograph one of the dance sequences.

In rehearsal, Coward found himself for the first time in charge of a company of nearly a hundred people, among them Sean O'Casey's future wife and Billy Milton who, cast as a young lover, remembered being told by Coward to 'play it very quickly and don't give them time to think'.

A great deal was at stake here – not only the £40,000 that Cochran was spending on *Bitter Sweet*, but also because this was Coward's first major work as writer, composer, lyricist and director; all went well enough in rehearsal, however, and when Cochran came to the final run-through, he was almost incoherent with joy at the effectiveness of it all. 'I would not,' he told the assembled company, 'part with my rights in this show for a million pounds.'

Noël Coward (second from left) with the impresario Charles B. Cochran and his
family on board the liner *Berengaria* at Southampton in July 1929, when they
sailed to the United States to start work on the Broadway production
of *Bitter Sweet*.

Coward for his part was in no doubt about the opportunity that
Cochran had at last given him after almost a decade of vastly more
fragmentary revues: 'DEAR COCKY,' read his telegram to the impresario on
the London opening in July, 'I HOPE THAT TONIGHT WILL IN SOME SMALL
MEASURE JUSTIFY YOUR TOUCHING AND AMAZING FAITH IN ME.'

Cochran's 'amazing faith' was indeed justified: though some reviews
proved to be distinctly cool (*The Times* wrote of 'a rather naive medley
for a man of Mr Coward's undoubted talents'), the first-night audience
rose to cheer a one-man English operetta the like of which had simply
never been seen or staged before. As James Agate put it in the *Sunday
Times*, it was 'a thoroughly good light entertainment'. The *Daily
Telegraph* was rather more enthusiastic: 'Crushing the serpent Jazz, Mr
Noël Coward has here created a work of art. *Bitter Sweet* has all the
essential qualities of its kind. The music flows with an easy grace, and
whether he borrows from Offenbach or Lehár, or dallies with some old
popular song, or gives us a waltz that owes Strauss for its ancestor, it is
always in the picture. The waltzes dominate the canvas, and Mr Coward
throws them off sometimes as if they were airy trifles, sometimes as if
they really were better than they sound. There is at least one number, the

officers' drinking chorus in the second act, which Offenbach would have been proud to write, whilst the ladies' sextet, mostly unaccompanied, in Act III is in the authentic tradition of the English part-song. Musically this operette is a remarkable production which starts a new chapter in the genre.'

Others were more grudging about Coward's orchestral 'borrowings' from the Viennese, and it was the *Telegraph* alone which pinpointed the importance of *Bitter Sweet* in the development of the English musical. Here for the very first time, teetering on the final edge of the 1920s, was a totally integrated show emanating from London with no discernible Broadway influence of any kind, save perhaps the presence of Peggy Wood. It was *Bitter Sweet*, and *Bitter Sweet* alone, which restored the London musical theatre to the confidence and pre-eminence it had lacked since the end of the Gilbert and Sullivan era some forty years earlier.

At the first night, one fashion correspondent noted 'tiara'd women clapped till the seams of their gloves burst; the older generation could say with more complacency than truth that this was the way they had fallen in love, and the younger generation were wondering if, in rejecting romantic love, they might not have missed something.'

The journalistic estimate was that *Bitter Sweet* would last six months at His Majesty's; in fact it lasted there for eighteen, then transferred to the Palace and ended its run in April 1931 after playing to cut-price audiences at the Lyceum. All in all, nearly a million people saw it during more than 750 performances in London, and counting subsequent American and French revivals as well as the film rights (it was twice shot, once in England with Anna Neagle and once in Hollywood with Jeanette MacDonald and Nelson Eddy) and the song royalties it would be fair to assume that *Bitter Sweet* made its author richer over the years by something in the region of a quarter of a million pounds. The published script was dedicated by Noël to Cochran, 'my help in ages past, my hope in years to come'.

The cover of a 1919 issue of *The Play Pictorial* featuring Beatrice Lillie in *Oh Joy!*,
the successful Jerome Kern/P. G. Wodehouse/Guy Bolton show which launched her
as a star of revues and musicals in the 1920s.

The American invasion
By the mid-1920s the West End musical scene was becoming increasingly dominated by shows imported from Broadway.

Above. Fred and Adele Astaire made their London début in *Stop Flirting* in 1923 (see p. 47), and George Grossmith and Irene Browne (*right*) starred in *No No Nanette* at the Palace Theatre in 1925.

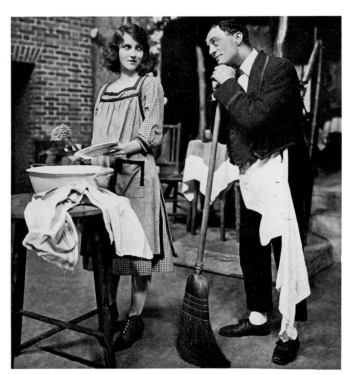

Opposite. Dorothy Dickson in the title role, with Leslie Henson as Constantine, in a scene from *Sally* at the Winter Garden Theatre (1921). *Above.* A scene from *Rose Marie*, which had a score by Rudolf Friml, Oscar Hammerstein and Otto Harbach; after an uncertain start at Drury Lane in March 1925, the show eventually ran for 850 performances.

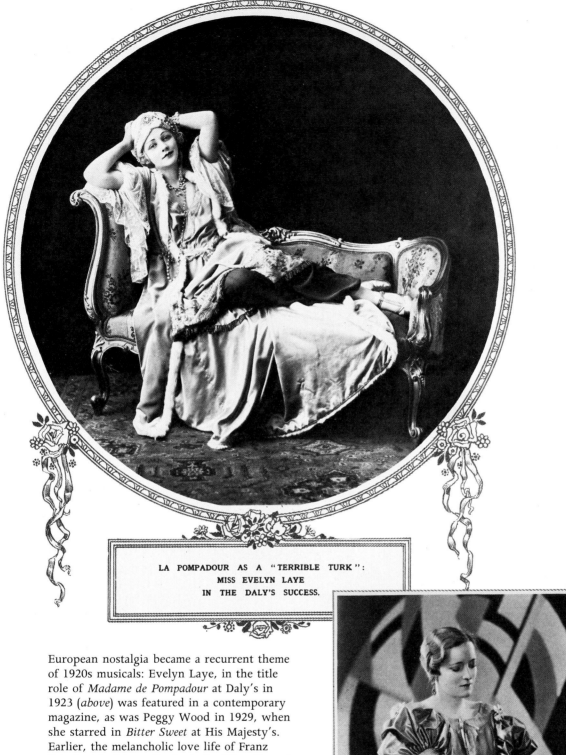

European nostalgia became a recurrent theme of 1920s musicals: Evelyn Laye, in the title role of *Madame de Pompadour* at Daly's in 1923 (*above*) was featured in a contemporary magazine, as was Peggy Wood in 1929, when she starred in *Bitter Sweet* at His Majesty's. Earlier, the melancholic love life of Franz Schubert had been the basis for *Lilac Time* at the Lyric (1922), with Courtice Pounds as the composer, seen (*opposite*) with Clara Butterworth.

1936

The Thirties

'ART MAY HAVE NO FRONTIERS but behind some frontiers there is precious little art,' wrote James Agate in 1929, dismissing yet another Germanic revival, this time of *The Student Prince*, and indeed there seems at the beginning of the new decade to have been a sudden critical and managerial realization that for too long the West End musical had been relying on overseas imports. If the Thirties were to be a time of economic retrenchment, they were also to be a decidedly more chauvinist and anglophile time in the London theatre. *Bitter Sweet* may have been set partly in a dear little Viennese café, and its second act may have ended in a duel, but it remained an all-English affair throughout and its success gave a new kind of confidence to writers and producers who had already spent too much of their time merely cobbling together English adaptations of European or American original scores.

Just as the Webber–Rice hits of half a century later were as important for the confidence they breathed into the British musical theatre generally as for their own merits, so *Bitter Sweet* spread a kind of confidence around neighbouring theatres. In these years, more than a decade before *Oklahoma!*, the resentment felt towards a Broadway invasion was already tangible; indeed it was Joseph Thorp, reviewing *Chu-Chin-Chow* in 1916, who had sounded the first anti-invasion battle cry. 'Oscar Asche,' he had written then, 'is no mere pilferer of other people's ideas and the unabashedly tuneful, pleasantly unsophisticated music of Mr Frederick Norton is Occidental in the frankest possible way *without being transatlantic or boisterously syncopated.*'

A great many of the musicals that followed *Chu-Chin-Chow* through the 1920s were of course both transatlantic and boisterously syncopated: but now, at the turn of the decade, altogether different sounds seemed to be emerging from the orchestra pits of the West End. The confidence of the Jazz Age had been replaced by an altogether more melancholy,

Opposite. Noël Coward, as the Duc de Chaucigny-Varennes, in his own *Conversation Piece* (1934), set in Regency Brighton; photo by Angus McBean.

yearning sound: that short mid-1920s period of *Rose Marie, No No Nanette, The Student Prince, Lady Be Good* and *The Desert Song*, all scores of tremendously upbeat confidence, had by now given way to softer strains and often impossible hopes. 'I Want To Be Happy' had yielded its place in the hit parade to 'Sometimes I'm Happy', and the line after that was of course 'Sometimes I'm Blue'. A kind of post-war confidence and brassiness had given way to the elfin waif-like figures of Jessie Matthews and Binnie Hale looking for a silver lining that often just wasn't there any more.

But the greatest problem for the British musical as it went into the Thirties was a curious lack of personnel: because it had been for so much of the Twenties an essentially second-hand business, with shows coming either from across the Atlantic or from Europe, much of the best local singing and dancing talent around the West End was still to be found in revue. It was only when musicals like *Bitter Sweet* began to be created in and for London that the climate changed, and some indication of that can be found in the original casting of the leading roles in the Coward operetta: Peggy Wood had to be tempted from New York and George Metaxa from Romania simply because the West End, even by 1929, had not yet bred artists of the talent required for an operatically scored, heavily plotted original musical.

Now, however, that all began to change, and very rapidly. In the theatre 1930 opened as one of the worst box-office years on record: 'Business bad,' read one report, 'due to Wireless, Daylight Saving Time, Motor Cars and Talkies' – and all these did indeed spell trouble. The two greatest threats to live theatre – radio and talking pictures – had come within five years of each other: summertime clock changes made for longer evenings spent in the garden, and car ownership meant (admittedly for only a few) an escape from the city and therefore also from its theatrical attractions. These were new problems, and they somehow had to be dealt with; moreover, the Depression of 1929 had suddenly put an end to the most lavish of the Broadway musicals, and that in turn meant that in 1930 there was not a lot for London managers to bring across the Atlantic. In a state of some shock, managements all along Shaftesbury Avenue now came to realize that they were out there on their own for the first time, and that prospects for the Thirties were already looking a lot chillier than they had in the Twenties.

Their first reaction was the perennial response of all theatrical managements in trouble: see if what has worked before will work again. Hadn't *Lilac Time* managed to link the life and music of Schubert and become a popular hit? Then *The Damask Rose* would surely do precisely the same for Chopin. Except that, for some unfathomable reason, audiences had wished to go to a musical life of Schubert but did not wish to go to a musical life of Chopin. Hadn't small-scale Charlot revues been the great success story of the West End in the Twenties, establishing the careers of Buchanan and Coward and Lawrence and Lillie? Then surely the recently opened Cambridge Theatre in Seven Dials should inaugurate 1930 with a lavish new Bea Lillie revue entitled *Charlot's Masquerade*? Except that, for some unfathomable reason, people didn't want to see revues any more. Hadn't the Gaiety had always done musicals? Then surely one entitled *The Love Race* and starring two popular comics, Laddie Cliff and Stanley Lupino, alongside two versatile young dancers, Madge Elliott and Cyril Ritchard, had to be a hit? Except that for some unfathomable reason nobody wanted to go to the Gaiety any more.

Until its closing weeks, therefore, 1930 was a year of comedies and thrillers and not a lot else; it was also the year in which musical-comedy audiences delivered notice to West End managements that they didn't really want any more of what had gone before, and would be staying at home with the new-fangled wireless or maybe even going to the talkies until Shaftesbury Avenue got its act together again.

Suitably enough, it was the most inventive and powerful impresario of the day who changed all that in December; Charles Blake Cochran already, thanks to Noël Coward, had, with *Bitter Sweet* and *Private Lives*, the two biggest hits in town. Now, turning his attention back to the modern musical, he was the first to realize that if the techniques that had been learnt in his own lavish revues – rapid changes of set and a fast-shifting sequence of sketches and songs – could actually be harnessed to some semblance of plot, then maybe audiences could be encouraged to give the British musical yet another chance.

They might, though, need something more than that to drag them back from the all-singing, all-dancing wonders of the new screen musical: what was needed was a flamboyant gesture of faith in stage spectacle, and Cochran found it in a comparatively simple device. His *Ever Green*, which opened at the Adelphi on 3 December 1930, was the first London musical ever built on a revolving stage. It was also a show of considerable delight: Richard Rodgers and Lorenz Hart, who had already written for several Cochran revues, were now sent by Cocky to Germany where a young dramatist, Benn Levy, was under contract to UFA, a major film production company. The plan was for the three of them to construct a plot which would show off the revolving stage to full advantage by allowing spectacular and frequent changes of setting, while also being slender enough to entertain those revue-minded audiences unable to retain details of characterization for more than a few moments.

Accordingly, Levy came with an outline story of a young woman who, in order to promote the fortunes of her beauty salon, exchanges her birth certificate with her mother's and then poses as a sixty-year-old rejuvenated by her own cosmetics. A storyline as undemanding as this allowed for the inclusion of huge Parisian cabaret numbers, as well as one entire fairground sequence on the revolve, and audiences were suitably impressed. 'A Feast of Colour,' headlined *The Times*, going on to note that 'here in this musical show, which is really a revue with something like narrative linking the different episodes together, is displayed once more that attention to trifles which makes for perfection. There is nowhere any fumbling or uncertainty of aim, and we get the impression that a knowledge of the end to which the piece is voluptuously moving has been drilled into everybody on the stage . . . the brain reels at such splendours, such quivering humanity, such a whirligig of principals, chorus and bystanders all set in motion as by a magic wand. And then there is music, music mercifully discreet, far from the all too violent vagaries of jazz.'

And such music: this last of the Rodgers/Hart London scores was also the greatest of all the Cochran musicals (it was later filmed with a drastically revised plot and score). It left one strong and lasting memory, perhaps the definitive musical image of these 1930s: Jessie Matthews, alone on stage in a pool of limelight, that eager, urchin, elfin face more than any other the symbol of the musical decade of which she was the brightest star, singing 'Dancing on the Ceiling', –

> *He dances overhead, on the ceiling near my bed,*
> *In my sight, through the night.*
> *I try to hide in vain, underneath my counterpane,*
> *There's my love, up above . . .*
> *I whisper go away my lover, it's not fair,*
> *But I'm so grateful to discover he's still there,*
> *I love my ceiling more, since it is a dancing floor,*
> *Just for my love . . .*

A score which had 'Dancing on the Ceiling' as just one of its outstanding numbers ('In the Cool of the Evening' was another) and which offered its audiences whole sequences set in the Royal Albert Hall (a beauty parade) and at the Neuilly Fair, not to mention scenes in the Casino de Paris and one of a religious festival in Catalonia, was unlikely not to succeed at the box-office, and indeed such was Cochran's confidence that he put Miss Matthews' salary up to an unprecedented £250 a week. 'I've spent tens of thousands of pounds on this show,' he told her reassuringly a few minutes before the curtain went up on the first night, 'so now it's all up to you.'

Backstage, though, all was not well: she was still in the midst of considerable matrimonial problems with Sonnie Hale, and her recollection of the staging of 'Dancing on the Ceiling' suggests already that the battle between star and management, a battle for supremacy that was to rage unresolved across footlights and orchestra pits on both sides of the Atlantic for the next fifty years, was already well under way. As

Jessie Matthews herself noted: '"Dancing on the Ceiling" was the big song and dance number in the show, and the way those men mauled it about! "She's too coy" said Benn Levy; "she isn't coy enough" said Rodgers. "Sweeter and lighter" said Hart. "I don't like it" said Cochran. I looked down at these four men so busy manipulating me. I felt like a puppet with tangled strings. Some demon took hold of me. What was I to them? Nothing but some image they had in their minds, an object, a bloody blueprint to scrawl their ideas on. I was sick and tired of letting four old men mess me about. What the hell did they know about love? How did they know how a girl in love really feels?'

In the end, she fell in with their wishes: '*Ever Green* was their creation, and even if I thought the storyline was corny and the character a mess, I was paid to play it.'

In her early resentment of the power-structure of the West End, or perhaps just in the fact that she was more intelligent than most of the ideas contained in the songs she was hired to sing, lay one of the greater difficulties that faced those who believed as early as this in the possibility of creating the genuine native West End musical. In this nobody would make a better star than Jessie Matthews: of her rivals, Evelyn Laye may have been more operatic, Gertrude Lawrence more comical, Cicely Courtneidge more farcical, Binnie Hale more winsome, Dorothy Dickson more stylish, Gracie Fields more popular. But Jessie Matthews alone seemed for a brief, shining moment to capture the bitter-sweet sexuality of the era: there was about her a vulnerability and a sense of triumph which perhaps Hollywood only ever found in Judy Garland, and intriguingly it was Jessie Matthews alone who for a while in the mid-Thirties managed to make a British musical cinema look like a distinct possibility. Her film director, Victor Savile, once summed up what it was that made Jessie Matthews special. 'She had a heart,' he said, 'and it photographed.'

This quality was also visible across the footlights to a quite remarkable degree, and it was the cause both of her stardom and her failure ultimately to celebrate or continue that stardom: in the end a traumatic private life overcame a chequered professional career and as early as *Ever Green* Jessie Matthews had in fact reached her peak.

But the failure was not hers alone: despite the genius of Cochran, despite the fact that writers like Coward, Novello, Benn Levy and Beverley Nichols were all working around the West End on plays and revues and occasional 'book' shows, it never seems to have occurred to anyone along Shaftesbury Avenue that the musical stars of the era would need to have scores created for them in the same way as, in America, composers were soon to start writing for legendary Broadway Babes like Ethel Merman and Mary Martin. In the 1930s nobody in England ever really sat down to write a show as a vehicle for Jessie Matthews or Evelyn

Laye: certainly Coward wrote for Gertrude Lawrence, but frequently in the straight theatre as he had no great opinion of her singing voice, and with reason. So by and large the stars of the era were simply shuffled into already existing scores, and because of that some of them began to seem dangerously interchangeable. Who now can be utterly certain without checking which scores of the early 1930s starred a dapper, jaunty Bobby Howes and which starred a dapper, jaunty Sonnie Hale?

Certain stars did of course carve out readily definable stage identities, but even then they seldom got beyond them: in a career of forty years and more than thirty musical shows, Jack Buchanan only ever starred in two (Jerome Kern's *Sunny* in 1926 and *King's Rhapsody* in 1951, when he replaced the composer on Novello's sudden death) that anybody anywhere in the world has ever bothered to revive. It was in 1931, however, that Buchanan established his partnership with Elsie Randolph, forming an ineffably elegant high-gloss dancing team who were to shuffle through the 1930s in the nearest equivalent to Fred Astaire and Ginger Rogers that was ever achieved on the London stage. The show was *Stand Up and Sing*, a characteristically mindless piece uncharitably referred to by one critic as 'Sit Down and Shut Up'; but a cast which included Anna Neagle in her first non-chorus job and Anton Dolin and Richard Murdoch by way of support ensured a long run at the Hippodrome, with Buchanan at his most casually charming in 'There's Always Tomorrow' (with Miss Neagle) and 'It's Not You' (with Miss Randolph), songs that he turned into definitions of his own infinitely laid-back style.

Down-market, it was a year of Gracie Fields in *Walk This Way* at the Winter Garden and Cicely Courtneidge rampaging through *Folly to be Wise* (which also boasted Nelson Keys doing impersonations of Maurice Chevalier). Beyond that, this was also the year that European operetta returned to London: the triumphant arrival of *White Horse Inn*, adapted from the German by Harry Graham, led directly to Richard Tauber in Lehár's *Land of Smiles* and, a week or two later, *Waltzes From Vienna* which the *Daily Telegraph* greeted as 'the Viennese Operetta in excelsis'. This musical story of Johann Strauss and his son was, reckoned *The Times*, 'a little too long, perhaps, as a biographical potpourri. But after the lightning largesse of Charles Cochran's splendours and the hustled song-and-dance work of the ordinary musical show, there is genuine relief in being allowed to sit back and savour a dallying fragrance instead of being forced to sit up and take notice of a thrill a minute.' Ivor Brown for the *Observer* thought that in the success of these tales from the Vienna Woods lay evidence that 'the Flight from Ugliness has begun on a wide front . . . here are charming ballets of the simplest elegance. No contortionist contorts, no acrobatic dancers make catapults of themselves to hurl audacious young women through the air like bullets.

70

The waltz and its mood are left to do their own work; the result has
infinite charm as well as the benefits of change from the tearaway
fashion.'

Away from Old Vienna, two other shows of 1931 were remarkable not
so much for themselves as for the pointers they offered to the future of
the West End musical: *Tantivy Towers* came from the Lyric Hammersmith
to the New (now Albery) Theatre as an introduction to the eccentric
world of A. P. Herbert, and *Hold My Hand* was an early score from the
greatest cockney-populist composer of the decade, Noël Gay, a man so
steeped in the British musical theatre that his *nom de plume* was actually
inspired by the poster for *London Calling*, a Charlot revue featuring Noël
Coward and Maisie Gay.

Born Reginald Armitage, and once a player in a dance band conducted
by Louis Mountbatten, Gay had started out as a classical musician but
graduated from the Cambridge Footlights to the revues of André Charlot
that were effectively the only training ground for all those involved with
the British musical between the wars. After several revue solos, he wrote
'Tondeleyo', the first song ever to be integrated into a British talking
picture, before finding his true métier as a composer for Bea Lillie, Cicely
Courtneidge, Jack Hulbert, Stanley Lupino and Lupino Lane, all of
whom saw in his novelty songs a welcome and popular alternative to the
chic of Coward or the Viennese schmalz of Novello and the Tauber
imports.

As for A. P. Herbert, although *Tantivy Towers* failed to take London by
storm, it did suggest that in a versatile satirist and (later) member of
parliament the West End had at last found a natural successor to W. S.
Gilbert. Herbert, too, was now working with a classical composer
(Thomas F. Dunhill) and like Gilbert before him was commendably
unafraid to bite the hands that were feeding him. At a time when West
End theatregoers were still drawn largely from the top social and
economic registers, when in other words most of them could reasonably
be expected to have places in the country and a certain interest in
hunting, shooting and fishing, Herbert gave them a rousing anti-
bloodsports chorus which began:

> *You fouled the charming country's breath*
> *With scent of blood and boast of death,*
> *While every spinney blushed for shame*
> *To be a partner in the game.*

Insofar as the West End musical of the Thirties ever had any kind of a
quirky social conscience, that conscience was A. P. Herbert's, and for
this reason his shows were still regarded as a mixed blessing by
audiences and critics alike. It was only fifteen years later, when Herbert
finally teamed up with a vastly more popular and hummable composer

than Dunhill, that he reached a sequence of hit musicals. That composer was of course Vivian Ellis, who started these 1930s as the most prolific and successful music man in town. Because of the huge triumph of his reversed-sex Cinderella, *Mr Cinders*, Ellis was now commissioned to write a cabaret musical for Sophie Tucker (*Follow a Star*), a Daly's score for *Little Tommy Tucker*, additional music for Buchanan's *Stand Up and Sing*, and a *Folly to be Wise* revue for Cicely Courtneidge, his contribution being hailed by Agate as 'the most knavishly witty music imaginable'. Then there was a Drury Lane disaster called *Song of the Drum* for Bobby Howes and a late Gaiety musical called *Blue Roses*. Nothing very memorable there, certainly, beyond a couple of numbers that might later prove useful for pianists to play at cabarets in smoke-filled rooms, but what matters is that Ellis was commissioned for all of these, indeed saw them all staged, within the 1930/31 season. After six such shows in only twice as many months, a gossip columnist noted waspishly that 'the single most remarkable thing about Mr Cochran's newly-announced revue for 1932 is that it will not have music by Vivian Ellis.'

In fact the 1932 revue for Cochran was to be another Coward show, *Words and Music*, which the two men conceived and staged as a radically small-scale alternative to their 1931 epic *Cavalcade*, arguably the most ambitious musical ever attempted even at Drury Lane. More than thirty years after the first (and for half a century the only) professional stage production in Britain of *Cavalcade*, Coward found himself at a fork luncheon in London the only man in possession of a knife. 'But of course, dear boy,' he explained to an impressed reporter (me), 'after all, I did write *Cavalcade*.' And if indeed Coward is to be considered in the light of any one single technical achievement in the theatre, then *Cavalcade* is undoubtedly the one. Not because it is an especially remarkable drama, not yet because it offers to the literature of the theatre any new or stunning insights, nor yet because of its chances of survival (which, until the 1980s revivals at Farnham and Chichester, and the Shaw Festival in Ontario, were considered wildly remote), but rather because of the massively impressive scale on which it was first conceived.

From a single theatrical notion, born one afternoon in 1930 in a London bookshop where Coward was leafing through some bound volumes of the *Illustrated London News* and happened upon a photograph of a troopship leaving for the Boer War, grew a grandiose show in three acts and 22 scenes covering thirty years of English upstairs-downstairs life. When indeed they came forty years later to make the television series *Upstairs Downstairs*, it was surely in tribute to Coward and *Cavalcade* that some of the principal characters bore the same names.

That first 1931 production of *Cavalcade* was to cost an almost unprecedented £30,000 to stage, and it was to keep a cast and backstage crew of three hundred people employed at Drury Lane for well over a

The set design for Gladys Calthrop for the pub scene in Noël Coward's epic
Cavalcade (1931) at Drury Lane.

year playing to a total box-office take of around £300,000. It was in short
an epic, and Coward's cable to Cochran from New York (when he was
appearing there in *Private Lives*) listing his principal technical and
musical requirements for the show ran to just over nine pages.

Among its many other firsts, *Cavalcade* was the first show to harness
its nation's musical past to its plot; the score contained only one major
new Coward song, but that too became a haunting echo of the times:

> *Blues, Twentieth Century Blues, are getting me down.*
> *Who's escaped those weary Twentieth Century Blues?*
> *Why, if there's a God in the sky, why shouldn't he grin?*
> *High above this dreary Twentieth Century din.*
> *In this strange illusion,*
> *Chaos and confusion,*
> *People seem to lose their way.*
> *What is there to strive for,*
> *Love or keep alive for?*

Elsewhere in this chronicle, Coward wrote loving parodies of
Edwardian musicals and quoted marching songs ranging from 'Soldiers
of the Queen' all the way through to 'Tipperary': not until Joan
Littlewood's *Oh What a Lovely War!* in 1963 would another London

musical attempt to tackle British history in terms of its popular music. But apart from two disappointing movie versions, all traces of *Cavalcade* then disappeared for half a century, and even the much-quoted toast 'that one day this country of ours which we love so much will find dignity and greatness and peace again' only finally resurfaced (unattributed) in a pre-election address on television by Margaret Thatcher.

The wonder of *Cavalcade* (and in 1931 most original reviews were more stunned than ecstatic) lay, however, in its breathtaking ambition: for Coward, only seven years after his initial London success with *The Vortex*, and still barely thirty, to have conceived something of this historical size and sweep was almost as though Neil Simon or Alan Ayckbourn were suddenly to have spent the middle 1980s writing and staging *Ben Hur* for the first time. But the original first night had its problems: the cast (which included the playwright Arthur Macrae and the youthful John Mills, as well as Binne Barnes and Mary Clare and the young Margaret Lockwood) all crowded on to one of the Lane's newly installed and revolutionary hydraulic lifts which Cochran had brought to London in the wake of his triumph with the revolving stage for *Ever Green*. During one set change the lift then jammed, and the orchestra had to play a particularly repetitive period waltz, 'Lover of My Dreams', over and over again for fully fifteen minutes until the lift was released and the show could go on.

That delay, and the feeling of suppressed panic that it caused among the company, affected the rest of the performance to such an extent that, despite the applause at the final curtain, Coward and his manager Cochran went home uncertain whether or not they had a hit. By ten o'clock the next morning, when Cochran tried to phone the Drury Lane box-office to see if they were doing any business, there was already a queue stretching about 200 yards, as far as the corner of the Aldwych.

So Coward had a triumph, but it was not for the reasons he had hoped: instead of being hailed for its spectacle of stage management (scenes ranged from Mafeking Night through the sinking of the *Titanic* to the General Strike, and Noël directed the first production by dividing a hundred extras into teams and colour-coding them across maps of the stage), *Cavalcade* was largely admired for its patriotic appeal in a difficult economic and social time. Reviews were headlined 'Coward's Call to Arms' or 'A Message to the Youth of our Nation', for what Noël had overlooked, in his usual total absorption in rehearsal and lack of political awareness, was that he was opening in October 1931, only a few weeks after Britain had come off the Gold Standard and a fortnight before a general election which was to bring about the return of a National Government in a mood of near-hysterical patriotism. His timing, though accidental, thus proved as immaculate as ever, and by making a curtain speech which concluded, 'it is, even in these difficult times, still a pretty exciting thing to be English,' Coward had clinched it.

Yet he had intended *Cavalcade* to be about a great deal more than a concept of unthinking jingoism or even patriotism. This is an epic devoted to a wider concept of duty, one that runs through much of Coward's other work, and somewhere in it can be found almost everything that mattered about Noël as a playwright and as a man. The sense of the past, the concept of duty and decent behaviour as being above all else, the brisk edginess of a forward-looking love scene set aboard a liner about to hit an iceberg, and above all a cascading sense of sheer theatre.

Cavalcade is not just about duty to nation: it's about duty to family, friends, circumstances and ideals, and in among the great processional crowd numbers is in fact a much smaller play, one entirely concerned with the fortunes above and below stairs of one archetypal English household from 1899 to 1929. But rather than leave it at a domestic convention he was later to explore in plays like *This Happy Breed*, Coward decided that a West End audience battered by the Depression might like to see something a little more lavish, hence whole nightclub sequences and a representation of Queen Victoria's funeral, not to mention a finale deliberately designed in sound and lights to rival the all-new wonders of the Hollywood musical.

Having watched all of that, plus a troop train pulling out of a stage replica of Victoria Station, the then manager of Drury Lane (George Grossmith) still complained that he saw nothing in the show to appeal to children during the Christmas holidays. 'By then,' replied Coward acidly, 'we shall have put in a Harlequinade' – and indeed that was about the only thing *Cavalcade* did not seem to have. Two weeks after the opening, on election night (28 October) King George V and Queen Mary with other members of the royal family were present, and the audience rose to join the cast in the national anthem: rumour even had it that Coward was, that night in the royal box, to become Sir Noël (though in the event he would have to wait another forty years before receiving that particular honour).

But the importance of *Cavalcade* was that, uniquely among stage musicals of the 1930s, it looked at the history of its own nation and raised certain questions about where that nation was now heading. It was to some extent a show about public and private morality, at a time when musicals were generally reckoned to be incapable of sustaining such ideas or any real themes beyond those emanating from a pianist in the pit.

The next year, 1932, brought Evelyn Laye in *Helen!*, an anglicized version by A. P. Herbert of Offenbach's opéra bouffe *La Belle Hélène*, given a production of stunning opulence by Max Reinhardt against the settings of Oliver Messel, including an all-white bedroom scene. Herbert and his new partner Alfred Reynolds, the resident conductor at the Lyric Hammersmith, then came up with *Derby Day*, an Epsom singalong which announced in its prologue precisely what its writers were trying to achieve:

> *We have defied the canons of the age*
> *And put the British people on the stage.*
> *Prepare your shoulders with the rough to rub:*
> *Most of the action centres in a pub.*

This was also the show which contained the immortal couplet 'Beloved horse, attend I pray; the Derby will be run today', but despite that, the *Sunday Times* review was a killer: 'There is not a single tune here which the commonalty will recognise as such.' European imports of the year included *Casanova* and *The Dubarry* and the Robert Stolz *Wild Violets*, while a number of old and reliable farces were now made over by various hands as 'plays with music'.

In a thin time, the only real smash hit came once again from Broadway: Jerome Kern's *The Cat and the Fiddle* was an attempt to adapt the conventions and traditions of operetta to a small-scale jazz setting, and a cast headed by Peggy Wood, Alice Delysia and Francis Lederer celebrated a score which included, among other evergreens, 'She Didn't Say Yes' and 'The Night Was Made For Love'.

The following year, 1933, proved more interesting, though largely because of just two Cole Porter scores shining through an otherwise dark theatrical and orchestral time. The first of these was *Nymph Errant*, which started out as a novel written by a young and then very junior keeper at the Victoria and Albert Museum by the name of James Laver: it told a simple but enchanting story of an English girl on her way home from school in Switzerland who falls in with a Frenchman and sets out with him on a series of adventures through which she travels wide-eyed, returning home at the last totally unaware of what she has just narrowly escaped in the way of sexual and other disasters.

Cochran and Gertrude Lawrence rapidly took the novel to Coward with a request for songs as soon as possible, to which Noël replied that though he would soon be writing for his old friend (in fact *Tonight at 8.30*), this would be something of his own devising; he was not, he added, the kind of hired hack who could simply be summoned to the piano whenever Miss Lawrence needed a vehicle for her talents.

Undaunted, Cochran and Lawrence next approached Cole Porter, who read the book in a single evening and was at work at his piano the following morning. What he had seen in *Nymph Errant*, according to his biographer Charles Schwartz, was 'the story of an English lass hell-bent on losing her virginity in such offbeat places as a sheik's desert tent, the Parisian follies, a Turkish harem and a nudist camp. Cole created an

Gertrude Lawrence as Evangeline, Iris Ashley as Madeleine and Austin Trevor as André in a scene from *Nymph Errant* (1933), a witty and sophisticated show with a score by Cole Porter.

extraordinary score for the show that not only kept pace with the heroine's global philanderings but added some wonderfully suggestive overtones of its own.'

Porter himself always said that *Nymph Errant* was his best score, although it remains, apart from its three great hits ('Experiment', 'The Physician' and Elisabeth Welch's great number 'Solomon'), among his least-known internationally, perhaps because the utter Englishness of the heroine denied the show an afterlife on Broadway or on film. But Cochran was determined to spare no expense on the only one of Porter's scores to have had a world premiere in London as the direct result of an English commission: he was already paying three writers (Laver, Porter and the actor Romney Brent) for the adaptation, and he now brought in Doris Zinkeisen to do the sets. Brent himself was directing, but most intriguingly there was also a revolutionary young American choreographer on her first major musical theatre assignment. Exactly a decade later, her choreography of *Oklahoma!* was to be seen on Broadway and a few years after that it was to send the British musical theatre into a state of shock from which, many would argue, it took fully thirty years to recover its confidence. But for now Agnes de Mille, niece of the first great Hollywood mogul, was content merely to send home to her mother extracts from a fascinating rehearsal logbook:

'Cole Porter is a small, finely boned and fastidious little man with a round doll head like a marionette's, large staring eyes and a fixed and pleased expression . . . he barely speaks, but make no mistake is the most powerful man in the theatre not excepting Cochran. His rhymes are fabulous, male, female, middle word which I suppose could be called neuter . . . Gertie on the other hand, although warm and charming, has been something rather special to deal with. Her art is built on instinct and improvisation: she disciplines her performance, I'm told, no more than her rehearsals, changing with whim and temperament and without warning. You expect Gertie downstage; she comes in centre back – even with the curtain up and a paying audience. You expect her to play grazioso and gently; she is allegro vivace and sharp. You expect her in a dark-green silk: she is in transparent gauze, but always fun.'

For James Laver, 'the combination of Cochran and Gertrude Lawrence was irresistible . . . on the [Manchester] first night of *Nymph Errant* I took her to the Opera House in a taxi. She sobbed in my arms, crying "I can't go on", but of course she did, and in two minutes had the audience at her feet . . . I suppose I shall never be involved in any capacity in a more glamorous affair. Manchester had suffered an invasion of fur coats and orchids and white ties and when we got back to the Midland Hotel, the stairs leading up to the dining room were lined five deep with people clapping and cheering Gertie.'

For Miss de Mille, more immediately involved in the show's mechanics than the author of the original book, disenchantment with Gertie's vagaries had come rapidly, as had disillusionment with the whole venture: 'The show began and it was as I'd suspected piffling. But the Porter songs are enchanting and the dances stopped the show. That's God's truth . . . Gertie breaks my heart because it is never my exact work she is performing but who cares? She sells tickets . . . she is funny, bright, touching, irresistible. When she walks, she streams; when she kicks, she flashes. Her speaking voice is a kind of song, quite unrealistic but lovely, and her pathos cuts under all, direct and sudden. Her eyes fill, her throat grows husky and she trembles with wonder. The audience weeps. She can't sing, but who cares?'

Some of the London critics, for a start: dismissing it as a 'pantomime for intellectuals', the *Observer* thought 'the piece is doomed to failure. In sentiment it is as parched as a pea, and the English public dotes on sentiment. Then again there is the deterrent of its unrelenting wit, the one quality of which the English public is uniquely shy.'

Nevertheless, *Nymph Errant* survived for six months and 150 performances, a respectable enough run, though admittedly less impressive than the other Porter show of the London autumn, *Gay Divorce*. This brought Fred Astaire back to the West End for the last time and offered a vastly more accessible plot about misunderstandings in a New York divorce court, plus a score featuring 'Night and Day', 'After You Who?' and 'I've Got You On My Mind' (this last sung by Fred to Claire Luce, his dancing partner in the brief interval between Adele's retirement and the discovery in Hollywood of Ginger Rogers and a whole new life for Astaire from which he was never to return to the stage).

But if 1933 was only retrieved for the London musical by young king Cole, 1934 could not even manage a Broadway transfusion. A desperately lacklustre year was in fact mainly notable for Frances Day and John Mills singing the Seesaw song from Vivian Ellis's *Jill Darling* and for another Jack Buchanan–Elsie Randolph soft-shoe shuffle, this one *Mr Whittington*, which took the old pantomime story (pantomime was still a major source of plots for musicals in a time that seemed remarkably bereft of writers able to think up original storylines for the linking of songs) and updated it to allow Dick to dream of himself as a policeman, a prospective parliamentary candidate, an Albert Hall boxer and a winner of the Derby. Leaving nothing to chance or audience imagination, the management also lowered a cinema screen during the show: on it the hero (Buchanan) could be seen making the winning hit in a Test Match, and victorious in both the World Billiards Championship and the Schneider Cup Trophy air race. There was also a minstrel show staged implausibly enough in the central chamber of County Hall (headquarters of the then London County Council) and Johnny Green was brought in from New York to write such Buchanan standards as 'Weep No More My Baby' and 'Like Monday Follows Sunday'.

But this was also the year of *Conversation Piece*, the first of Coward's two 1930s attempts to repeat the success of *Bitter Sweet* with yet another lavish, romantic and escapist musical. During the summer of 1933 Noël had been thinking about a possible vehicle for the French singer Yvonne Printemps, undisturbed by the fact that at that time she spoke barely a word of English. Watching her on stage in Paris, Coward had been enchanted by her voice and he felt sure that she could now learn enough English to cope with whatever plot he could devise. The result, some weeks later, was a sentimental comedy with music, set in Regency Brighton; but the central theme did not come easily, as Coward later recalled when describing the difficulties he had experienced while working at Goldenhurst, his farmhouse in Kent: 'I had completed some odd musical phrases here and there but no main waltz theme, and I was firmly and miserably stuck. I had sat at the piano daily for hours, repeatedly trying to hammer out an original tune or even an arresting first phrase, and nothing had resulted from my concentrated efforts but banality . . . I sat gloomily envisaging everybody's disappointment and facing the fact that my talent had withered and that I should never write any more music until the day I died . . . I didn't care if I became fried as a coot, so I gave myself another drink and decided to go to bed. I switched off the light at the door and noticed there was one lamp left on by the piano. I walked automatically to turn it off, sat down and played 'I'll Follow My Secret Heart' straight through in G flat, a key I had never played in before.'

The rest of *Conversation Piece* didn't work out so happily, however: a large cast included two men who subsequently became Hollywood stars, George Sanders and Louis Hayward, and Coward himself stepped into the lead only days before the premiere when Romney Brent decided that, as a youngish American comedian, he had been somewhat miscast in the role of a bitter and cynical middle-aged French adventurer. A subsequent recording suggests that Coward's accent was not a lot more convincing, but in production *Conversation Piece* stemmed from and then revolved around the personality of Yvonne Printemps who, like Evelyn Laye in the American premiere of *Bitter Sweet*, carried it through on the first night to a tremendous success which started on the personal level and then radiated out to the rest of the company. Without her it is doubtful whether *Conversation Piece* would have survived at all: the plot is less conspicuous than in Coward's earlier musical romance and rambles still further; the songs (with the memorable exception of 'Secret Heart') are also not up to the standards of *Bitter Sweet*, and there was little that other members of the cast could have done to fill out underdeveloped characters. In the lead, Noël was efficient but wooden; he himself also noted later that his plot bore some pretty remarkable anachronisms, not least an English packet-boat sailing blissfully for France at the height of the Napoleonic Wars.

But the reviews that mattered at the box-office, the ones in the popular dailies, were all excellent, and before long *Conversation Piece* was breaking theatre records, playing to standing-room only and taking almost £1,000 a night. Yvonne Printemps' English did not improve spectacularly during the season, but it was no mean tribute to her that by the end of it the rest of the company spoke with a convincing French accent. About eight weeks into the run, Noël began to suffer from a grumbling appendix and his usual restlessness brought on by playing a single part night after night for any length of time; he left the cast, to be replaced by Pierre Fresnay, who had the advantage of correct nationality for the part and a close offstage friendship with his leading lady.

An interesting row had, however, now developed between James Agate, still the leading theatre critic of his day, and Coward's producer Charles Cochran; in his notice of *Conversation Piece*, Agate had objected to an excessive amount of French being spoken on an English stage. 'I have timed with a stop watch,' replied Cochran in an indignant letter to the Editor of the *Sunday Times*, 'the amount of French spoken in *Conversation Piece* and it totals 3 minutes 57 seconds in a play which not counting intervals lasts for 2 hours and 20 minutes. I am not afraid of French on the English stage, indeed whole scenes of *Ever Green* and *Nymph Errant* were spoken in that language. I find that the upper parts of the house understand it and laugh at exactly the right moment. The laughter of drama critics and others in the Stalls usually follows a few moments later.'

There was not a lot more to be said for 1934 in the musical theatre, unless one counts a show called *She Shall Have Music*, about which the surprise was not the songs (ideas like 'Splashing in the Sea', 'You Must Be Very Careful In Love' and 'I'll Snatch the Man from the Moon' were lyrically not uncommon at the time), but the man who wrote them, the young Christopher Fry. But it was in December of that year, suitably enough in a most theatrical restaurant, the Ivy, that Harry Tennent, Cochran's only real rival at the head of the West End management hierarchy, was lamenting the dearth of really good new American musicals now worth transporting across the Atlantic.

The man he happened to be talking to was Ivor Novello, for many years since World War I a songwriter ('Keep the Home Fires Burning') and now also a playwright, actor, film star, director and manager. Novello was acutely aware that Coward, with whom he regarded himself as being in perpetual but friendly rivalry, had achieved in *Bitter Sweet* the one thing that he had not yet managed: a fully-fledged theatrical score rather than a batch of random numbers as material for another revue. This Novello clearly had also now to attempt, and, in Tennent's despair at what to do with a vacant Drury Lane in 1935, Ivor saw his chance.

The answer, suggested Ivor at that lunch at the Ivy, was not to go on forever looking hopefully out over the Atlantic or even across the Channel in the hope of finding new scores: nor was it to depend as other managements were on the likes of Coward (and A. P. Herbert, whose lyrical track record was decidedly patchy). Instead, the answer surely was to commission a show specifically for Drury Lane. Ivor was now forty-one, and had not written a note of music for ten years. On the other hand Drury Lane had not had a success since *Cavalcade* closed there in 1932, and the theatre's current run of an American musical (*The Three Sisters* by Jerome Kern and Oscar Hammerstein) was proving so disastrous that Tennent had not a lot to lose by listening to Ivor's plan: this was for the Drury Lane management to entrust him with an orchestra of forty, a cast of 120 and total autonomy to write, direct and star in a new musical of his own devising.

Unlike Coward, Novello was never a lyricist: however, he did have, in the company performing his current thriller *Murder in Mayfair*, a young poet called Christopher Hassall, and he took eagerly to the idea of writing lyrics for Novello's brand of lilting, lush music. Novello himself, however, took responsibility for the plot of the show that was to be called *Glamorous Night*, and this had at least the virtue of immediately establishing that the plot was not the reason why people went to a Novello show. In essence, *Glamorous Night* concerned a young television inventor who is paid £500 by Lord Radio to keep the process secret. Using the money to holiday in the mythical kingdom of Krasnia, he saves the life of a gypsy singer (female) who happens to be engaged to the local king. Undaunted by such arrangements, she follows the inventor to his ship, shortly to be wrecked; emerging from the waves, the inventor and the gypsy marry, only then to discover that if Krasnia is to be saved, she will have to return and become its queen, leaving the inventor to go back to London and watch her coronation on the screen he has invented.

Give or take one or two minor changes of detail and locale, such was to be the essential plot of almost all Novello's later shows. Even so, from *Glamorous Night* through *Careless Rapture*, *Crest of the Wave*, *The Dancing Years* and *Perchance to Dream* to *King's Rhapsody* (which was running at the time of his sudden death in 1951), Novello was to remain the most consistently successful British stage composer of his time. His success served as a sharp reminder that in those days it was quite difficult to overestimate the intelligence or desire for novelty of the average audience at a musical.

What Novello alone had tapped here was the middle of the market: between the cockney singalongs of Noël Gay and the urban chic of Coward and Buchanan, there lay a vast uncharted stretch which only foreign shows seemed attuned to: when Novello began to offer tales of the Vienna Woods filtered through the Welsh valleys of his childhood, he struck a chord in predominantly middle-aged and female audiences that no other composer ever quite managed to find. That this was to some extent a cynical operation is indicated by the alternative titles that he and his gay circle gave these lavish romantic spectacles (*The Prancing Queers*, *Careless Rupture*, *Perchance to Scream*); yet there is no doubt that for a largely innocent audience, unaware of the gap between Ivor's true sexuality and the dashing lovers he always played on stage, these shows provided some of the happiest theatregoing nights of their lives, and this despite the fact that, unlike Coward, Ivor virtually never sang in his own shows – a few words spoken across the keyboard to his leading lady while she was in mid-aria was about the most he would trust his own voice to deliver in time to any of his own music.

To star in *Glamorous Night*, Ivor enticed Mary Ellis, the original Rose Marie, back to London from Hollywood: he also began then to build up what was effectively his own personal West End repertory company of musical players, on stage and in the pit, who would follow him from

Characters from Ivor Novello's *Glamorous Night* (1935) sketched in cartoons by Nerman: (*left*) Ivor Novello as the English adventurer and Mary Ellis as the gypsy singer, and (*right*) Minnie Rayner as her companion.

show to show in the course of the next fifteen years. He did of course bring to his first Drury Lane musical a considerable personal following: unlike the infinitely more experimental Coward, Ivor had always specialized, even in the non-musical theatre and cinema, in a line of romantic adventurers. Through most of the 1920s and early '30s he had been the West End's answer to Valentino or John Gilbert, playing a sequence of destitute princes (*I Lived With You*) or starving composers going blind (*Symphony in Two Flats*) or handsome adventurers (in *The Truth Game*) which could now be seen as superb preparation for him and his matronly fans as they moved on to Drury Lane and an accompanying orchestra.

But Ivor had also learnt from *Cavalcade* that what worked best at the Lane was spectacle: having wrested a sizable budget out of H. M. Tennent, he now gave his customers gypsy weddings, shipwrecks, assassinations and all that in a single show, *Glamorous Night*. One or two critics recognized this extravaganza for what it really was: 'inspired punk' thought *The Tatler*, though James Agate solemnly opined that 'one left Drury Lane wondering why we should bother about a National Theatre when we have this'. Leontine Sagan, one of the first women to direct major musicals in Britain, and her designer Oliver Messel had spent several weeks in and around Budapest seeking ideas for authentic sets and costumes, and their lavish arrangement of Ivor's heart-wringing romance left not a dry eye in the house, but ensured £100,000 in advance box-office takings by the end of the first week.

There was just one major snag: Drury Lane had always been committed to putting on a Christmas pantomime, and the deal for 1935 had been signed by Harry Tennent shortly before *Glamorous Night* opened there in early May. Since the show was too big to transfer, and too costly to hold over, this meant that after barely six months of standing-room-only performances, despite the fact that it had easily earned back its £25,000 costs and was now running at a considerable profit, *Glamorous Night* would have to close. Furious at this prospect, Novello went to the Drury Lane board and offered them all the money he could then raise, £8,000, to cancel the pantomime; the board did its sums, estimated that the pantomime was already costing them £10,000 and asked Ivor for that. He refused to raise the balance, and *Glamorous Night* duly closed in November to mass outrage both backstage and at the box-office.

Feeling somewhat abashed, however, the board did hold out an olive branch: as soon as the pantomime was over in 1936, they agreed, they would much like to have Ivor return to the Lane with a new musical of his own devising. Just before *Glamorous Night* closed he therefore, within about a week, came up with a script and score for a new musical to be called *Careless Rapture* and read it to the assembled board at what he had now begun to think of as his theatre. The board listened politely and in total silence, leaving Harry Tennent to break it to Novello that though they did indeed want him back at their theatre, they really didn't want him back there with *Careless Rapture*.

As a result, 1936 opened in the London theatre with no prospect of another Novello musical and not a lot else around either: in the closing months of the old year Jack Buchanan had suffered a rare flop with a Parisian circus musical called *The Flying Trapeze*, and – apart from the ill-fated *Glamorous Night* – the only other really successful musical in town was Cole Porter's *Anything Goes*, in which the French star Jeanne Aubert played the role that had already made a Broadway star of Ethel Merman. The book was the work of P. G. Wodehouse, Guy Bolton, Howard Lindsay and Russel Crouse, and for the London production Wodehouse slipped in a few local references. With a Porter score that featured not only the catchy title song but also 'You're The Top', 'I Get a Kick Out Of You', 'Blow Gabriel Blow' and 'All Through The Night', it was perhaps not altogether surprising that English composers still regarded the American presence in the West End with a mixture of resentment and sheer awe.

With Novello still deep in the gypsy dancing of Krasnia, only one English stage composer could challenge Porter and the Americans from a position of anything like comparable strength, and he of course was Noël Coward. Noël spent the year writing and directing and starring in not just one, but a sequence of nine new one-act plays and musicals under the overall title *Tonight at 8.30*, written for himself and Gertrude Lawrence. They both welcomed the chance to play in three different shows every night, this being a wide-ranging sequence of dramas, comedies and romances, among which was the one that was later to achieve lasting fame on film as *Brief Encounter*. Of the musicals, *Red Peppers* was an acid satire about the tacky music-hall tours that had been so much a part of Gertie's musical apprenticeship, and *Shadow Play* was a haunting echo of *Private Lives* in which another couple faced with a broken marriage try in song and flashback ('Small talk, a lot of small talk, with quite different thoughts going on behind') to recapture their first meeting. Ivor Brown for the *Observer* noted of Coward that 'a man who used to write very slight long plays is now composing very full brief ones', but the melancholy significance of *Tonight at 8.30* was that it would mark all too soon the end of the Noël and Gertie partnership that had started in the Charlot revues a decade earlier. They were never again to appear together on a London stage, and without the oddly haunting music of their clenched, bitter-sweet partnership the London stage was never again quite the same.

Apart from *Tonight at 8.30*, this was the year of the last big Jack Buchanan/Elsie Randolph dance marathons, *This'll Make You Whistle*, but now, with the break-up of the Noël and Gertie and the Jack and Elsie partnerships, as all four moved on to other partners and other shows (none of which ever quite recaptured the elusive magic of their teamwork), there was already a feeling that an era was coming to an end. Admittedly this was abdication year, too; but spiralling costs, ever-more impressive Broadway expertise and a desperate paucity of composers and lyricists were making the brief early-'30s flowering of the London stage musical look like the result of freak conditions in a hothouse.

Such was the climate in which the management of Drury Lane realized they could not, after all, survive without Ivor Novello; having rejected his *Careless Rapture*, they had gone into the pantomime and then put on a Binnie Hale musical called *Rise and Shine*, which signally failed to do either and closed after less than fifty performances. Now, having nothing else remotely ready to fill that large and expensive stage, Tennent's management went sheepishly back to Ivor and said that they would in the circumstances be prepared to reconsider the merits of *Careless Rapture*. Novello now had them over a barrel: in return for his return to the Lane, he was able to negotiate a no-pantomime clause in the run, full artistic autonomy over sets, casting and even budget, and generally to take charge of a kingdom where he was to rule unchallenged for the next ten years, surviving even a short prison sentence to return to his faithful flock. 'His knees,' once wrote St John Ervine waspishly, 'his shins, even his thighs and his dear little wiggly toes cause palpitations in the pit and sighs of satisfaction in the galleries.'

On *Careless Rapture* Novello had managed to cut himself in for three-quarters of the production, and to his credit this did not mean any saving on the sets: audiences were this time treated to a Chinese Ballet in which Ivor himself danced, a cockney busking scene set during a fair on Hampstead Heath, and an all-white finale set in a Chinese Temple, with Dorothy Dickson waiting at the altar for Ivor to burst in all hot and tattered from a nasty encounter with yet another band of brigands. *Careless Rapture* also featured an earthquake scene and a happy ending, this last written in response to the complaint made by George V who, after attending a performance of *Glamorous Night*, had told Ivor backstage that the Queen had been brought to tears. As Queen Mary was not a drama critic, this must have been on account of its downbeat ending, something Novello took care to rectify this time around, although alas too late to please the King, for he had died in the meantime.

To listen now to the early Novello scores is to realize how close he was as a composer to the Kalman of *Countess Maritza* or to countless other minor Lehárs of the period: though Hassall's lyrics tend to have a plodding banality which makes these works largely unrevivable today, the music does swoop and soar in all the right places and *Glamorous Night* did offer in 'Fold Your Wings' and the title song a couple of numbers that were to keep palm court orchestras at English seaside resorts happy for several years to come. Even so, it is hard to say the same for any single number from *Careless Rapture* unless one counts 'Bridge of Lovers', sung by Olive Gilbert in the finale. One of the enduring problems about Novello's music was that because he always cast himself as a non-singing hero, and because his experience of heterosexual love was, to say the least, limited, he could only ever write love songs for a single female voice: the duets were something else altogether, and something he never entirely conquered until the very end of his life when, with Alan Melville as lyricist, he suddenly broke away from all the Straussery and wrote instead a wickedly funny backstage musical called *Gay's the Word* which suggested – only a month or two before his death – that he was about to embark on a whole new style of songwriting, one that owed more to *42nd Street* than to the Vienna Woods.

Careless Rapture ran on through 1937 until it was replaced by the third of the Novello shows, *Crest of the Wave*, at Drury Lane, but this Coronation Year was otherwise notable for two musicals which at either end of the social and national spectrum more or less defined the state of the art. At its lowest but perhaps most immediately enjoyable level, a whole succession of revues and musicals starring the likes of Cicely Courtneidge and Leslie Henson and Nelson Keys had over the last two or three seasons suggested that there was a real market for low-life singalongs having none of the pretensions of the middle European or American musical. In 1937 one of these really caught fire; it was called *Me and My Girl*.

The composer of *Me and My Girl* was Noël Gay, working with Douglas

Furber and Arthur Rose, and together they had already achieved a number of hit novelty numbers in revues and musicals. This, however, was something else entirely: another variation on the old Cinderella story which had served Vivian Ellis so well for *Mr Cinders*, it was all about a Lambeth barrow-boy finding himself suddenly among the aristocracy. Lupino Lane, the greatest cockney singer-comedian of his generation, played the lead and though the production got a mixed critical reception and was slow to catch on, it was saved when a BBC radio unit had to cancel a planned visit to an outside broadcast location and decided instead to relay some of the show live from the Victoria Palace. It was the first time that a West End show had been broadcast in a live-audience situation, and when listeners at home heard Lane 'Doing the Lambeth Walk' to cheers of delight, they decided that they too had to visit the Victoria Palace. As a result, *Me and My Girl* ran for the next five years, despite being bombed out of two theatres early in World War II, and the 'Lambeth Walk' became everything from a coronation anthem in 1937 to a marching song in 1942. (In the mid-1980s *Me and My Girl* returned to the West End to considerable acclaim in a production devised by Noël Gay's son Richard Armitage, and from there it went on to make its California and Broadway debut; its success in New York rivalled even that of *Cats* and the *My Fair Lady* it faintly resembled.)

The triumph of *Me and My Girl*, much like that of the antics of the Crazy Gang (also deeply identified with the Victoria Palace theatre), was its immediacy and its accessibility: Noël Gay wrote the kind of songs that people not only sang in their baths but also imagined they could write in their baths. Sunny, optimistic, patriotic numbers that seldom taxed brain or pen were his speciality: indeed Gay's most quintessential and popular song is the one with the simple chorus refrain 'Run, rabbit, run, rabbit, run, run, run'.

But if in 1937 the West End took *Me and My Girl* to its coronation heart, revelling in its aura of Lambeth folksiness and the carefully rehearsed impression that the whole affair could have been just another knees-up around the piano in a south London pub, there was something distinctly more chilly about the way that critics and audiences greeted the other great musical of the year. Rodgers and Hart's *On Your Toes* was, on Broadway as in London, the first musical ever to incorporate ballet into its plot and staging: the story of a contest between classical and modern dancers leads up to the whole of 'Slaughter on Tenth Avenue' and an elaborate pastiche called 'La Princesse Zenobia', both choreographed by the great Balanchine. All that, and a score which also featured 'There's A Small Hotel', failed to save *On Your Toes* and it managed a West End run lasting less than a hundred performances. As the editor of *Theatre World* icily noted, its mistake was to have a coherent plot and great dancers at a time when 'in order to succeed, the West End

Vera Zorina and Jack Whiting in the 'Slaughter on Tenth Avenue' ballet from *On Your Toes* (1937), as seen through the eyes of cartoonist Tom Titt in *The Tatler*.

musical play should be pointless to the verge of inanity, with a plot that enables the chief comedian to lose his trousers, hide in a grandfather clock, dress as a woman, burst into mock operatics and fall over at least a dozen times.'

Either it needed such qualities in order to succeed, or else a score by Ivor Novello: his third offering, *Crest of the Wave*, found Ivor doubling up as an impoverished Duke and a Hollywood villain in yet another complex plot of the utmost inanity. This one, however, included at least one great hit song (the massively patriotic 'Rose of England') and although there were some dissenters, not least the critic of the *Observer* who noted that 'one staggers out of Mr Novello's latest musical sated and a trifle stunned, observing with a bloated species of relief as at the end of a long Christmas dinner with the family that this occasion is mercifully over for another year,' Novello achieved another six-month run followed by a very long and lucrative provincial tour.

In the year that now remained before the outbreak of World War II, only two musicals of any real distinction opened in the West End and predictably one of those was by Ivor Novello, the other by Noël Coward. Once again a period of considerable economic and political uncertainty had driven most other composers, stars and audiences back to the easier world of revue, where topical allusions could quickly be put into sketches and the running order of songs altered to accommodate ever-quickening changes in public musical taste. Somehow the amount of time, energy, money and coherent thought that had to be invested in a new musical before there was any way of gauging its possible success or failure served to make the form ill-suited to the times. Revues were quicker and easier to stage, and talents such as those of Beatrice Lillie, the Hulberts and later the Hermiones – Gingold and Baddeley – found they could have a lot more fun with a novelty song or a quick satirical sketch than they could with the labour of building one entire character part over an entire evening. Just as Coward and Lawrence had turned back from *Private Lives* to their earliest revue training for the quick-change plays that made up *Tonight at 8.30*, so the rest of London now began to prefer the idea of something changeable and speedy to the more cumbersome operettas of old.

Which, paradoxically, was precisely the moment when Coward decided to try his luck with another operetta. *Operette*, the second and last attempt that Noël made to follow the nostalgic success he'd had with *Bitter Sweet* almost a decade earlier, was also one of the least successful musicals he ever wrote, and it served only to underline how triumphantly Novello had now invaded and conquered that particular corner of Coward's much wider theatrical territory. It was the story of an imaginary Gaiety Girl in the early 1900s who achieved stardom overnight but then had to sacrifice her love life to her career, and within its two acts and seventeen scenes Coward left no cliché of backstage life unturned. There was the understudy who took over at a few moments' notice after the star had a tantrum, the actress in love with the young aristocrat whose stiff-backed dowager mother ordered her to give him up, and the star who staggered on with the show in the face of overwhelming grief and in response to lines like 'Go on and act . . . act better than you have ever acted in your life.'

But as Coward himself later noted, the main trouble with *Operette* was that it was overwritten and undercomposed, so that in production the plot became an elaborate and top-heavy affair which the songs were unable to carry. This was where the structure that had served *Bitter Sweet* so well tended to collapse, and with the one great exception of 'Stately Homes of England' there were no showstoppers at all. The action of *Operette* switched rapidly between the play-within-a-play and the backstage lives of those involved in it, a device which considerably confused many theatregoers. On the first night, Coward leant out of his stage box only to see bewildered theatregoers furtively striking matches and rustling through their programmes in a frantic effort to find out where they were and what the hell was supposed to be going on.

By now it was too late to rescue *Operette* anyway, and the notices were unusually bleak: 'I can stand any form of criticism,' said Noël once, 'as long as it's unqualified praise.' On this occasion it wasn't, and *Operette* staggered through a run lasting barely three months.

The collapse of *Operette* left Ivor Novello at Drury Lane, and the Lambeth Walkers at the Victoria Palace, in sole charge of the West End musical as World War II loomed. Following the lengthy tour of *Crest of the Wave*, Ivor had promised a new musical not only to his Drury Lane management and regulars on both sides of the footlights, but also to a new singer, Roma Beaumont, who had taken over from Dorothy Dickson on that last tour.

This new musical was to prove the greatest of all Novello's successes and the best of all his scores: where his previous caution in doling out the hit numbers had meant that Drury Lane audiences were lucky if they got one per show, *The Dancing Years* introduced 'Waltz of My Heart' and 'My Dearest Dear' and 'I Can Give You The Starlight' and the Edwardian pastiche 'Primrose' among half a dozen others. It also even had a moment of topical social comment (a protest against German treatment of Austrian Jews), which was all the more courageous in early 1939 for the fact that it was saved until the finale, though the theatre management insisted on the deletion of all specific references to Hitler and the banning of Nazi uniforms on stage.

But by celebrating the world from which he had always borrowed his best themes and ideas, and by having as the hero of *The Dancing Years* a starving young composer (played of course by himself) torn between an innkeeper's daughter (Roma Beaumont) and the star of the Vienna Opera (Mary Ellis), Novello managed to combine *Mayerling* with *The Waltz King* for an evening of unadulterated nostalgic sentiment. Even Christopher Hassall rose to the occasion, with lyrics that seemed not just to represent but also to summarize and bid farewell to a whole light-operatic Central European tradition that was about to vanish, swept away by the events of World War II:

> *My dearest dear,*
> *If I could say to you*
> *In words as clear*
> *As when I play to you,*
> *You'd understand*
> *How slight the shadow that is holding us apart.*
> *So take my hand*
> *I'll lead the way for you,*
> *A little waiting, and you'll reach my heart.*

Ivor Novello in *Glamorous Night* (1935) at Drury Lane; this was the first of a series of musical successes that were to establish him as the last of the great West End matinée idols.

Dorothy Dickson with the chorus (*left*) in Ivor Novello's *Careless Rapture* (1936) and (*right*) with Novello himself in the Drury Lane production. Shortly before the outbreak of World War II, Novello continued his run of successes there with *The Dancing Years*, appearing as a starving young composer, seen (*below*) with Mary Ellis as a star of the Vienna Opera.

Of all the leading ladies of the 1930s Jessie Matthews was the most romantically vulnerable, endowed with a wistful little-girl-lost quality (*left*) which contrasted with the brittle glamour of the others; she is seen (*below*) on stage with her then husband Sonnie Hale in Rodgers and Hart's *Ever Green* (1930), the show which included her solo performance of 'Dancing on the Ceiling', the sheet-music cover of which is shown (*bottom, left*).

The elegant Jack Buchanan (*right*) was the nearest the West End came to producing a British-born rival to Fred Astaire.

A cover illustration of *The Play Pictorial* shows Jack Buchanan with his regular dancing partner, Elsie Randolph, in *Mr Whittington* (1934) at the Hippodrome (*above*), and the two stars are seen together (*right*) on stage in *This'll Make You Whistle* (1936) at the Palace Theatre.

Nymph Errant

This Cole Porter show, the programme cover for which (*left*) shows the façade of the Adelphi Theatre in the Strand, ran there for six months in 1933; its leading lady, Gertrude Lawrence, dancing with her leading man, Walter Crisham (*opposite*), found herself in a variety of exotic locations in the course of her travels (*below*).

Act ONE   WALTZES FROM VIENNA   Act TWO

Scene 1   Outside Ebeseder's Pastry-Cook Shop
Scene 2   ...   .   The Garden
Scene 3   ...   .   The Sitting Room

All the following Scenes occur in Doumayer's Gardens
Scene 1   ...   .   The Ballet
Scene 2   ...   .   The Pavilion
Scene 3   ...   .   The Gardens
Scene 4   ...   ...   Another part of the Gardens
Scene 5   ...   .   The Ballroom

MUSICAL NUMBERS
The Orchestra under the direction of WALFORD HYDEN

1.   ...   .   RADETSKY MARCH
2.   "Morning"   ...   .   RESI
3.   "Look before you Leap"   ...   RESI and LEOPOLD
4.   "You are My Songs"   ...   RESI, STRAUSS and CHORUS
5.   "Love will find you"   ...   RESI and STRAUSS
6.   "On love alone"   ...   BRIDE and BRIDEGROOM
7.   "Like a Star in the Sky"   ...   COUNTESS and STRAUSS
8.   "With all my heart"   ...   RESI

INTERVAL

MUSICAL NUMBERS

9.   "Night"   ...   .   CHORUS
10.   ...   .   BALLET
11.   "To-day"   ...   ...   RESI and LEOPOLD
12.   "One Hour"   ...   ...   STRAUSS
13.   "We Love You Still"   ...   COUNTESS
14.   "While You Love Me"   ...   RESI and STRAUSS
15.   "Love and War"   ...   LEOPOLD and CHORUS
16.   ...   .   QUADRILLE
17.   "The Blue Danube"   ...   RESI and ENTIRE COMPANY

Music arranged by
E. W. KORNGOLD, JULIUS BITTNER
G. H. CLUTSAM and HERBERT GRIFFITHS

European operetta on the London stage in 1931: (*above*) inside spread from the programme of *Waltzes From Vienna* at the Alhambra; Richard Tauber as Prince Sou Chong in Lehár's *Land of Smiles* at Drury Lane (*opposite, top*); and a scene from *White Horse Inn* at the Coliseum (*opposite, below*).

Towards the end of the decade, Noël Coward made his final attempt to repeat the magical nostalgia of *Bitter Sweet* with *Operette* (1938) at His Majesty's; the main inspiration for his score had been a desire to lure the great Fritzi Massary, seen (*right*) with Coward, out of European retirement, but the show as poorly received and closed after a three-month run.

Me and My Girl

The 'Lambeth Walk'
line-up, with the star
of Noël Gay's 1937 hit,
Lupino Lane, at the
Victoria Palace.

The Forties

'WHEN THE SECOND WORLD WAR began in 1939 I decided,' wrote Noël Coward, 'with tight-lipped patriotism to renounce all creative impulse for the duration and devote myself hook, line and sinker to the service of my country. This gesture, admirable as it appeared to me at the time, turned out on more mature consideration to be rather a silly one.' Nevertheless, it was far from his alone: the declaration of war on 3 September not only brought about a temporary closure of London's theatres, it also froze any desire to create new musicals.

A couple of weeks into September some theatres did, however, reopen for daytime performances, and the West End therefore went to war with *Me and My Girl* (one of the very first shows to reopen) now well into its third year at the Victoria Palace and *The Dancing Years* well into its first at Drury Lane. But there was not a lot else around, and although an ailing and aging Charles Cochran firmly announced to the press that 'my collaborators and myself will continue to prepare for the day when we are told to turn on the tap,' there was no sign of when that day might come or indeed of what audiences were expecting to pour out of the tap.

In fact, the bomb that fell on West End musicals did not come from an enemy power at all: it was first detonated on Broadway in March 1943, in the shape of *Oklahoma!*, but its impact would not be felt in London until four years later. In the meantime, the first reaction of theatre managements in 1939 was that World War II might prove only to be part two of World War I, providing a climate in which the same shows might work again. A revival of *Chu-Chin-Chow* was soon tried, and another of *Young England*; *Blossom Time* and *Old Chelsea* were duly taken out of mothballs too. But the radical changes that had come about in popular taste during the 1920s and '30s, the glimpses of the new musical world that Broadway had to offer, and the alternative forms of entertainment now provided by the radio and the talking picture (both easier to sustain

Opposite. Mary Martin modelling one of her gowns for Noël Coward's *Pacific 1860* (1946), watched by the designer Gladys Calthrop and the composer.

in wartime) meant there was no longer much interest in what had kept the home fires burning a quarter of a century earlier.

More than ever, this was a time of revue: just as the quick-change format had suited the roaring Twenties and the turbulent Thirties, so now shows like the Crazy Gang's *Little Dog Laughed* and *Black Vanities* and *Shephard's Pie* (the title derived from the name of its impresario, Firth Shephard) proved a lot more suitable to theatres that might at any moment be blitzed out of existence and to potential audiences who no longer knew how much time was left to them on earth, let alone in a theatre. A musical was still a sustained gesture of economic defiance and (sometimes) intellectual development of thought, and that was not a guarantee of success in 1940.

The catalogue of new musicals staged in London during the war years is thus a short and generally dismal one: even Novello was forced to clear out of Drury Lane to make the theatre available as a headquarters for ENSA (the armed services entertainments organization informally dubbed Every Night Something Awful) and *The Dancing Years* thus camped out in more senses than one at the Adelphi. Elsewhere, few managements deprived of resources and military-age casts were likely to risk a new musical when an old one might do a lot better; these were therefore the years when the West End saw again not only *Chu-Chin-Chow* but, in 1942 alone, *White Horse Inn*, *The Maid of the Mountains*, *Rose Marie*, *The Belle of New York* and *Lilac Time*. The following year brought back *The Merry Widow*, *Show Boat*, *The Vagabond King* and *The Desert Song*, while 1944 saw the return of *The Quaker Girl*. Many of these productions were cut-price wartime economy versions, suitable for touring afterwards to entertain the troops.

The idea of a new musical specifically written for or about World War II seems to have appealed to remarkably few people on either side of the footlights, though it is true that in 1943 Harold Purcell and Harry Parr-Davies had a modest success at the Hippodrome with *The Lisbon Story*, which had a contemporary espionage plot and a leading lady shot down in a dramatic finale. But audiences who could accept the wartime romanticism of *Casablanca* in the cinema did not seem to want any of that on stage, and as a result West End musicals remained locked in a pre-war time-warp.

There was also a distinct lack of composers or lyricists around the West End: with Coward abroad for the duration, first in a propaganda office in Paris and then on countless troop tours, and both A. P. Herbert and Vivian Ellis serving in the Royal Navy, only Novello was left of the first division team, though at the head of the second division (where I would group those composers less interested in the overall shape of a show than of an individual number) Noël Gay kept Lupino Lane going at the Victoria Palace through the war with shows like *La-di-da-di-da* and

Meet Me Victoria, which while never living up to the success of the original *Me and My Girl* yet managed to echo something of its cockney charm. But Lane's only true rival now in the world of popular musical comedy was Bobby Howes, who had survived the 1930s in a succession of minor Tunbridge and Waller scores like *Yes Madam* and *Please Teacher* and *Bobby Get Your Gun* and now spent the war largely on tour in revue and seasonal pantomimes, while further up the cultural ladder (though not a lot) Eric Maschwitz's chief contribution to the era was a haunting revue song, 'A Nightingale Sang in Berkeley Square', which Judy Campbell launched in *New Faces of 1940*. From there Maschwitz went on to *Waltz Without End* (1942), which featured the life and music of Frédéric Chopin and drew fire from Agate in the *Sunday Times*: 'To alter a composer's rhythms, key and tempi is to murder that composer, and to make voices sing words that are the acme of tawdry nonsense is to destroy an exquisite reputation.'

Richard Tauber ran into no such trouble with *Blossom Time* (1942), set by Rodney Ackland to the music of Schubert, nor yet with *Old Chelsea* (1943), which had a score − by Tauber himself − that was so close to Schubert as to run the same critical risks. Tauber was, however, a law unto himself: a great star of classical opera and minor operetta, he would now stride down to the footlights and hurl his numbers out into the auditorium where they were gratefully received by the same kind of fanatically loyal audiences who would later devote themselves to John Hanson on tours of *The Desert Song* and *The Student Prince*.

So by 1943, the year of Tauber's *Old Chelsea* and Lupino Lane's *La-di-da-di-da*, London had seen no shows from Broadway in almost four years and for obvious reasons no shows from continental Europe that were not revivals. There had been no new scores from Coward or Novello or Herbert/Ellis, no first night of any major new musical of any but the most farcical Lupino Lane/Cicely Courtneidge variety. When therefore it was announced that in November 1943 there would be a new Novello show at the Phoenix, considerable hopes were raised. Admittedly, Novello himself would not be in the cast, since he was still playing *The Dancing Years* at the Adelphi, but members of his regular repertory company like Mary Ellis, Peter Graves and Elisabeth Welch were all cast in *Arc de Triomphe*, a musical biography loosely based on the life of the American prima donna Mary Garden. 'Nobody wades through his own tosh with quite the confidence of Ivor Novello,' noted Ivor Brown, and here Peter Graves was left to struggle with the tale of a starving young actor falling in love with an opera star (Mary Ellis) but then getting killed in World War I. Though set a few decades earlier, this plot did allow Miss Ellis to sing 'France Will Rise Again' to topical cheers, and it even ended with a mock-opera in which another Novello regular, Olive Gilbert (still playing a few streets away in *The Dancing Years*), arrived for the finale.

Reviews were, however, only mildly enthusiastic, and the run of *Arc de Triomphe* was not much helped by the fact that in April 1944 Novello was sentenced to eight weeks in prison on a charge of misusing his wartime petrol allowance for private purposes. It was a curious charge, brought – many thought at the time – to discourage others from flouting petrol rationing of the period, and after the sentence was halved on appeal Novello in fact returned to *The Dancing Years* 'as if,' said Eddie Marsh, 'he had been to Normandy and won the VC instead of doing a spot of time', such was the cheering from Ivor's devoted fans. *Arc de Triomphe*, being somewhat less invincible, failed to survive his incarceration.

As if to remind London audiences that there was still another world out there, the great Irving Berlin American GI's revue *This is the Army* played the Palladium towards the end of 1943, but 1944 brought nothing more than a couple of topical revues while 1945 opened in the depths of nostalgia with *Three Waltzes*, an Evelyn Laye musical built around themes of Oscar Straus, and *Gay Rosalinda* which turned out to be a leaden English version of *Die Fledermaus*.

It was therefore once again left to Novello to get the West End out of the Vienna Woods, and this he did with *Perchance to Dream*, which was to run for more than a thousand performances across the next three years. This time he was a dashing Regency highwayman wagering to seduce an unknown cousin (Roma Beaumont) and then falling in love with her only to die as the curtain fell on Act I. But audiences who had had enough of first-act hero deaths in *Arc de Triomphe* need not have worried: by the second act Novello was reincarnated to pursue his love across the centuries in one of the most unashamedly schmalz-ridden plots that even he had ever conceived. Yet this was the score that offered its entranced audiences 'We'll Gather Lilacs', perhaps the quintessential Novello song in its combination of soaring strings and lyrics of extreme banality, as well as 'Love is My Reason', and a cast of the regulars much improved by the addition for this one show of the redoubtable Margaret Rutherford.

Even Agate admitted himself defeated by the romance of it all: 'Perchance,' he wrote in the *Sunday Times*, 'I dreamed at the first night of Mr Novello's new Hippodrome show. Anyhow, the following is what the lighter stage's most popular magician induced me to believe I saw. A Regency buck, who is also a highwayman. A cad who will wager £5,000 that he will seduce an unknown cousin within twenty-four hours of her stay under his roof, doubled with a verray parfit gentil knight prepared to wager a hundred-thousand pearl necklace at the feet of Purity Unsullied. A cutpurse who dies babbling of reincarnation. Did I spend the rest of the Dreamtime watching what gross and vulgar spirits would call "subsequent developments"? Yes. Was time punctuated by aeons and aeons of Ballet? Yes. Was there a very, very, very great deal of lush romantic music, scored principally for harp after the manner of that popular composer Herr Mittel Europa? Yes. Or so these things seemed, for I vouch for none of them. Is all this a trifle grudging, even bordering on the ungenerous? I think it may be, and I hasten to say that the curtain, when it went up, took with it the entire audience which remained in seventh heaven until, after three hours and a half, the curtain descended and automatically brought the audience down with it.'

As the West End began in the summer of 1945 to emerge from the effects of a long and debilitating war, Novello alone seemed professionally sure of what he was doing: across ten years, a long series of triumphant musicals (few of which had lasted less than a couple of years in London and the same again on tour) had established an empire as secure as that of the father-and-son Strauss family. Alone among writers in post-war England, Novello would also now go on totally unperturbed by the shock waves that were coming from over the Atlantic as word of *Oklahoma!* spread abroad. Novello knew exactly what his audience wanted, and went on giving it to them until his death six years later: he was the last heir to the music of Vienna, and he went out still wearing the crown of half a dozen of the most commercially successful musicals in the entire history of the West End. But as an act his proved unrepeatable: a Novello show was a Novello show, a law unto itself and no longer any real guide to the general state of the British musical.

Such as it was in 1945: Coward still concentrating on revue (*Sigh No More*), Jack Hulbert and Cicely Courtneidge doing a knockabout (*Under Your Hat*) which could have been written at any time over the past decade, and elsewhere nothing but a small paragraph in the *Sunday Times* one September weekend announcing that A. P. Herbert, back from the war, had delivered a new comic opera to Charles Cochran. Happily, the story was spotted by Vivian Ellis's sister; there was as yet a book, but no score. In fact Cochran had already approached William Walton, who declined the task: it thus fell to Ellis to start composing *Big Ben*, the first British musical in several years to show any real sign of having been written in the country and decade of its first production.

Herbert was of course essentially a satirist, and his plot about the love of a Tory hero and a Socialist heroine who come together to stop a parliamentary bill which would prevent the sale of alcohol in Britain was really just another of his jokey attacks on some of the greater lunacies of the Palace of Westminster, where he had for so long served as an Independent MP.

Allied to Ellis's lilting music, Herbert's book and lyrics had a certain spikey charm, but the choice of a parliamentary theme allowed for rough critical comparisons with Gilbert and Sullivan and, especially, *Iolanthe*: in that league, Herbert and Ellis did not stand much of a chance and *Big*

Ben barely survived three months in the summer of 1946. But it had at least established, and not before time, the presence in the West End of a new musical partnership which was soon to go on to greater things.

Meanwhile, the American invasion was already under way: to a London which had in the whole of the war heard only two relatively lacklustre Cole Porter scores (*Du Barry Was a Lady* and *Panama Hattie*, neither of which ever sounded quite right without the 'golden foghorn', Ethel Merman, for whom they were written and by whom they were created on Broadway) now came *Song of Norway*, the Grieg musical by Wright and Forrest which, while admittedly no *Oklahoma!*, was already a sharp reminder of how far the American musical had moved beyond the lumbering Vienna shows like *Three Waltzes* that were still fresh in the West End memory.

But there was still enduring London faith in the operetta tradition: certainly it had done Novello no lasting harm, and with both *Perchance to Dream* and *Song of Norway* the big musical hits of an otherwise uninspiring post-war period, it was perhaps not surprising that Coward too should now embark on what would be his last attempt to recapture the glamour of *Bitter Sweet*.

The title for his new score was *Pacific 1860*, and by the beginning of 1946 it was taking hesitant shape in his mind as a love story about a world-renowned singer and the young man she meets on Samolo, a mythical island in the South Seas that was to recur in much of Noël's later writing as an odd mix of Hawaii and Jamaica. Originally, he planned the operetta for His Majesty's, a theatre that would have been ideally suited in size for the kind of entertainment that Noël had in mind. But when that proved unavailable, the impresario Prince Littler offered Coward the chance to reopen the Theatre Royal Drury Lane which, after being bombed in 1940, had served only as the headquarters for ENSA.

Though Drury Lane was technically far less suited to *Pacific 1860* than was His Majesty's, Noël realized that this was not a theatre to be lightly turned down, even if it did mean expanding his show to a much larger scale and taking the chance that the bomb damage would not be repaired in time for it to reopen in the autumn of 1946. It was now clear that his score would once again need a leading female singer capable of carrying most of the numbers in the way that Peggy Wood and Evelyn Laye (in the London and New York premieres of *Bitter Sweet*) and Yvonne Printemps (in *Conversation Piece*) and Fritzi Massary (in *Operette*) had carried the Coward operettas of the past. But this time the need was for a different kind of star: still a romantic heroine, certainly, but one capable of playing in a lighter and more cheerful convention.

Not for the first time, Noël's eyes strayed across the Atlantic: though she had resolutely turned down *Oklahoma!* and was only just out of a rare Broadway flop called *Lute Song*, Mary Martin had already established an

Vivian Ellis, A. P. Herbert and Charles Cochran at work on the parliamentary satire *Big Ben* (1946), together with the star of the show, Carole Lynne, at the Adelphi Theatre.

enviable reputation in *One Touch of Venus* and with Cole Porter's *My Heart Belongs to Daddy*, and Noël now decided that a breath of the new Broadway vigour was what his show most needed. After some hectic transatlantic cables Miss Martin agreed to make her London debut, and Noël, together with his resident designer Gladys Calthrop, began to tailor the production to their newly acquired star.

Work on *Pacific 1860* continued through the spring and summer, though Noël then had to greet Mary Martin and her entourage off the boat at Southampton with the gloomy news that a permit to repair the bomb damage at Drury Lane had been unexpectedly refused, and that there was now very little likelihood of opening there before the very end of the year at the earliest. By approaching Aneurin Bevan (Minister of Health in the post-war Labour government) in person, Noël did manage to get the permit through, but at the cost of delaying all rehearsals for a month.

At the beginning of November, Coward now started to direct a company of nearly a hundred in the show that was due to open at Drury Lane just before Christmas; but from the first week of rehearsal onward, everything that could possibly go wrong with *Pacific 1860* proceeded balefully to do so. Even in ideal conditions, this would not have rated as the best of the Coward musicals, but many better scores would have collapsed similarly under the problems that it would have to face during the coldest winter of the decade. Rehearsals were constantly interrupted by the need to repair and replace various parts of the stage, the seats were only put back into the auditorium three days before the first night, and Coward's ambitious plans for a full week of dress-rehearsals (which had been feasible fifteen years earlier for *Cavalcade*, his only other experience of working at the Lane) had to be abandoned as totally impracticable. Nor was it possible to open *Pacific 1860* anywhere outside London in the hope of polishing some of its rougher moments during a tour, since regional theatres were by now well into the pantomime season and a musical of this scale was in any case already proving prohibitively difficult to travel.

Worse still, during the last week of rehearsals Noël and Mary Martin both gradually began to realize that, even for an entertainer of her undoubted and flexible talent, she was hopelessly miscast and was having to struggle with a part originally conceived for a heavier-voiced soprano. Rows about her costumes developed into more serious arguments about the show itself, and a feeling of impending doom began to permeate Drury Lane. In the bitter cold, since permits to reinstal the theatre's heating system had also been withheld in the chaos of post-war bureaucracy, the company struggled through two hasty and sketchy dress-rehearsals which served only to leave a frozen and depressed author-director with the conviction that there were still a thousand things wrong with *Pacific 1860* and that he had neither the time nor the opportunity to get even a dozen of them right in the few remaining hours before the first night. But if Coward was chilled in the stalls, the company on stage, appropriately dressed for a nostalgic love story set in the tropical heat of the South Seas, could barely manage to make themselves heard above the chattering of their teeth.

For Noël, the last few days of rehearsal were one of the unhappiest periods he had ever known in the theatre, and the notices after the first night on 19 December 1946 bore out his premonitions of absolute disaster. *Pacific 1860*, which might just have scraped by in easier times, had everything going against it, not least the icy weather which made any enjoyment at Drury Lane distinctly hard to find. Listening today to a contemporary recording of the only Coward musical never to have been revived anywhere in the world, I find that it emerges as a light, lyrical score enchantingly sung by Miss Martin and Graham Payn with at least a couple of numbers ('Bright Was the Day' and 'I Saw No Shadow on the Sea') which would have been a credit to the best of his hit shows, and a couple of others ('Uncle Harry' and 'His Excellency Regrets') that were to prove more than useful in his subsequent cabaret routines at Las Vegas and the Café de Paris.

But in production *Pacific 1860* was, in Noël's own considered opinion, 'really rather a bore', and the operettta was not much helped by great expectations. Here, after all, was the show that was to reopen London's greatest musical theatre, Drury Lane, after a six-year gap and audiences and critics alike were expecting something pretty splendid. What they got was an innocuous, vaguely pleasant entertainment strong on its score (which was the last of Coward's post-*Bitter Sweet* attempts to return the light musical theatre to the glory of his own childhood memories) but rather weaker on its book, lyrics and minor performances. The songs did indeed have an undeniably nostalgic charm, but reviews of *Pacific 1860* were characterized by an almost resentful disappointment. The most that any morning paper could find to say of the music was that it was 'vaguely reminiscent of Novello' and one Sunday reviewer decided unhelpfully to couch his plot summary in the language of Damon Runyon: 'It's all about a prima donna who takes a number of peeks at a guy living in the Pacific who takes a number of peeks back at her: obviously when a doll and a guy get to taking peeks back and forth and he is already engaged and she keeps travelling back to concerts in Europe, well there you are.'

Nevertheless the advance booking had been strong, and for the first few weeks a respectable number of people turned up to shiver each night at Drury Lane; soon, however, the effects of the reviews and the continuing fuel crisis began to take their inevitable toll, and though Mary Martin played on doggedly through the next four months, the last two were in Noël's phrase 'more of a convulsive stagger than a run'. The production lost a total of just over £28,000.

Coward himself rapidly closed his mind to a resounding and unfortunate flop, a discipline of mind that he had cultivated from his very earliest days in an unpredictable business. The failure of *Pacific 1860* did Mary Martin no lasting harm, and a few years later she was to return to that same stage in triumph as the Nellie Forbush of *South Pacific*; but Noël's post-war image had undoubtedly been severely tarnished by it. His reputation was suddenly made to seem both dated and shaky and he himself an irrelevant survivor from a bygone era; indeed the crash of this musical marked the beginning of a slump in Coward's professional standing from which he did not totally recover until the National Theatre revival of *Hay Fever* eighteen years later. But long before *Pacific 1860*, Noël had become largely immune to most press reaction, whether good or bad: 'If I had really cared about my notices,' he wrote to a friend in 1946, 'I would have shot myself in the Twenties.'

And quite apart from Coward's failure with *Pacific 1860*, symbolic though that was of the change that the war had wrought in public musical taste, the West End generally was now living in an extraordinary time-warp. On Broadway, not only *Oklahoma!* but also *Carousel* and *Annie Get Your Gun* had all opened by the time the last of the Coward operettas reached Drury Lane in 1946; yet because the war had

The culmination of the American invasion: a scene from *Annie Get Your Gun* at the Coliseum (1947).

effectively severed all transatlantic theatrical traffic, and because post-war economic conditions in London meant for a while that American shows simply could not be afforded, only occasional rumours were reaching London of the total change that had come over the stage musical during the New York 1940s. These were still the days before the invention of the long-playing record: soundtracks did not travel any more frequently than audiences across the ocean, and as a result the Drury Lane changeover in April 1947 from *Pacific 1860* to *Oklahoma!* came as the collision of two worlds, one lost and the other so new that critics reeled back in some amazement.

Harold (Howard) Keel, who had replaced Alfred Drake in what was originally called *Away We Go* and only a few nights before the Broadway premiere retitled *Oklahoma!*, now led the English company and they were greeted by London audiences as if they were a liberation army. The effect on the West End of *Oklahoma!* was in fact much more violent than could be accounted for even by one of the greatest scores in the whole history of the Broadway musical or by the revolutionary nature of Agnes de Mille's choreography, which for the first time merged the dance numbers into the action of the plot. As W. A. Darlington noted in retrospect, 'London was in 1947 still convalescent after the war strain: wartime restrictions were still in force but without the wartime incentive to bear them cheerfully, and a bureaucratically minded Government was doing its tactless utmost to make them seem burdensome. Its supreme folly, which must have cost it dear at the next election, had been to allow the country to run short of fuel just as the coldest months of the year arrived. It had happened that these months at the beginning of 1947 had been exceptionally cold. All sections of the community had gone shivering and cursing about their avocations; and none chillier or more maledictory than playgoers who were suffering from a *ukase* that no theatre should be heated . . . about the impact of *Oklahoma!* on a public thus beaten down into a depression of mind largely artificial and unnecessary, there was something apocalyptic. It was the vigour of the performance, its energetic gaiety, its insistence on the simple pleasures of life that lifted the hearts of its audience. Never in the history of the theatre can a show have been better timed: "Oh What A Beautiful Morning" was just what we needed to hear just then. The sense of uplift was physical as well as spiritual; as I sat there a sudden sense of well-being swept over me and I remembered what the dreary unimaginativeness of our food-rationing had made me forget for so long, what it felt like to be well fed.'

As a result of the instant sunshine that *Oklahoma!* brought to end this English winter, critics and audiences alike simply fell in love with it, and that was the start of a love affair with the American musical which was to continue across many more post-war years, at first a largely uncritical affair. American musicals were welcomed with the same eagerness as were other American inventions like Coca-Cola: certainly, these transatlantic productions might rot the brain or the teeth if taken to excess, but for sheer professional perfection Britain had nothing to match the American musical, so lie back and enjoy. And if that was the typical reaction of a European prostitute in the face of an army of liberation bearing cigarettes and chewing gum, then so be it: the West End had been rationed long enough, the old operettas patently weren't working any more, and the British had almost nothing else of their own to offer.

So when, five short weeks after the opening of *Oklahoma!*, Dolores Gray raised the roof of the London Coliseum as the Annie Oakley of *Annie Get Your Gun*, the American invasion was complete and unchallenged. Inside barely a month, after seven years of musical isolation from Broadway, London had been introduced to not just 'Oh What A Beautiful Morning' but 'Surrey With the Fringe on Top', 'People Will Say We're In Love', 'Out of My Dreams', 'Kansas City', 'Doin' What Comes Natur'lly', 'I Got the Sun in the Morning', 'The Girl That I Marry' and, suitably enough, the anthem of all American musicals, 'There's No Business Like Showbusiness'. Faced with the arrival of a song catalogue like that in less than five weeks, the wonder is that any British composers ever went back to the piano again.

Happily they did: indeed one was already there, and 1947 was not only the year of the great Broadway invasion, for it also brought *Bless the Bride*, a lyrical period piece by A. P. Herbert and Vivian Ellis that might almost have been designed as a riposte to the Great American Outdoors typified by *Oklahoma!* and *Annie Get Your Gun*. If the English could hardly manage the country-and-western magnificence of Rodgers and Hammerstein or Irving Berlin in full cowboy cry, then it would be hard to think of any American who could have managed the gentle cross-Channel elegance of *Bless the Bride*, which achieved a run of 886 performances at the Adelphi as against 1,304 for *Annie Get Your Gun* and 1,543 for *Oklahoma!*; not in the same league, perhaps, but beaten among home-grown musicals at this time by only three others – *The Maid of the Mountains*, *Chu-Chin-Chow* and *Me and My Girl* – though soon also challenged by Novello's contemporary *Perchance to Dream*.

Just as the idea for *Cavalcade* had begun with Coward leafing through bound volumes of the *Illustrated London News*, so *Bless the Bride* resulted from A. P. Herbert looking through back numbers of *Punch*, the magazine to which he had contributed so much of his best verse and prose over the past twenty years. There he found drawings of the 1870s conjuring up a world of European wars (the Franco-Prussian War, to be precise) while on English vicarage lawns vicars' daughters still played croquet. The book that Herbert now wrote for Vivian Ellis to score was thus far removed from their last Westminster satire: instead it was an unashamedly sentimental tale of an English girl falling in love with a French soldier who is then reported killed in battle. Reports of that death turn out at the last to have been somewhat exaggerated, however, and all ends happily at the altar, by which time a cast headed by Lizbeth Webb and George Guetary had been able to charm their way through such haunting love songs as 'Ma Belle Marguerite' and 'This Is My Lovely Day'.

Even with a score like that, Cochran as manager still had his doubts about whether any English musical could ever again please the critics, and he chose to open it on a Saturday night, thereby allowing at least a little time for any favourable reaction to be spread by word of mouth before the Monday papers could do their worst. He was right to be nervous: one critic wrote of 'less plot than would fit easily on the back of a sixpence', and *The Times* called it 'musically sugary and undistinguished', while acknowledging 'all the charm of an ornate valentine painted and lavendered by artists whose taste commands respect'. Harold Hobson, setting all in perspective for the *Sunday Times*, noted that 'Sir Alan Herbert and Mr Vivian Ellis in "Ma Belle Marguerite" and "This Is My Lovely Day" prove that Englishmen can still write songs as well as any people in the world, and *Oklahoma!* proves that Americans can do it as well as Englishmen.'

Whatever the respective, and very different, merits of these shows, there was no doubt that they had changed the climate of the West End drastically and suddenly: a year that came in with nothing more than the flop of *Pacific 1860* and an aging Novello in *Perchance to Dream* reached midsummer with three brand-new smash hits, *Oklahoma!* and *Annie Get Your Gun* and *Bless the Bride*, all full to bursting with songs that could be sung all over London.

By October there was also *Finian's Rainbow*, over from Broadway with a stunning Harburg-Lane score ('How Are Things in Glocca Morra?' 'Look to the Rainbow', 'Old Devil Moon', 'If This Isn't Love', 'When I'm Not Near The Girl I Love'), and though it barely survived three months in a West End that preferred the open optimism of *Oklahoma!* to the more cynical politics of *Finian*, it too gave palm court orchestras all over the country something to enliven their repertoire.

A year of such untold wealth was bound to be followed by one of anti-climax, and with at least four major musical hits now running happily side by side in the West End (Novello and Herbert/Ellis scoring for Britain while Berlin and Rodgers/Hammerstein played for America), it was not for another fifteen months that their number was increased by another Broadway hit, *Brigadoon*. In the meantime, 1948 brought *Lute Song* which had failed on Broadway, despite the presence of Yul Brynner and Mary Martin and the future Mrs Ronald Reagan (Nancy Davis), and did no better in London without them. But the year did also bring a rare eccentricity in the form of Noel Langley's *Cage Me a Peacock*, a musical about a Roman harlot sent into exile in a Britain as yet untouched by civilization of any kind, and the promise that the decade would end, as indeed it did, with another lush and lavish return to the world of Ivor Novello.

King's Rhapsody, which opened at the Palace Theatre in September 1949, was the last musical Ivor wrote for himself, and it outlived him in its original run by several months. The only one of his shows that I ever saw with him playing the lead, and I was ten at the time, it lingers in my memory almost forty years later as a kind of summary of everything that Novello and his productions must always have been all about. There was indeed a moment at the very end when he knelt on the altar steps of a deserted cathedral to pick up an abandoned rose while the orchestra built up to some kind of crescendo and women wept openly in the stalls, and one realized even as a schoolboy that one had been present at some bizarre but mystical religious rite shared by thousands of theatregoers, especially at matinées.

Critics by now accustomed to a tougher diet of American open-air rodeos were, however, appalled by the sentimentality of a musical, loosely based on the abdication of Edward VIII, which had Ivor as a Ruritanian Crown Prince (Nikki of Murania) marrying out of duty, but then exiling himself to be with the Woman He Loves. The rose on the altar steps had been left there by the Woman He Loves after the coronation of the boy King to whom Nikki has ceded the throne.

And that was by no means all: *King's Rhapsody* also had peasant uprisings, gypsy dancing and a cast-list that read like a roll-call of the Novello faithful: Vanessa Lee, both Zena and Phyllis Dare, Olive Gilbert and Robert Andrews. Given all that, plus one of the best of all the Novello scores (including 'Fly Home Little Heart', 'Take Your Girl' and 'A Violin Began To Play'), it was perhaps ungrateful of my predecessor at *Punch* to refer to 'a vast insipid musical in which Mr Ivor Novello has pulled out most of the known stops in the organ of easy sentiment', though Milton Shulman was in full agreement: '*King's Rhapsody* drips with cloying sentiment, its situations are contrived and ludicrous, and it is practically empty of wit.'

By now, however, Novello was virtually critic-proof, and audiences attended *King's Rhapsody* much as crowds attended any other royal event: it was Queen Mary herself who noted in her later years that Ivor was the only actor she had ever seen able to give 'an adequate indication of what it means to be royal'.

But, with *King's Rhapsody*, an end was coming to that Novello reign and to something more than just another decade: before the 1950s were two years old, three of the founding figures of the modern British musical (Ivor himself, the impresario Charles Cochran and the actress Gertrude Lawrence) were all to die suddenly, taking with them the last vestiges of a romantically un-American world. Nor was it clear, at the end of the 1940s, quite who or what would take their place: Coward had yet to recover his reputation after *Pacific 1860*, while Herbert and Ellis had followed the triumph of *Bless the Bride* with a 1949 catastrophe called *Tough at the Top* which concerned a Pomeranian Princess falling in love with an English boxer at the turn of the century, a cumbersome plot mainly designed so that Herbert could invent what must then have seemed a ludicrously improbable government office, that of Minister for Sport.

If, therefore, the 1950s were not to see the total death of the West End musical, new composers would have to be found: and as yet there was no sign of a single one.

Opposite. Mary Ellis as the opera star (*above*) in Ivor Novello's *Arc de Triomphe* at the Phoenix Theatre (1943); and (*below*) a scene from *Song of Norway* (1946), based on the life and music of Edvard Grieg, which enjoyed a two-year run at the Palace Theatre despite having to compete with Broadway hits such as *Oklahoma!* and *Annie Get Your Gun* from mid-1947.

The Vivian Ellis/A. P. Herbert partnership at the Adelphi progressed from *Big Ben* in 1946 (*left*) to their greatest hit, *Bless the Bride* (1947), a lyrical period piece in which Betty Paul (*opposite*) was one of the stars, but two years later their *Tough at the Top* (*below*), a tale of a Pomeranian princess and an English boxer at the turn of the century, failed to repeat the success.

The longest-running of all Ivor Novello's musicals was *Perchance to Dream* (1945) at the Hippodrome (*below*); the Regency highwayman played by Novello appears on the sheet-music cover of one of the show's hit songs, 'Love is my Reason' (*left*). Four years later, *King's Rhapsody*, a musical echo of the Abdication, was staged – with Novello in the leading role (*opposite*) – as a farewell to Ruritania.

The Fifties

〜〜〜〜〜〜〜〜〜〜〜〜〜〜〜〜〜〜〜〜〜〜〜〜〜〜〜〜〜〜〜〜〜

We're blue without
Can't do without
Our dreams just won't come true without
That certain thing called the Boy Friend.

Sandy Wilson, *The Boy Friend*, 1953

〜〜〜〜〜〜〜〜〜〜〜〜〜〜〜〜〜〜〜〜〜〜〜〜〜〜〜〜〜〜〜〜〜

THE 1950s BEGAN with the West End borrowing heavily not only from the Novello past but also from other media: the first big musical opening of the decade was indeed a revue at the Prince of Wales called *Take It From Here* and lifted largely, as that title suggested, from a radio hit series of the era. The musical of the year was undoubtedly Rogers and Hammerstein's *Carousel*, which reached Drury Lane in June with a largely American cast fully five years after it had first opened on Broadway. The Crazy Gang were still going strong at the Victoria Palace in the latest of a long line of knockabout revues (*Knights of Madness*), but elsewhere almost nothing of any significance was happening bar a long backstage pause while local managements tried to consider their position in the light of the continuing Rodgers-and-Hammerstein invasion.

As ever, there were only really two schools of thought: one, held by the older Littler managements, reckoned that the only real hope for the English musical was to head back into areas that Broadway either couldn't or wouldn't touch. Hence the re-emergence in 1950 of Harry Parr-Davies, like Novello a Welshman, but one whose only real success thus far had been the wartime *Lisbon Story*. In 1950, however, he came up with two new musicals, the first of which was an adaptation of J. M. Barrie's tale of the young army officer and the two maiden aunts, *Quality Street*. Retitled *Dear Miss Phoebe* and set to the words of Novello's most faithful lyricist, Christopher Hassall, this achieved a moderate success at the Phoenix, but was followed only a few weeks later at His Majesty's by another Parr-Davies score of a very different kind. This, *Blue For a Boy*, was a farcical musical romp which mainly sold on the strength of its posters, huge photographs of the massively overweight comedian Fred Emney dressed in baby clothes, but it ran for more than six hundred performances to demonstrate the West End's continuing demand for

Opposite. Anne Rogers as Polly Browne, supported by Maria Charles, Anne Wakefield and Joan Gadsdon, all sporting 1920s fashions in Sandy Wilson's *The Boy Friend* (1953) at the Players' Theatre.

123

low-comedy musicals far removed from the slick professionalism of the Broadway imports.

The other school of thought, and intriguingly the one subscribed to by both Coward and Novello, who had done most to give the English stage musical its own character over the past two decades, was that lessons from Broadway now had to be learnt if the West End was to survive as anything more than just another date on touring schedules for Broadway originals. Both men had of course worked in the United States (Novello had indeed briefly been a scriptwriter in Hollywood, while Coward had frequently played on Broadway), and both shared an admiration for and understanding of the American theatre which were still not widespread among their West End colleagues.

It was Coward who moved first: his 1950 musical would, he decided, be as far removed as possible from the period-crinoline world of *Pacific 1860* or *Operette* or *Conversation Piece*. It would be set in a latterday nightclub, and it would concern at least in part a jewel robbery: effectively it would be his answer to *Guys and Dolls*, a Damon Runyon text that was to reach Broadway as a musical just four months after Coward's *Ace of Clubs* reached the Cambridge.

But the year, and a faint similarity of gangster plot, was all the two shows had in common: *Ace of Clubs* had an attractive score (with numbers like 'Chase Me Charlie', 'I Like America', 'Why Does Love Get In The Way?' and the comic 'Three Juvenile Delinquents') charmingly sung by Pat Kirkwood and Graham Payn and Sylvia Cecil, but its plot was desperately sketchy and for the third time in his life (the other two had been 1920s plays) Noël was actually booed by an audience on the first night. His diary for Friday, 7 July 1950 tells the tale: 'The theatre in the evening tingling with suspense and tension. I got the usual ovation when I went into the box. The show went magnificently, and everyone gave a beautiful performance. Sylvia Cecil stopped the show with "Nothing Can Ever Last". The "Delinquents", too, tore the place up. Graham had a rip-snorting triumph with "America" and Pat got them roaring with "Josephine" and "Charlie". The whole thing went marvellously all through, and when I walked on to the stage at the end there was a lot of booing. I must say I was both surprised and angry. I stood still and waited while a free fight broke out in the gallery. It was very unpleasant and excessively silly. Finally I silenced them and made my speech and that was that. It was a cruel bit of crowd exhibitionism and made me feel bitter because it took the edge off the success and made everyone gossip. I am disgusted with the filthy manners of the galleryites.'

The morning notices were, Noël further noted, 'patronizing, irritating, badly written and silly, as usual,' but despite them *Ace of Clubs* achieved a run of over two hundred performances, not altogether a disaster and a

Characters from Noël Coward's *Ace of Clubs*, the gangster musical which ran briefly at the Cambridge Theatre in 1950, sketched in a cartoon by Tom Titt published in *The Tatler*: Pat Kirkwood and Graham Payn are seen in the foreground.

considerable surprise to the Tom Arnold management which had staged the show over their own considerable doubts about its chances of survival. Noël however remained indignant enough to add in a letter to his secretary and lifelong friend, Cole Lesley, 'I am furious about *Ace of Clubs* not being a real success, and I have come to the conclusion that if audiences no longer care for first rate music, lyrics, dialogue and performance they can stuff it up their collective arses and go to see *King's Rhapsody* until *les vaches se rentrent . . .*'.

In a somewhat more thoughtful summary of the problems now facing Coward in particular and the West End musical in general, Anthony Cookman wrote for *The Tatler*: 'There is disconcertingly little of Mr Coward in his new musical *Ace of Clubs*. That is perhaps why the polite applause given for his company on the first night was broken into by some quite vehement booing as soon as he appeared on the stage. Possibly his appearance reminded people of a certain quality which they had expected to find in their entertainment and had not found. Mr Coward has now reached a rather critical point in his development as an artist. It is a long while since he established himself as the voice of the generation which had survived World War I. So sympathetic to the ears of his contemporaries was that bright staccato voice that it could often speak to them in tones of shrill reproof, and they liked it all the more. It comprehended the fascination of the gleaming social vortex; and if sometimes it sang of the muddy depths beneath with a sort of moral fury ("Dance, dance, dance little lady") those who hummed the tunes appreciatively excused the fury because they realised that it sprang from the same despair at the futility of life that they themselves felt. But that generation grew up at a rather faster rate than Mr Coward. His rage at the futility of life continued to simmer under the flippant surface of his plays long after his contemporaries had rid themselves of this particular obsession and had come to some sort of middle-aged compromise with life. Coward's anger was an anger which belonged to the 20s, and he shows no instinctive understanding of the youngsters of the 50s now that he too seems to have come to some sort of middle-aged terms with life. No doubt they are terms satisfactory to him as a private person, but whatever they are they appear to have deprived the artist of a point of view. The wit masking a desperate cynicism in an immense flippancy has given place to an enormously expert man of the theatre who does not quite know what the big public would really like him to be expert about.'

And as for Coward, so for the West End at large; nobody, no manager, no composer, no lyricist, no director, no choreographer, no star, really knew any longer what musicals were supposed to be about. Certainly they were supposed to last about three hours, and be about glamour maybe, and include memorable songs: what nobody seemed to have was a theme, a book worth exploring or even adapting. There was not just a lack of home-grown product, there was also a chronic lack of plot.

Meanwhile the blitz from Broadway continued: show after show that had been stored up in New York during the late 1940s awaiting more favourable economic conditions along Shaftesbury Avenue now opened to audiences and critics still open-mouthed with wonder at the sheer expertise and joy of hit-packed scores. A succession of new arrivals brought, in 1951, *Kiss Me Kate* and *South Pacific*; in 1952, *Call Me Madam* and *Love From Judy* (a world premiere, but from the American Hugh Martin) and the long-awaited London opening of Gershwin's 1935 opera *Porgy and Bess*; and in 1953, *Paint Your Wagon*, *Guys and Dolls*, *The King and I* and *Wish You Were Here*. In the face of such sustained competition, what was the West End to do?

Firstly, decided Ivor Novello in 1950, it must escape from its own past, a past that he himself had done so much to condition. At the height of the Ruritanian triumph that was still *King's Rhapsody*, he chose to start work with an altogether new lyricist, Alan Melville, on an altogether new kind of Novello musical. Where his usual lyricist, Christopher Hassall, had been essentially a romantic poet, Melville was a sharp and waspish satirist from the world of witty revues. Together, Novello and Melville now began to write a backstage musical for Cicely Courtneidge which was to be nothing less than a West End answer of sorts to Broadway's

42nd Street: the story of a stout-hearted, pert-tongued actress who, forced by theatrical failure to open a memorably incompetent drama school, yet manages to get herself back before the footlights in time for a wonderful parody by Novello of almost all his own Ruritanian romances. *Gay's the Word*, perhaps because of its title alone, has proved unrevivable in the thirty-five years since it was first staged. Yet in there somewhere is not only the West End's only true marching song ('Vitality') but a score featuring some of the most enchanting music that even Novello ever wrote: if there's a better lament for lost love than 'If Only He'd Looked My Way', it certainly was not to be heard in any other musical of the 1950s.

Yet the real virtue of *Gay's the Word* was noted by the MP and critic Beverley Baxter for the London *Evening Standard*: 'It is a pity that television does not stretch as yet across the Atlantic: if it did, we could let our American sympathisers and critics (now practically equal in numbers) look in at the Saville Theatre where Miss Cicely Courtneidge is convulsing the town with Ivor Novello's jolly affair *Gay's the Word*. All that Americans now read about us in the papers consists of gloom piled upon gloom, with an occasional disaster to give it spice. Influenza, floods, smallpox, Festival of Britain strikes, meat shortages, gales and Socialist majorities in the House of Commons. Poor old merry England. Like the nigger [*sic*] in the song, we're tired of living and scared of dying. At least that is what it must look like from Over There. Think then what a delightful shock it would be for the Americans to hear an audience laugh until its buttons burst . . . once more Ivor Novello proves that he is immortal without being divine. No Cole Porter or Richard Rodgers or Irving Berlin can dethrone him. He has the gift of bringing happiness to the British breast. He robs us of a sigh and charms us to a tear. It is time that some official recognition was shown of his achievement in keeping the British flag flying over Ruritania and giving so much pleasure to so many.'

In fact Novello's brief wartime prison sentence, not to mention a distinctly gay private life, was to deny him any such 'official recognition' as a knighthood, and sadly he was to prove rather less than 'immortal': three weeks after *Gay's the Word* opened in London, on 5 March 1951 he played as usual the evening performance of *King's Rhapsody*, had dinner with his old impresario friend Tom Arnold, returned to his flat in the Aldwych and died in the night of a coronary thrombosis at the age of 58. The crowds who lined the streets for his funeral were mourning not just an actor-composer, but the man who, almost single-handed, had kept the British musical alive through the years leading into and out of World War II.

With Novello gone, Coward badly wounded by the flops of *Pacific 1860* and *Ace of Clubs*, and Cochran also dead after being trapped in a bath of scalding water at his London home in January 1951, champions of the British musical were getting distinctly scarce. Gertrude Lawrence was already on Broadway rehearsing *The King and I* and showing no sign of a desire to move back to London: Jack Buchanan, who was going to Hollywood to film *The Band Wagon*, had already appeared in his last London musical and was also to die long before the close of the 1950s. Sonnie Hale and Bobbie Howes would just about survive the decade, but largely in straight plays or creaking revivals on tour; Howes made his last major London musical appearance with his own daughter Sally Ann in the 1953 London premiere of Lerner and Loewe's *Paint Your Wagon*.

Among the women who had once been the brightest stars of West End shows, Jessie Matthews made no appearance in a new London musical between *Wild Rose* (itself a reworking of Kern's *Sally*) in 1942 and *The Water Babies* in 1973. The 1950s were kinder to Evelyn Laye, who had one musical West End hit with *Wedding in Paris*, but Cicely Courtneidge went back from *Gay's the Word* to a succession of revues and light comedies, only once again to appear in a new musical – the 1964 Coward adaptation *High Spirits*. Her 'Vitality' now seemed like a lament for a world well and truly lost:

Do you remember Gertie Millar? You wouldn't, I'm afraid.
Marie Lloyd, Vesta Tilley's swagger cane?
Lily Elsie as the Widow, Jose Collins as the Maid?
Dear old Robey, Billy Merson at the Lane.
Some gone, and some who still
Are the tops of any bill.
Give me Gracie Fields in place of any crooner,
Hetty King, still debonair,
Phyllis Dare and Zena Dare,
G. H. Elliott in the 'Lily of the Laguna' . . .
Vitality: the stars who gained their immortality
Knew with finality
The practicality
Of something that's lacking in us:
They all had vitality plus . . .
They had vigour, they were bigger, they had wonderful attack,
They were workers, never shirkers, never blasé, never slack,
They could thrill you, they could fill you with their energy and verve,
They were servants of the public and by golly did they serve . . .
They were zealous, they were jealous of the fame that they had won,
They were vitally entitled to their stardom and they were fun.

As a summary of a generation that had now gone forever, that could hardly have been bettered, and as a parting message from Melville it had a kind of chilling finality: stars like that just didn't seem to exist around

Cicely Courtneidge in *Gay's the Word* (1951) at the Saville Theatre; this satirical piece was written for her by Ivor Novello and Alan Melville, in a style which suggested that – had Novello lived to write another musical – any later works would have been closer to the acid Broadway vein than to the Ruritanian past.

the West End any more, and through the 1950s we signally failed to find any transatlantic substitutes for the Broadway Babes of the Ethel Merman/Mary Martin generation, around whom entire shows were now being built elsewhere.

But if the British could no longer aspire to challenge Broadway on its own terms or within anything approaching its own production scales and values, perhaps there was something altogether different they could try? It was Vivian Ellis who thought of it first. After the failure of *Tough at the Top*, still his own favourite score, and after the death of Cochran, Ellis decided to work independently for a while, temporarily interrupting the partnership with Herbert to try something entirely on his own. In his autobiography he recalled: 'Small is beautiful, and in contrast to the lavish productions of Cochran, everything about *And So To Bed* was to be small. Cast, the orchestra of ten under Mantovani, even the theatre which was the New . . . Leslie Henson, like the comedian who wants to play Hamlet, had long nurtured the idea of playing Samuel Pepys. We'd once been next door neighbours, and in 1950 he thought of me to adapt J. B. Fagan's play, words and music, the lot. Pepys was by way of being a song writer. Indeed the opening phrase of one song, ''Beauty Retire'', words and music, were his. I persuaded Wendy Toye, director of all three of my Cochran shows, to stage it. To his everlasting credit, Leslie Henson resisted all temptation to play the fool with Pepys. Betty Paul (Susanne in *Bless the Bride*) as Mrs Pepys had never sung better, likewise a young Australian called Keith Michell as Charles II, understudied by another youngster, Denis Quilley. For some unfathomable reason, a somewhat mature American actress Jessie Royce

Landis was engaged at considerable expense to play King Charles's trollop Mistress Knight. Looking old enough to be Keith Michell's mother, she appeared to give the King an Oedipus complex.'

The importance of *And So To Bed*, though its softly enchanting score has now disappeared into almost total oblivion, far outlived the 330 performances that the musical lasted in the West End. Not only did it introduce a new generation of leading men (Michell and Quilley) who were across the next thirty years to be mainstays of the West End musical scene, both finishing up during the mid-1980s in post-Broadway revivals of *La Cage Aux Folles*. It also introduced the 'small is beautiful' notion of an English musical which could be true to its origins while never having to venture into the more dangerous territory of the big-band extravaganza complete with its chorus lines and huge budgets. And another thing: it established the importance of going back to a tried-and-tested success, whether dramatic or literary. *And So To Bed* had been a proven straight-play triumph of the late 1920s and therefore the book presented none of the problems with which Coward and Novello and A. P. Herbert had so often had to struggle on their way to another number. This was a vehicle which had already proved itself to be in good working order: all Ellis had to do was give it songs.

In its scale, in its origins and in its attitudes to the musical theatre, *And So To Bed* was to give a lead which would be followed by other composers and other shows throughout the decade: and for that Ellis has curiously never been given the credit that rightly goes also of course to Julian Slade and Sandy Wilson, all of them masters of the small-scale two-piano format which was so soon to overtake the West End now in search of an alternative to Broadway lavishness.

In sharp and steep contrast, the 1951/2 season also saw a return to the rather less elegant low-life musicals of a kind which had once been the province of Noël Gay and Lupino Lane: *Zip Goes a Million*, which starred George Formby (and, following his death, Reg Dixon) at the Palace, and Arthur Askey's *Bet Your Life* (which also starred Broadway's Julie Wilson) at the Hippodrome were attempts to win back audiences from the already dying music-hall circuit with knockabout shows in which the slapstick was of vastly greater importance than the score. But even here, some new lessons were being learnt: where once a Formby musical would just have consisted of his own hits cobbled into a paper-thin storyline, *Zip Goes a Million* was in fact (like the Vivian Ellis *And So To Bed*) a careful setting to music of an already established comic hit (*Brewster's Millions*) while for *Bet Your Life* the management brought over the Broadway expertise of Miss Wilson to strengthen an otherwise all-English company. Nevertheless they were still in trouble: 'crude and derivative', began one of the more generous reviews of *Bet Your Life*, and this must have been the last musical in world history to have tried to

Characters from the Vivian Ellis musical *And So To Bed* (1951), a small-scale work based on Pepys' diaries: Leslie Henson, Betty Paul, Jessie Royce Landis and Keith Michell – attired in period costume – were sketched by Emmwood for *The Tatler*.

improve its box-office chances after a few months by cutting forty minutes off the running time and playing it twice nightly instead of once.

The new year, 1953, therefore opened with half a dozen major Broadway musicals still playing in the West End, from *Paint Your Wagon* all the way back through *Carousel* to *Porgy and Bess*, and the news that Anna Neagle was coming to the rescue of the home-grown product with *The Glorious Days*. This, last of the Parr-Davies musicals, was in fact an arrangement of a collection of old song hits, from 'Soldiers of the Queen' through to 'K-K-Katie', which would allow Miss Neagle to move gracefully through her island story, pausing along the way to represent such characters as Nell Gwynne and Queen Victoria in a series of tableaux, some not terribly vivants.

It was Kenneth Tynan, reviewing *The Glorious Days* for the *Observer*, who noted that 'the gap between knowing what the public wants and having the skill to provide it is infinitely wider than most English producers ever dream,' and he entered the fray with an entirely justifiable attack on an appalling show and its star performance: 'There was heated division of opinion in the lobbies during the interval but a small, conservative majority took the view that it might be as well to remain in the theatre. There was always the chance that Miss Neagle might come bowling on as Boadicea with a knife between her teeth . . . as it was, she spent Part Two playing her mother, characterised by Miss Neagle with remarkable ferocity as a well-meaning diseuse of remarkably limited technique'. Though widely disliked within the profession at the time, these sentiments in fact did more than anything else to drag the West End musical into accepting the reality of Broadway expertise and talent in a year when there was precious little of it around Shaftesbury Avenue.

But off the Avenue, just six weeks after the opening of the vastly more heavily publicized and budgeted *Glorious Days*, the Players' Theatre underneath the arches between Charing Cross Station and Hungerford Bridge gave the world premiere of *The Boy Friend*, a musical that was to go on to two thousand performances at Wyndham's and to show, at home and abroad, precisely what the English could still do quite superbly. Like *Journey's End*, another small-scale piece with unknown actors which went on to achieve worldwide success, this was in fact to be one of those miracle shows which even its director Vida Hope had difficulty analysing:

'Early in 1953 my very good friends at the Players' Theatre asked me if I would produce a new small musical by Sandy Wilson, and having accepted I went round to Sandy's flat one bleak February morning to look at the book and hear the music. He was no stranger to me as I had already produced a late-night revue that he had written previously, and we had found we got on well together. He looked pale, seemed over-anxious that I should like it, and as always when he is nervous played his own composition shockingly. But never mind: I saw, I heard and I was conquered. Over coffee I declared my love for *The Boy Friend*, told Sandy I wanted to do it as a serious reproduction of a period and not a burlesque . . . we started rehearsing in March, and I well remember haranguing a rather young company that we were to present a show that would be witty, elegant, charming and tender, and that in no circumstances would I tolerate any attitude of laughing at the Twenties.'

Precisely because *The Boy Friend* was a tribute to that period and not a burlesque, precisely because it was staged by a director with one eye on back numbers of the *Play Pictorials* of the era, it had a charm and confidence which was to carry it far beyond that opening season at the Players'. The show was never intended, as Sandy Wilson has noted, to be a reply to *Oklahoma!*; it was simply, he added, 'a loving salute to those far-off days of the cloche hat and the short skirt, a valentine from one postwar period to another'.

Despite the loss of a leading lady (Diana Maddox) forty-eight hours before the first performance, *The Boy Friend* opened to considerable triumph: true, *The Times* didn't care for it, but most other papers did and Kenneth Tynan, scourge of *The Glorious Days*, at last found a London musical he could welcome unreservedly. Even so, its transfer from the Players' to Wyndham's was to take nine months (during which time West End managers complained that the Wilson show was too short, too dated and too starless; one even suggested that it could do with a comic like Norman Wisdom to liven it up).

The brilliance of the original *Boy Friend* lay in its passion for historical accuracy and its understanding that small is beautiful: where the plot has worked less well over the last thirty years, as in the Broadway transfer and a 1983 Old Vic revival and a catastrophic Ken Russell movie, it has been because either that original passion or that original understanding has been somehow compromised. *The Boy Friend* is, like Rattigan's *French Without Tears* (also set in a French finishing school for young English ladies), a perfect miniature period piece, and its score, ranging from the hauntingly romantic 'Room in Bloomsbury' to the splendidly comic 'Never Too Late To Fall In Love', is one that any composer of the 1920s would have been proud to acknowledge. 'There are,' Coward told Sandy Wilson soon after the opening of *The Boy Friend*, 'only three good lyricists left: you, me and Cole.'

It was *The Boy Friend* that made a star of Anne Rogers (taking over at forty-eight hours notice at the Players' Theatre) and of Julie Andrews (in the original New York production) and of Twiggy (on film), and it was *The Boy Friend* which suggested that there were once again creative forces at work in the London musical. But by the time it reached the West End in 1954, by way of another season at the Players' and a Christmas stint at the Embassy and a certain amount of expansion, Sandy Wilson's reputation as the hottest, if not the only, young theatrical composer in town had been faintly tarnished by his next complete score: *The Buccaneer* was a tale not of pirates but of boys' magazines in Britain and the problems they were having in fending off competition from the more garish imported American comics then flooding the market. Originally seen at the New Watergate in September 1953 and then tried again at the Apollo in 1956 and the Lyric Hammersmith in 1958, this was one of those shows that (to judge from its score) ought to have worked but somehow never did, and indeed no show in Mr Wilson's subsequent career has ever quite rivalled 'that certain thing called *The Boy Friend*'.

And yet the oddly grudging way that even *The Boy Friend* was originally handled, not by critics or audiences certainly but by commercial managements, underlined still another problem facing the composers of West End musicals in the 1950s: there was no backstage machinery of any kind to support them. In earlier and easier times both Coward and Novello had managed to build up their own teams of designers, choreographers, orchestrators and indeed actors who would move with them from show to show. But now, with the death of Cochran, no West End manager was taking any real interest in new musicals: showbiz impresarios tended instead to be of the vastly less creative Val Parnell generation, men whose main hope was to book a big Hollywood star into the Palladium for a short revue season. It was indeed Parnell who had turned down, perhaps rightly, Coward's last score – provoking from Noël the bitter comment 'that at any stage of my career, let alone this one, Mr Val Parnell's opinion should be of the remotest importance is indeed gloomy news.'

Nevertheless, with Parnell looking across the Atlantic and the Littler brothers looking so far back over their musical shoulders as to be in imminent danger of breaking their necks, the fact remained that nobody along Shaftesbury Avenue had the remotest interest in or knowledge of the contemporary British musical and for that reason hardly any existed. The dedication that Hugh Beaumont of H. M. Tennent was putting into classic revivals at the Haymarket, or that Anthony Quayle was already putting into Shakespeare at Stratford, or indeed that the Crazy Gang were still putting into revue at the Victoria Palace, was totally lacking in the world of musicals. When therefore a composer like Sandy Wilson or a musical like *The Boy Friend* left the relatively cloistered confines of a small and eminently suitable club theatre like the Players', they found themselves in a commercial jungle run by and for managers who had no real idea what to do with a musical if it didn't come across the Atlantic already laden with American success and stars.

But nor did London managements really know what to do with the few stars they had managed to create in musicals: the year that *The Boy Friend* opened was also the year that Evelyn Laye was turned down for the lead in *The King and I*: the role went instead to a Valerie Hobson, who, it was vaguely hoped, might mean more to filmgoing audiences. The idea of looking after, or even creating stars who could then be cherished by managements and nurtured by composers (as was now happening in America to the likes of Ethel Merman and Mary Martin) simply never seemed to occur to anyone in London. Where Coward and Novello would once write for themselves and a chosen band of loyal supporting players at least, the notion now that somebody might like to sit down and construct a new musical for Evelyn Laye or Jessie Matthews, or that after the tremendous success of Anne Rogers in *The Boy Friend* it might make sense for some London management to work on her career, appears not to have been anywhere within the scope of West End thinking. Nobody actually planned a musical or a musical career: they just occasionally happened, usually from the other side of the Atlantic, and largely at random.

One or two theatres, certainly, began to develop a musical policy: the London Coliseum, no longer able to generate its own ballets and overwhelmed by the sudden triumph of *Annie Get Your Gun* there, now began a run of Broadway shows including *Kiss Me Kate* (1951), *Call Me Madam* (1952), *Guys and Dolls* (1953), *Can-Can* (1954), *The Pajama Game* (1955), *Damn Yankees* (1957) and *Bells Are Ringing* (also 1957). But this was a matter of importing as many Americans as the unions would allow and cobbling the rest together in London as one more stop on a bus-and-truck tour: as a general rule, London tended to get the star of the Chicago rather than the New York productions.

Locally, however, the Wilson triumph with *The Boy Friend* was soon followed by another small-scale blockbuster: seven months after the

Players' company moved up West to Wyndham's, there opened at the Vaudeville the other great British musical hit of the decade, a show which was to exceed the run achieved by *The Boy Friend* by two hundred performances. *Salad Days* had started out at the Bristol Old Vic and its composer/pianist was, though six years younger than Wilson, in many ways his mirror image; educated at Eton and Cambridge, whereas Wilson had gone to Harrow and Oxford, Julian Slade was a barrister's son who started out by writing Cambridge undergraduate revues. From there he graduated as an actor to the Bristol Old Vic, where he and his leading lady, Dorothy Reynolds, began composing a sequence of Christmas musicals designed essentially to let the fundamentally classical company have a bit of fun around the piano. The first two of these seasonal entertainments, *Christmas in King Street* (the address of the theatre) and an adaptation of *The Duenna* remained just that. But the show they devised for Christmas 1953 was something else: *Salad Days* is the tale of two nostalgic college graduates coming out into a real world and encountering instead a tramp with a magic piano capable of making all who hear it break into dance routines.

The London first night prompted Ivor Brown, often the most acerbic of critics, to write 'while jet planes crashed the sound barrier, a piano tinkled and we suddenly took this to be the music of the spheres', though admittedly Milton Shulman for the *Evening Standard* took a dimmer view, noting that 'those best qualified to enjoy this would be an aunt, uncle or some other fond relative of a member of the cast.' Nevertheless, for five and a half years it remained at the Vaudeville, outlasting and overtaking *Chu-Chin-Chow* and *My Fair Lady* and *The Boy Friend* to become the longest-running musical in the history of the British theatre until, a decade later, its record was in its turn overtaken by the run of Lionel Bart's *Oliver!*

But like *The Fantasticks* in America, *Salad Days* came out of nowhere and like *The Boy Friend* it led nowhere: it didn't belong to the much more lavish Coward/Novello tradition, nor did it have much to do with the big-band sound of the Bart shows that followed it. Slade himself was just 24 when it reached London, and was amiably to reconcile himself to the fact that, like Wilson, his first success would be far and away his greatest.

Thirty years after the original Bristol opening, I asked the composer to think back to the events of 1953–4. *Salad Days* was originally put together in six weeks for a Bristol run meant to last no more than three: 'in those days,' recalled Slade, 'London managements didn't automatically send scouts out looking for promising material, but word-of-mouth spread and during our second week one or two people came down on the train from London to have a look at us.'

Of those managements who did express any interest, most insisted (as they had done with *The Boy Friend*) that it would have to be recast with

'West End' names: Slade managed nonetheless to keep most of his original company intact, and he himself went on playing the piano in the pit for the first eighteen months of the London run. But essentially he was still the 'house composer' for the Bristol Old Vic, and like Wilson he worked best in the Players'-like surroundings of a small non-West End theatre with a semi-permanent company:

'You had to work with the people you'd got at Bristol, but at least that meant you knew exactly what everyone was best at and what they enjoyed doing, even before you started to write a score. My difficulty ever since then, living in London, has been that when one starts a new show one never really knows who it is for, how many people one is supposed to have in the cast, what kind of budget or indeed management it will end up with. So one works in a kind of vacuum, hoping for the best; I've always been a great believer in knowing your own limitations – I know I'm never going to be the English Stephen Sondheim, any more than I was ever the English Rodgers and Hammerstein. I work best on a much smaller scale, preferably when I know exactly which actors and which theatre I'm writing for.' As for Slade, so for Wilson and the English musical theatre generally in the 1950s: the two composers were at once its greatest asset and a definition of its limitations.

But they were not of course working in a total vacuum: 1954 was also the year of *Wedding in Paris*, a banal Hans May/Sonny Miller score which achieved a certain success by bringing back Evelyn Laye and Anton Walbrook to the considerable number of their fans, even though it did only allow them one song each in an otherwise deeply unmemorable evening. And it was the year in which Noël Coward began his very last musical to receive its world premiere in London rather than in New York: *After the Ball*, an adaptation of Oscar Wilde's *Lady Windermere's Fan*, to which well-made comedy Noël had turned in some desperation after being vilified for his own plotting in *Pacific 1860* and *Ace of Clubs*. The Wilde play had always worked as a classic comedy, why should it not now benefit from some beautifully crafted period songs? In practice, largely because they slowed up the action, bringing it to a virtual standstill. Though Noël felt totally at home in the 1890s period, and had (in the view of Cole Lesley) never been so happy with a score, the fact remained that Coward and Wilde were an uneasy mix and reviews were generally dismissive: 'restless' and 'untidy' were among the adjectives used by Noël in his diary entry for 1 April 1955, when describing the Bristol opening night. In the next eight weeks before the London opening, the Robert Helpmann production did not improve hugely on the road, and though it survived a couple of hundred performances at the Globe, it then disappeared forever, taking with it some of the most lyrically nostalgic of all Coward's songs and leaving their composer with the determination henceforth to take all his scores across the Atlantic for proper professional treatment from the musical authorities around Broadway.

During the next two years, the Broadway invasion of the West End continued unabated (*Pal Joey, Can Can, Wonderful Town, Kismet, The Pajama Game, Plain and Fancy, Fanny*), and London continued to celebrate *The Boy Friend* and *Salad Days* while elsewhere retreating into a world of eccentric small-scale revue characterized by Bea Lillie and by Michael Flanders and Donald Swann. Very occasionally, a new English musical (usually derived from a classic source) would peer over the parapets of Shaftesbury Avenue, only to be blasted by critics and disappear again. Thus, *A Girl Called Jo* was a wan musical version of Louisa May Alcott's *Little Women*, while *Summer Song* was by Eric Maschwitz out of popular classical pieces by Dvořák; attempts at totally new musicals tended to be whimsically fey romances like the Pat Kirkwood *Chrysanthemum*, or *Wild Thyme* which had a famous opera star passing through a London railway station and taking off with one of the porters. Then there was *Wild Grows the Heather* (a musical based on J. M. Barrie's *Little Minister*), and by the time Harold Rome's entrancing Broadway musical of the Pagnol trilogy *Fanny* reached Drury Lane in the autumn of 1956, audiences seemed to have wearied even of good musicals from America, let alone the usual bad ones from home. Indeed, the only real musical highlight of the mid-1950s had been a Royal Court staging of the Brecht/Weill *Threepenny Opera*, with a remarkable cast led by Georgia Brown and Warren Mitchell.

There was, admittedly, one other show in this period that deserves to be recalled, though, by the time of its premiere at the Winter Garden in August 1955, it too seemed like an echo from some altogether different world: *The Water Gypsies*, the last of the A. P. Herbert/Vivian Ellis musicals, was an utterly enchanting adaptation of Herbert's own novel about the life of the barge people of England's canals, but as a stage show it had come just too late. *The Boy Friend* and *Salad Days* had accustomed audiences to a musical world where nothing could be taken too seriously: Herbert, like J. B. Priestley, still expected his audiences to care about the fate of his characters, and though the Ellis score is to my mind the best he ever wrote, the problem with the book was summarized by Tynan's theory that 'instead of measuring by miles the way *The Water Gypsies* fails as a modern musical, we should consider the inches by which Herbert and Ellis have failed to turn out a matchless museum piece. Their enterprise, beyond doubt, was to write a cockney pastoral which derived from Dickens and reached, in the *Punch* cartoons of the 1880s, a state of flawless unreality in which Sir Alan has striven to preserve it. And how nearly he has succeeded in making us believe in Hammersmith as a rural hamlet peopled with quaint bargees whose joys are homely and whose destiny is perforce obscure.'

The music of Vivian Ellis, conceded Tynan (though whether in praise or blame I have never been entirely certain), 'chimes like cowbells over the meadow' but it was not loud enough to overcome a general critical clamour that cockney pastorals were unlikely to point the way ahead to a future, if any, for the British musical. It was against this chilly background that a new score – *Grab Me a Gondola* – opened at the Lyric Hammersmith a few months later, followed by a swift transfer to the other Lyric on Shaftesbury Avenue; and, though not the greatest of scores or even the greatest of successes, this one does, I believe, deserve a credit it has never been given as the first coherent and confident attempt in the 1950s West End to stage a new musical which could just possibly be recognized as such on Broadway.

Certainly *The Boy Friend* was now to run there triumphantly, in fact the only British musical to thrive there in the thirty years that separated *Bitter Sweet* from *Oliver!*, but it had crossed the Atlantic as a period piece and it is still possible to meet countless Broadway theatregoers who believe that Wilson's show dates from the mid-1920s, so perfect was his sense of that period.

By contrast, *Grab Me a Gondola* never reached New York at all; yet it was surely the first English musical of the 1950s to betray any sign that its creators, cast and production team were even vaguely aware of what had been going on in New York during the decade since *Oklahoma!* Essentially a parody of the then headline-grabbing antics of British starlets at the Venice Film Festival, *Grab Me a Gondola* was written by Julian More and James Gilbert for a cast headed by Joan Heal and Denis Quilley, and there was an immediate edginess about it which suggested the start of a new generation of musical writers and players far removed from the ones who had been for so long enmeshed in what Agate called 'musicals richly endowed with the kind of thing their public likes best – complete vacuity of thought, combined with a lavish dispensation of everything else'. Indeed, the number called 'Cravin' for the Avon', in which Miss Heal as the dumb blonde announced her Shakespearean ambitions, might not have disgraced the score of *Kiss Me Kate*.

While James Gilbert was to leave the West End for a successful life in BBC television comedy, Julian More went on to write (often with Monty Norman and/or David Heneker) a wide range of the most interesting London stage musicals of the next thirty years, from *Expresso Bongo* all the way to *Songbook*: it is indeed some reflection on the way the British musical has been chronicled that because Julian More has had no major transatlantic hit, and because he is in no way as readily classifiable as Slade or Wilson or Bart, his career is still largely unchronicled in stage histories. Yet it was More who went on, through the 1960s and '70s, trying to push back the barriers of the small-scale domestic product and open it up to the influences of both Europe and America.

The year of his *Grab Me a Gondola*, 1956, was of course also the year that saw the most dramatic change in the straight theatre since the arrival of Bernard Shaw at the Royal Court in Sloane Square where, half a century later, John Osborne's *Look Back in Anger* was now to be seen. But musically the big hit of the season was nothing as ambitious as *Grab Me a Gondola*, nor did the Broadway/Marseilles of Harold Rome's *Fanny* appeal much to London audiences, despite a cast headed by Robert Morley who, before Paul Scofield and Rex Harrison, was the first non-singing star to attempt to take on a full-scale modern musical in the West End, albeit with rather less than total success. The big musical hit, which opened on the very last day of 1956, was instead a show that consisted of two men, one in a wheelchair and the other at a piano, singing amiable comic ditties of their own composition: Flanders and Swann in *At the Drop of a Hat*.

Nor did 1957 open promisingly for those who wanted their musicals to come with scenery and costumes and plots and perhaps rather more than two sedentary people: the first big show of the New Year was a uniquely disastrous fantasy called *The Crystal Heart*. Almost everything that could go wrong with a London musical did so here: it was an ambitious and, for its time, extremely expensive show, coming in to the Saville on a budget of £30,000. For it my grandmother Gladys Cooper, in a plot of such stunning banality that I have managed to forget all traces of it, was required both to sing and to dance. The fact that she had done neither in public since her days as a Gaiety Girl fully half a century earlier seemed not to alarm anyone, least of all Gladys. On the pre-London tour, during a strenuous dance routine, she sustained a cracked rib and this meant that when she opened at the Saville she was on painkillers. The first night was not a success: indeed it was one of those rare post-war occasions on which a West End show has been resoundingly booed not only at curtain fall but a long time before it. 'Like watching Christians thrown to the lions,' wrote Shulman in the *Evening Standard*; 'What a lovely afternoon,' said Dilys Laye, on stage, 'but not a very lovely evening' added a voice from the gallery. The cast battled on regardless; Gladys did a song about a Bluebird (a singularly unfortunate choice for a show that was already getting the bird) and finally won the evening on points, though it was a close thing. 'Gladys Cooper,' wrote Harold Hobson in the next issue of the *Sunday Times* (by which time the show had closed after only five performances), 'responded to the jeers and catcalls with magnificent venom. At the close, such victory as there was lay with her for the tremendous curtsey, defiant, lovely and imperial, with which (like a spirited Miranda kneeling to Caliban) she provocatively challenged the audience.'

Already, however, the flops in the West End musical theatre were more interesting than the hits: hits tended to come prepackaged from

New York but already slightly travel-weary, whereas the local productions had at least the merit of being built around subjects which would never get as far as a first-rehearsal read-through on Broadway. One such at this time was *Zuleika*, based by two Cambridge undergraduates (one of whom, James Ferman, went on to a long and successful career as secretary of the British Board of Film Censors) on the Max Beerbohm tale of a Victorian beauty causing mass suicide at Oxford. The production was not much helped, however, by the disappearance from the title role shortly before the opening night of Diane Cilento, of whose replacement (Mildred Mayne) it was noted by at least one critic that 'she is competent in a role where competence is alas not enough.'

That, too, was true enough of the English musical in general at this time: it relied mainly on charm and respectable pedigree in an era when both *My Fair Lady* and *West Side Story* had already indicated on Broadway that if you were to plunder Shaw and Shakespeare you had, in your adaptation, to be at least as good as the original instead of merely faintly reminiscent of it.

The great Lerner/Loewe and Bernstein/Sondheim scores were, however, not to reach London for another eighteen months, and in the meantime such shows as were coming across the Atlantic (*Bells Are Ringing* and *Damn Yankees*) had suddenly started to fail in the West End, leaving managements to turn back in some desperation to Julian Slade. With *Salad Days* still safely installed at the Vaudeville, surely the Strand would benefit from putting on another small-scale singalong across the road at the Savoy? Sure enough, *Free As Air* was to survive for four hundred performances, despite reviews complaining that the original unspoiled magic of innocence that was to be heard in *Salad Days* had now become somewhat affected: 'where their first success was a spring song about youth,' wrote Anthony Cookman of Slade and Reynolds now, '*Free As Air* is Arcadian whimsy.' Then again, London audiences had always liked *The Arcadians*.

But the *Free As Air* plot might almost have served as a metaphor for the state of the English musical at this time: essentially it concerned a mythical and of course unspoiled and rustic Channel Island which had managed totally to avoid the perils of modern sophistication and civilization. The best song of a patchy score was indeed 'Let the Grass Grow Under Your Feet', and its recurrent theme was that outsiders with modern methods and money spelt nothing but trouble. Such was indeed the general thinking around a rusty if not actually rustic West End about the threat of Broadway: English musicals of the period were expected to be small, cheap and fundamentally amateurish, preferably with a faint air of collegiate entertainment. The only trouble with *Free As Air* was, as Cookman noted for *The Tatler*, 'that Slade's songs, though catchily sentimental, tend to monotony. They celebrate the joy of breathing early morning air, the wisdom of forgetting what is painful to remember, the happy calm of being where there is nothing but sea and sky and suchlike simple delights. It is a pleasant piping of songs of innocence, but the pleasantness begins to cloy as the suspicion grows that such innocence is more of a literary affectation than real.'

While Slade was to continue at least until *Vanity Fair* (1962, Sybil Thorndike then inheriting from Gladys Cooper the mantle of the Old Lady Who Still Dances) trying to repeat the *Salad Days* formula with ever-diminishing returns as the salad lost its freshness and wilted in shows like *Follow That Girl* and *Hooray For Daisy* and *Wildest Dreams*, at least Sandy Wilson abandoned the 1920s territory of *The Boy Friend* for an altogether more dangerous idea. For 1958, his *Valmouth* was a musical of considerable courage and ingenuity based on the 'scandalous' novels of Ronald Firbank. Here, far from the purity of *Free As Air*, was a world of dancing cardinals, homosexual sailors and sex-starved aristocrats all of whom had private lives of distinct and often hilarious kinkiness. To that world, Wilson brought what is in my view not only his finest score but also one of the most impressive, varied and lyrical in the whole post-war history of the British theatre.

Though no critic went so far as to note this in print, *Valmouth* contained the first sexually ambivalent duet ('You're my friend, Jack, aren't you? Yes I am, Dick'), as well as a range of other numbers that was the most impressive in the thirty years that separated *Bitter Sweet* from *Oliver!* – from the title song through 'Magic Fingers' and 'Big Best Shoes' all the way to 'Cathedral of Clemenza' and 'I Will Miss You'. But though the original Hammersmith production made a star of Fenella Fielding and gave Bertice Reading (later replaced by Cleo Laine) some spectacular moments, the trouble was always the book. Though Wilson brought in Cardinal Pirelli from an altogether different Firbank novel to boost the second half, plots were never that author's strongest suit – nor, as any synopsis of *The Boy Friend* might indicate, have they ever been Sandy Wilson's either.

What audiences therefore got were some marvellous characters and superlative songs in search of a central focus: the dialogue, especially when spoken by Fenella Fielding (who was, even at that stage of her career, already so far over the top as to be almost out of sight) sounded like Evelyn Waugh rewritten by Oscar Wilde, and you couldn't ask for much more than that when dealing with high-camp Catholicism run riot. But Firbank himself was a master of the unlikely ('Order me,' he once commanded my godfather Sewell Stokes when they were supposed to be having tea at a Lyons' Corner House, 'herons' eggs whipped with wine into an amber foam.') and where else in the world but in *Valmouth* did characters ever amuse themselves by smacking the hermaphrodite?

The year of *Valmouth* and the London premieres of *My Fair Lady* and

West Side Story was also the year when two Julian More scores indicated that there was indeed now such a thing as the London musical which was neither small-scale, high camp nor imported from Broadway. The irony of *My Fair Lady* and *West Side Story* was of course that both were, in their original Shavian and Shakespearean form, essentially English properties: *My Fair Lady* is indeed the only musical with a setting only a stone's throw from the Theatre Royal Drury Lane, where it played for five years and, unlike *West Side Story*, opened with an all-English cast. The Julian More shows were certainly in nowhere near the same sort of league, but they did suggest that, left to itself, the West End could still manage to attract major talents from more classical spheres.

The first of these, opening at the Saville in April 1958, was *Expresso Bongo*, based by Wolf Mankowitz on his own short story satirizing the then new phenomenon of the teenage crooner, precisely the same theme as would be tackled on Broadway two years later by Charles Strouse and Lee Adams in *Bye Bye Birdie*. Of the two, there can't be a lot of doubt that *Expresso Bongo* was the better musical, albeit staged on a fraction of the budget and with minimal choreography. Yet here, for once in a very long while, was the West End actually giving Broadway a lead: where *Birdie* was essentially showbiz-soft at its centre, *Bongo* was, as Milton Shulman noted, 'a raucous, rhythmic paean of disgust aimed at the shoddy side of the entertainment business. In its misanthropic tour of the gutters of the West End, it washes up an unsavoury flotsam of sharp agents, talentless artists, love-starved women, greedy managers, shady café proprietors and dim debutantes. If they had a redeeming virtue among them, it would be stolen off their backs.'

And where *Birdie* had the bland Dick Van Dyke as the crooner's reluctant manager, *Bongo* had Paul Scofield making his first (and, thus far, only) appearance in a musical hot from classical triumphs at Stratford and the Phoenix but now turning in a Tin Pan Alley performance of such weary, disillusioned venom that his solo numbers still burn off an increasingly scratchy disc.

Bongo was also the show which started the career of Millicent Martin and which established a mood of seedy despair closer to *Pal Joey* or *Guys and Dolls* than to any English musical that had ever preceded it; perhaps the first genuinely adult musical to have opened in London and been written there, it memorably bit the West End hand that was feeding it while resembling nothing so much as a musical answer to the music-hall bitterness of Osborne's *The Entertainer*, then also playing in a city which seemed at last to have woken up to the darker realities of the show-business dream.

Within three months of the opening of *Expresso Bongo* (which Julian More had written with Wolf Mankowitz and David Heneker and Monty Norman) there followed at the Lyric his English adaptation, again with

Heneker and Norman, of a very different though also unusually dark musical drama, this one in his own view 'the first in the *Threepenny Opera* manner to capture the louche glamour of the Paris backstreets, the world of Jean Gabin, Edith Piaf and René Clair with its small-time crooks and good-time cocottes living out their lives in sleazy bars to the accompaniment of a nostalgic accordeon waltz.'

It was in fact another classical visitor to the West End musical, Scofield's long-time Stratford and Phoenix director Peter Brook, who first alerted More and his collaborators to the notion of converting Marguerite Monnot's *Irma la Douce* into English, and More still had his doubts: 'After several versions had been thrown into the wastepaper basket we eventually hit on the right way to present Irma to English audiences, which was to avoid the use of Bronx or Cockney slang equivalents, but to use instead a few French terms in the original and to adapt the lyrics freely . . . having had little or no trouble with the Lord Chamberlain, who apparently had no objection to good clean sex, we opened *Irma la Douce* at the Pavilion Theatre, Bournemouth, and though many of the Aunt Ednas in the audience could not believe their hearing aids at some of the lines, our fear that the show would prove too shocking was belied by a tremendous reception from a seaside clientele.'

That was echoed when *Irma la Douce* moved with Keith Michell and Elizabeth Seal to London, where Tynan hailed 'a bold, blue musical' and Richard Findlater wrote of 'a bold and surly extravaganza', while another critic claimed that it was 'the most adult, enjoyable and artistic musical since *The Beggar's Opera*'.

Suddenly, it seemed the West End musical no longer had to be either soft-centred or sugar-coated: a whole new generation of angry, grainy, unglamorous shows was ending the decade in a blaze of activity unknown in the more tranquil past of nostalgic Shaftesbury Avenue singalongs. And in the final year of the 1950s – a year notable in terms of imports only for a catastrophic attempt to stage Bernstein's *Candide* in London – an entirely new centre for the British stage musical opened up at Stratford East. Joan Littlewood's Theatre Workshop, which had hitherto only gone as far down the musical path as Brendan Behan's *The Hostage*, decided in 1959 that part of its populist brief for audiences in the area would be a musical about East End life and the sleazier crooks and whores and bent coppers who inhabited it.

Frank Norman, author of *Bang to Rights* and himself a man with some first-hand knowledge (since he had recently served two years in jail for bouncing cheques), was commissioned to write the book of what would be *Fings Ain't Wot They Used T'Be*, and a young local lyricist called Lionel Bart, who had just scored a pop-song success for Tommy Steele, was asked to write the score. Norman himself was less than happy with the improvisational methods by which Littlewood and her Stratford cast would regularly alter shows in rehearsal, but *Fings* opened in February 1959 to such acclaim that cast salaries were immediately raised to £20 per week. Bernard Levin acclaimed 'a musical of brilliant, bawdy irreverence', though in *The Tatler* its critic noted in some alarm that 'Banished are now the musicals such as came from Lehár and Novello: love, kindness, hope, faith and common decency are no longer the thing.'

Others thought that the East End was no place to sing comic songs about villains, but *Fings* anyway soon moved up West to the Garrick where it ran for over two years, thereby guaranteeing Littlewood's company some rare financial stability at their home base but also raising uneasy questions about whether this was the kind of work Theatre Workshop had been formed to perform. As Lindsay Anderson saw it, 'the chief problem was a kind of intellectual limitation: while much of what was produced at Stratford was subversive, because of the knees-up quality of the style it could just be seen as a nostalgic variety show. The problem with Joan was that her belief in popular theatre often fought with the dissident element, so that you got a strong traditional music-hall influence and all that rather regrettable and banal comedy.'

But with *Fings* and *The Hostage* both playing in the West End, Littlewood embarked on a major refit of the Theatre Royal complete with new chandelier, and in October 1959 it reopened with another low-life London musical, this one set in the Portobello Market. *Make Me an Offer* had already been a bestselling first novel, a television play and a Peter Finch movie by the time Wolf Mankowitz turned it into a musical with the help of Monty Norman and David Heneker, and the strongly Shaftesbury Avenue casting (Daniel Massey, Dilys Laye, Sheila Hancock) at Stratford East suggested that they already knew they had here another guaranteed West End transfer. At this time, of course, that was not necessarily the key to a goldmine: in 1959 Stratford's total profit from the West End runs of *Fings* and *Hostage* was just under £10,000. Mankowitz, like Frank Norman before him, was distinctly unhappy with what Littlewood and her troupe had done with his book on stage, but *Fings* was to go on to win the first *Evening Standard* Best Musical award while *Make Me an Offer* was acclaimed by Harold Hobson in the *Sunday Times* as 'the best musical now playing in London', and this at a time when both *My Fair Lady* and *West Side Story* were among the competition. The Lord Chamberlain still had grave doubts, however: a year after *Fings* opened at the Garrick, in response to 'numerous complaints against the play', he insisted that such lines as 'Don't drink that stuff, it will rot your drawers' and 'Excuse me dear, red plush, that's very camp that is' be instantly deleted. He also insisted that the actor playing a builder's labourer should carry his plank at a less erotic angle. 'The Lord Chamberlain,' concluded a letter from the official censor of the period, 'wishes to be informed of the manner in which the plank is in future to be carried.'

The Garrick Theatre in the West End, to which Joan Littlewood's production of Lionel Bart's low-life musical *Fings Ain't Wot They Used T'Be* transferred in 1959 from Stratford East.

But if modern musicals were still to be censored, there was a kind of refuge in the classical past: it was on 28 May 1959 that the first theatre in the City of London to have opened in three hundred years offered delighted audiences a boisterous and bawdy musical romp which had the added virtue of being based upon Henry Fielding's *Rape Upon Rape*. This too now had a score by Lionel Bart (lyrics only, music by Laurie Johnson) and, as *Lock Up Your Daughters*, was to ensure the safe launching of Bernard Miles' Thames-side Mermaid Theatre at Puddle Dock. Hy Hazell as Mrs Squeezum singing 'When Does The Ravishing Begin?' and Stephanie Voss leading the company in the title song will remain among the great musical memories of those of us lucky enough to have been at the opening of a show which has proved too local to export and oddly tricky to revive. But the real stars of *Lock Up Your Daughters* were the director Peter Coe and his designer Sean Kenny: here and together, they devised a kind of half-timbered classic musical setting which was to point the way to their next joint venture and the greatest British musical success of the 1960s, Lionel Bart's *Oliver!*

The West End musical thus ended the 1950s in a rare and unrepeatable blaze of East End celebration (*Fings* and *Make Me an Offer*), period City randiness (*Lock Up Your Daughters*) and black rage, this last being provided by John Osborne in a short-lived and commercially catastrophic musical about Fleet Street called *The World of Paul Slickey*. Prompted, many thought, by the way he had himself been treated by gossip columnists after his sudden success with *Look Back in Anger*, this was a somewhat hazy attack on tabloid diary columns at a time when the one in the *Daily Express* was signed 'William Hickey' and the one in the *Daily Mail* 'Paul Tanfield'. Osborne's musical was about the men who wrote the diaries and the sleazy aristocracy who inhabited them, and it opened at the Palace to what Milton Shulman reckoned was 'the most raucous note of displeasure heard in the West End since the war . . . it is inconceivable to me that Osborne's experience did not warn him that this potpourri of indignation and aimless abuse would not fit comfortably into the innocuous framework of a musical comedy.'

Christopher Whelen's score came in for some grudging praise, but even after *Fings*, audiences at the Palace were not yet ready for a musical in which a crucial development of the plot was a sex change by one of the leading players. Osborne himself once put together, without comment, a wonderfully funny scrapbook of the abuse that was poured on him at the time, starting with the entry dated 5 May 1959 in Noël Coward's diary ('never in all my theatrical experience have I seen anything so appalling . . . interminable long-winded scenes about nothing, and above all the amateurishness and ineptitude, such bad taste that one wanted to hide one's head.') and finishing with his own dedication to the text as published: 'I dedicate this play to the liars and self deceivers; to those who daily deal out treachery; to those who handle their professions as instruments of debasement; to those who, for a salary cheque and less, successfully betray my country; and to those who will do it for no inducement at all. In this bleak time, when such men have never had it so good, this entertainment is dedicated to their boredom, their incomprehension and their distaste.'

Quite far down the cast-list of *Paul Slickey*, for the few weeks that it survived at the Palace, playing an aged and eccentric aristocrat, was an actor called Harry Welchman who at Drury Lane in 1927 had created, and for several decades thereafter toured, the role of the Red Shadow in *The Desert Song*. As Lionel Bart was now so accurately observing at a nearby theatre, things were not what they used to be.

Opposite. Stage comedians, faced with the demise of the music-hall, were more inclined, in the 1950s, to turn to full-scale musicals which would still allow them some freedom to exploit their old routines: (*top*) George Formby in *Zip Goes a Million* (1951) at the Palace Theatre; (*below, left*) an advertising handout for *Bet Your Life* (1952), starring Arthur Askey; and (*below, right*) Fred Emney as the oversized baby in *Blue for a Boy* at His Majesty's (1950).

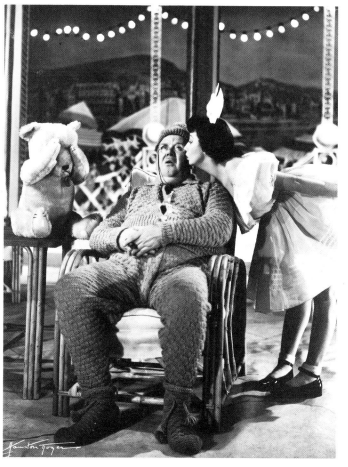

Two outstanding British challengers to the American invasion were Julian Slade with *Salad Days* (1954) at the Vaudeville (*above*), and Sandy Wilson with *The Boy Friend* (1953) at the Players' Theatre, their success proving that small-scale musicals could still compete with Broadway blockbusters. Later, Wilson came up with a brilliant score for Ronald Firbank's exotic *Valmouth*, staged at the Lyric Hammersmith in 1958, allowing Bertice Reading and Fenella Fielding (*opposite*) to give flamboyant performances as Mrs Yajnavalkya and Lady Panzoust.

Above. The cast of *Grab Me a Gondola* (1956) on stage at the Lyric Hammersmith, and (*inset*) Joan Heal and Denis Quilley, who took the leading roles in this satire on the behaviour of publicity-seeking starlets at the Venice Film Festival.

Left. A scene from the last and most lyrical of the Vivian Ellis/A. P. Herbert collaborations, *The Water Gypsies* (1955) at the Winter Garden Theatre: from left to right are seen Dora Bryan, Pamela Charles and Wallas Eaton.

Musicals of the later 1950s included: at the Lyric, *Irma la Douce* (1958), a Parisian folk tale of prostitution and prison, with Keith Michell, Elizabeth Seal and Clive Revill (*above*); at the Saville, *Expresso Bongo* (1958), starring Paul Scofield in his musical debut as a seedy Tin Pan Alley agent (programme cover, *below left*); and, at the Palace Theatre, *The World of Paul Slickey* (1959).

The Sixties

IN THE MUSICAL THEATRE as elsewhere around the West End, the 1960s opened in a mood of considerable confusion; the sudden burst of late-1950s activity, much of it happening far away from the traditional confines of Shaftesbury Avenue, had proved that most of the old theories about the musical could now be abandoned. Audiences were apparently prepared to pay good money to see shows without great stars or lavish settings, and they were prepared to celebrate the arrival, not before time, of a new generation of local composers led and symbolized by the abrasive cockney cheerfulness of Lionel Bart, a London music man about as far removed from Ivor Novello and Noël Coward as you could reasonably hope to get within one century and continent.

But managements who believed that the triumph of Bart's *Fings* and *Lock Up Your Daughters* meant a kind of Brechtian change, whereby audiences would be prepared to accept extremely unglamorous low-life musicals with maybe also a social message, soon came to realize that the situation was rather more complex than that. The crucial warning had been contained in Lindsay Anderson's comment about Stratford East: the music-hall element was at the same time a key to success and a denial of anything too overtly political or downbeat.

In 1960 shows like *The Lily White Boys* (at the Royal Court) and *Johnny the Priest* (at the Prince of Wales') rapidly established that musicals with a message and not much else were, like satire, what closed on Saturday night. A year that was mainly notable elsewhere for a headlong flight back to Julian Slade (*Follow That Girl*, *Hooray For Daisy*, the titles tell you all you need to know) and to Rodgers and Hammerstein in their most sentimental vein (*Flower Drum Song*) was also to be rememberd as the one in which Terence Rattigan turned his classic play *French Without Tears* into a musical called *Joie de Vivre*; it lasted all of four nights at the Queen's.

Opposite. Ron Moody in his memorable role as Fagin in Lionel Bart's *Oliver!* (1960) at the New Theatre.

153

Had it not been for *Oliver!*, then, the British stage musical in 1960 would have been in no better shape than it had been in 1950; a short golden period in 1958/9 had come to a rapid halt because there was no back-up system, even at Stratford East or the Mermaid, which would allow the successes of *Fings* or *Lock Up Your Daughters* to point the way ahead. Hit musicals in London were still regarded as lucky accidents that came out of nowhere and went nowhere; the idea of having a support system of the kind that Broadway has always given its musicals and that in the British theatre has only ever been given to Shakespeare at Stratford, the idea of a continuous policy of training and reviving and rehearsing, is still oddly alien to the world of musicals and it was not until twenty years after *Oliver!* that Bart's one true successor as a sole creator of hit musicals which could also make an impact on Broadway, Andrew Lloyd Webber, would begin even to think about the possibility of a permanent London musical theatre company.

But *Oliver!* had in fact emerged from the work that Bart, Coe and Kenny had done on *Lock Up Your Daughters*: here too they were working with a long-established classic, and here too they had the advantage of a plot which was at one and the same time a celebration and a criticism of the city where and about which it was written. Above all, it had a working plot: whereas Julian Slade's contemporary *Follow That Girl* reached its climax with a rousing chorus number solemnly entitled 'Shopping in Kensington', *Oliver!* was actually about something. It was about poverty and murder and revenge and theft, much like *The Threepenny Opera*, and for it Bart crafted a score of rousing brilliance: Georgia Brown's 'As Long As He Needs Me', the Artful Dodger's 'Consider Yourself At Home' and above all Ron Moody's closing soliloquy ('Reviewing the Situation') became part of the history and the fabric of the English musical theatre as soon as the show opened at the New Theatre on 30 June 1960.

Indeed, Ron Moody's Fagin still stands alongside Topol's Tevye in *Fiddler on the Roof* and Angela Lansbury's Rose in *Gypsy* as one of the very few performances created in a West End musical (rather than one transferred there from New York) which can truly stand comparison with Channing's *Dolly*, with Mary Martin's Nellie Forbush in *South Pacific*, or with Streisand's *Funny Girl* at the very head and heart of great acting in big-band shows. Moody will never do anything in his career that is better than that Fagin, and there will never be a musical Fagin that good: the part defines the career and the career is dominated by the part, one he also happily immortalized in the film version (far and away the best ever made of a British musical and also – the two do not always go so neatly together – the most successful at the box-office).

The figures for *Oliver!* spoke for themselves: Donald Albery's management at the New Theatre saw the curtain rise on the first night for an outlay of just under £15,000, and by the next morning had done a ticket-agency deal worth £22,000; within a month Bart had been offered £700,000 for the film rights alone. In terms of the Bart bank balance (though ironically he sold out all rights in the show some years later and no longer benefits from its frequent revivals) and of West End morale in general, *Oliver!* was a miracle: but all it really led to was a series of other and decreasingly successful Dickensian plunderings, while other music makers seemed ever more desperately in search of a theme. Early in 1962, Wolf Mankowitz even tried a musical life of the mass-murderer Dr Crippen (*Belle*), which got ritually dismembered by critics and found little favour with the public.

By the end of 1961 *Salad Days* was already being revived, and in the face of a renewed onslaught from Broadway (*The Music Man, The Sound of Music, Bye Bye Birdie, Do Re Mi, The Fantasticks* all in that year) local developments were again on a more intimate scale: *Beyond the Fringe* effectively killed off revue competition forever, but the only new English musical of real interest was *Stop the World, I Want to Get Off*, with a book, music and lyrics by Leslie Bricusse and Anthony Newley, who also starred and directed. Newley, who had himself started out as a boy actor in the film of *Oliver Twist*, and Bricusse, who was to go on to such Hollywood scores as *Dr Doolittle* and *Goodbye Mr Chips*, were an intriguing team who seemed for a while to be offering a real alternative to the Dickensian nostalgia or the East End jollity that was everywhere around them. Both men had been steeped in show business from an early age, and their scores (of which far and away the best, *Roar of the Greasepaint, Smell of the Crowd*, has never had a proper London hearing) were essentially backstage fables of one kind or another.

Stop the World was set in a Sean Kenny circus tent, and concerned a penniless boy becoming a millionaire but losing himself somewhere along the way: it too went on to a long Broadway life much aided by a hit number called 'What Kind of Fool Am I?' Essentially, Newley and Bricusse had written here a lightweight musical *Peer Gynt*, but Kenny's minimal-chic set, Newley's pop-record stardom and some intelligent management on both sides of the Atlantic assured them runs of five hundred performances in both cities; neither of their subsequent musicals (*Roar of the Greasepaint* and the catastrophic *Good Old Bad Old Days* ten years later) could repeat that initial triumph, however, and once again the immediate prospects for the English musical appeared to be entirely confined to the talents of one man, Lionel Bart, though even his career was already beginning to falter.

It would perhaps have been optimistic to expect that a man who had in less than three years had three of the biggest hits in the whole of the post-war British musical theatre (*Fings, Lock Up Your Daughters* and *Oliver!*) was not now heading for some sort of a fall, and though his next show

155

achieved a thoroughly impressive run of more than five hundred performances, its costs had been so exorbitant and its reviews so generally grudging that *Blitz!* cannot overall be considered an unqualified triumph. Essentially, this – at the time the most expensive British musical costing around £50,000 – was an attempt to do for World War II what Coward's *Cavalcade* had done for the years surrounding World War I. It was an epic about London families living under constant German bombing, but it emerged, as had *Cavalcade*, from a Londoner's desire to get local musicals out from under the dominance of Broadway. As Bart himself explained at the time: 'The American musical, having been influenced over the years by British [writers and] composers like Gilbert and Sullivan, finally broke into their own territory with *Oklahoma!*, but then they too became stereotyped and the only real departure has been *West Side Story* which is a brilliant marriage of drama and dance, a revolutionary step but totally lacking in heart. There's no way we could do a show like that over here, but what it has taught me is the importance of truth on a stage. What I want to do now is to get back to English folk groups, English street cries and English nursery rhymes. I'm a Jew, so there are Jewish things in there too, and I use jazz because it's unavoidable, because it means either civilisation or decadence. I'm not a musical scholar, but I've a good ear and in *Blitz!* I've tried to use music as period pastiche and as dramatic statement.'

In fact, the real star of *Blitz!* was undoubtedly Sean Kenny's amazing exploding set, the kind of spectacular you only ever get to see now in a Lloyd Webber show. In its review *The Times* pinpointed an essential problem here: 'The most expensive British musical to date turns out to be a theatrical hybrid: it sets out as a panorama of life in the East End during the bombing, and then narrows its focus to the fortunes of one family. What promises at first to be a tribute to plucky Little England in the traditions of the Rank cinema turns into a no less sentimental story of the Jewish community. This sounds a frail idea to support an elaborate entertainment, and indeed it is; nor is there much in the characterisation, dialogue or music to divert attention from the banality of a plot which, after opening speciously with a microcosm of wartime London, is finally tied up when a Jewish deserter gives himself up to the authorities and a Gentile boy capitulates into marriage with a blind Jewish girl. However, as in the case of his previous *Oliver!*, Mr Bart is saved by a stage set of quite staggering magnificence, and once again it is by Mr Sean Kenny. It consists of four immense mobile units representing the streets of the East End; in addition to these, there is a huge platform the full length of the stage which in the opening scene soars up into the flies, disclosing an Underground station in which the cast are bedding themselves down for the night.'

The comments made by the late Kenneth Tynan were in a similar vein, and he ended with a warning of possible things to come: '. . . I have a fearful premonition of the next show Mr Kenny designs. As soon as the curtain rises, the sets will advance on the audience and summarily expel it from the theatre.' Such a nightmare concept was to become a reality some twenty years later in the rock musical *Time*, but any show in which the sets attract all the attention is – as *Mutiny!* was also to demonstrate in the 1980s – a show in trouble; had the score of *Blitz!* been a little better as a whole (one number alone, an evacuees' marching song, 'Going to the Country', lives with me still) or had the post-*Oliver!* expectations been a little lower, the show might have received a more rapturous welcome. As it was, the last word went as usual to Noël Coward, on emerging from the first night at the Adelphi: 'Just as long as the real thing,' he murmured, 'and twice as noisy.'

Coward was in fact in London to attend the opening, on the opposite side of the Strand at the Savoy, of what was to be his last West End musical and his first not to receive its premiere there. Asked why, Noël – then in New York – had said: 'Because critics there [in London] never even notice the music in a musical. Here in New York light music is treated properly, taken seriously, and given a whole production expertise backstage which is still totally unknown in London. We just don't have the choreographers, the orchestrators, the dancers, the technicians to cope with the complexities of a big musical.' And this, in a nutshell, was the problem that was to bedevil the West End musical for yet another fifteen years until the arrival of *Cats*, years in which local musical activity was once again to drop to the usual London low.

Ironically, however, the London production of *Sail Away*, which Noël himself directed from his own book and lyrics about the life and loves of a luxury liner's cruise hostess (hauntingly well played by Elaine Stritch in what I consider has been the greatest performance of her career) was treated rather better by critics than the original Broadway staging. An otherwise English cast sharpened the contrast between the passengers and their all-American guide, while the notices displayed an eagerness to welcome Coward home now that critics had seen what generally happened to the London musical scene in his absence. Indeed, the playwright John Whiting, who was then also drama critic of *The London Magazine*, used *Sail Away* as the starting point for an affectionate essay about Noël: 'We have had him with us now for sixty glorious years; we had better accept him. That extraordinary piece of landscaping which he uses for a face, and the dying dove which he pretends is a voice, are always hinting nowadays that he is forgotten, old-fashioned and unloved. That he is forgotten is demonstrably untrue; that he is old-fashioned is another matter. *Sail Away* is the bluntest thing to have struck the West End for many a year. But is he unloved? Speaking as one twenty years his junior, all I can ask is: who doesn't love his youth? For that is what Coward is to men of my age: *Private Lives, Conversation Piece, Operette, Tonight at 8.30, The Scoundrel* and all those songs we sang to our girls driving back in the red MG from the Thames pub on a summer night in 1936.'

Few of Coward's critics, or his admirers, ever put it better; but Noël himself now knew, looking at the brave new world of Lionel Bart and Anthony Newley, that his musical epoch was lost forever: as Stritch sang night after night at the Savoy, 'When you feel your song is orchestrated wrong, why should you prolong your stay? On the wings of the morning with your own true love, sail away, sail away, sail away.'

The rest of that year brought nothing more exciting then the prospect of Dame Sybil Thorndike kicking up a heel in Julian Slade's otherwise fairly unagile musical *Vanity Fair*, though there was also, just in time for Christmas, the premiere of *Cindy-Ella*, an amiable if sketchy attempt by Ned Sherrin and Caryl Brahms to turn *Cinderella* into a kind of black-face revue, one which was to enjoy a long life in seasonal revivals here and there.

By 1963, however, it had been generally decided that despite the failure of *Vanity Fair*, classic texts set to music were about the only safe bet in the West End's orchestra pits, the result being that we got Tommy Steele in *Half a Sixpence* (based on H. G. Wells' *Kipps*), Harry Secombe in the title role of *Pickwick* (a long way after Dickens), and *Virtue in Danger* (based by Paul Dehn on Sir John Vanbrugh's *The Relapse*). Even the Broadway imports of the year were the classically-derived *Boys From Syracuse* and *A Funny Thing Happened on the Way to the Forum*.

Both *Half a Sixpence* and *Pickwick* went to Broadway in the wake of *Oliver!*, though neither stayed there as long, since a law of diminishing returns about chirpy period British singalongs had already started to apply. Moreover, so far from advancing the cause of the British musical, save perhaps in economic terms, these shows were actually setting it back into a cosy historical past from which Julian More and Anthony Newley had at least tried to drag it into the second half of the twentieth century. A new musical in London now usually meant an old book, safely out of copyright, to which somebody had managed to add a few songs. New musicals that started from scratch were now as rare as a good dance director, and it was therefore not surprising that the one truly great musical of the year was in fact an anthology of songs from World War I that had originally been cobbled together as a radio documentary.

Oh What a Lovely War!, which opened at Stratford East in March before moving on to a two-year run at Wyndham's, was an evening of wartime songs, dance, a few battles and a few jokes. It was also a memorably savage attack on the generals' management of affairs in the Great War, though in Ewan MacColl's view its success meant the end of the Joan Littlewood dream of a people's theatre: 'The wrong kind of good

Tommy Steele and Marti Webb in *Half a Sixpence* (1963) at the Cambridge Theatre, as seen by Punch cartoonist Bill Hewison.

write-up from critics produced a situation where you couldn't get near the theatre for Bentleys and Mercedes, with the result that working-class people in Stratford East felt "this is not for us" . . . here was an anti-war show with retired generals in the audience, and instead of fury it left the audience with a rosy glow of nostalgia. It was at this point that we could say farewell to the dream of creating a working-class theatre.'

Yet, as the Richard Attenborough film went on to demonstrate with equal clarity, *Oh What a Lovely War!* was an angry and unforgettable reworking of nostalgia, though admittedly one which got softened on its way up West. On the original Stratford East first night, the show ended with Victor Spinetti alone on stage delivering one final speech of anti-war fury; by the time it got to Wyndham's, audiences were being sent out into the night with a closing reprise of all the great songs. But this was still a devastating attack on the officer class, a diatribe in which the men who served under them were seen going to their deaths amid the merry songs of the day: 'We don't want to lose you, but we think you ought to go.' Upstage a neon light spelled out the message of the musical: 'Passchendaele: British loss 135,000 men in the first day. Gain: 100 yards.' The War Office solemnly complained that the sign should have read 'officers and men': Joan Littlewood, the Mother Courage of East End theatre, replied simply: 'We have done your officers the honour of calling them men.'

Like most of what has always been best about the British stage musical, *Oh What a Lovely War!* was unbeatable and unrepeatable: it would never have worked with a new score, or a book that was much more than a scrapbook, but precisely because it took the music of the period and then looked beyond the nostalgia at the wartime carnage, it remains the most powerful and haunting evening I have ever spent in the British musical theatre. As some Mermaid shows and *Side by Side by Sondheim* were later to prove in gentler vein, producers in Britain have often been very good at putting together old songs in new and intelligent formations capable of saying something about their composers and the period in which the songs were first written.

The next year, 1964, saw a lot of apparently safe ideas proved extremely unsafe in production: one of the hardest lessons for British musical impresarios to learn has been the one about not going back to precisely the same well twice. Just because *Lock Up Your Daughters* had triumphed at the Mermaid, there was no guarantee that *Virtue in Danger* would work as well, even with such Dehn delights as 'Hoyden Hath Charms' and a cast featuring John Moffatt and Patricia Routledge who, a decade later at that theatre, would go on to play the classic *Cowardy Custard*. Equally, and at opposite ends of the musical market, *A Kayf Up West* was a catastrophic attempt at Stratford East to do another *Fings Ain't Wot They Used T'Be*, while at the Players' *Divorce Me Darling* was a better-written but no less disastrous attempt to do another *Boy Friend*. In both cases the original authors (Frank Norman and Sandy Wilson) were working at their original theatres with their original directors: but their sequels were not to be similarly rewarded, and by now even the Lionel Bart bandwagon was losing its momentum. Bart's 1964 musical *Maggie May* had a book by Alun Owen and a remarkable performance in the title role by Rachel Roberts: a pre-Beatles fable of Liverpool life, it was originally written by Bart for his *Oliver!* star Georgia Brown, who turned it down. This show, which earned back the £60,000 invested in it, opened to vastly better reviews than *Blitz!* but yet somehow never managed to generate the same degree of public enthusiasm as *Oliver!* or *Fings* had done.

Nevertheless, Kenneth Haigh and Rachel Roberts gave two vocally and dramatically strong central turns and Sean Kenny had a field day recreating huge dockland settings: if anything, the show was perhaps too local to Liverpool folklore to capture the imagination of what was now an increasingly international London theatregoing audience, and apart from the title song the score was not as strong as the great Bart triumphs. Of all his shows, though, *Maggie May* is the one I would most like to see revived and, *Oliver!* apart, the one that could now best stand up to reconsideration, despite Milton Shulman's belief in 1964 that 'whatever there was authentically Liverpudlian in the story of a navvy and a tart with a heart of gold has been dissipated by the attentions of a Canadian director [Ted Kotcheff], an Irish designer and a Jewish songwriter.'

The most intriguing musical of 1964 was perhaps an Oxford

undergraduate satire on the hypocrisy surrounding the then-topical capital punishment debate (*Hang Down Your Head and Die*, which came briefly to the Comedy), but elsewhere a headlong flight back to safe and well-tried texts led to the big London musical hit of the mid-1960s, Ronald Millar's adaptation of Besier's *The Barretts of Wimpole Street* which, as *Robert and Elizabeth*, was to survive two years and more at the Lyric. This was the show with just about everything to guarantee success in a London musical: a familiar story of familiar people (Robert Browning and Elizabeth Barrett) in familiar romantic difficulties, it starred June Bronhill (who was then at the height of her operetta fame) opposite Keith Michell who, alongside Denis Quilley, had remained the only impressive leading man of the post-war West End musical. For good measure it also had John Clements (and later Donald Wolfit in his last performance) going memorably over the top as Elizabeth Barrett's father. Ronald Millar's book was a perfectly adequate *Reader's Digest* concertina version of the original creaky incest melodrama, and Ron Grainer's score sounded as though it had been soaked in minor Novello rhapsodies for several decades. All in all a perfect formula for a musical theatre in a decade where the other longest runs were to be achieved by *Charlie Girl* and *The Black and White Minstrel Show*.

That same year, Dave Lee and the drama critic Herbert Kretzmer came up with a more impressive but less successful attempt to bring J. M. Barrie back into the musical theatre: *Our Man Crichton* offered Kenneth More as the admirable butler in what was now the Rex Harrison tradition of 'spokesinging', but more importantly this was the show that made a star of Millicent Martin who alone – had West End conditions been more favourable – might have been able to do for the London musical what Ethel Merman and Mary Martin and Carol Channing had already done for its Broadway equivalent.

But conditions weren't that favourable, and indeed 1965 was to prove a nadir year even by Shaftesbury Avenue standards: only three new English musicals, two of which (*Passion Flower Hotel* and Lionel Bart's *Twang*) were disasters of epic proportions while the third, *Charlie Girl*, was the kind of inexplicable triumph that had in 1953 had drama critics puzzled over *The Glorious Days*, which by no small coincidence also starred Anna Neagle.

The late Dame Anna always was a law unto herself and at her best in appalling surroundings: certainly there were enough of those here. Billed as 'a story conceived by Ross Taylor', *Charlie Girl* had already been worked on by three other writers (Hugh and Margaret Williams and Ray Cooney) before reaching the stage of the Adelphi, only to be acclaimed by Bernard Levin as 'harmless trash, somewhere between perfectly frightful and dead 'orrible'. 'It takes place,' he went on, 'in a stately home equipped with Adam ceiling, Jacobean panelling and a low Gothic

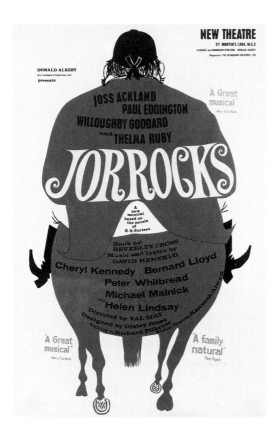

Poster for the New Theatre production of *Jorrocks* (1966), a musical adaptation of the Victorian hunting-field stories by Robert Surtees; and the programme cover for *Sing a Rude Song* (1970), an essay in nostalgia based on the backstage life of the music-hall star Marie Lloyd.

staircase, down which last in the fullness of time there comes an Early English Neagle in a remarkable state of preservation and a hired tiara to preside over some of the weediest revels to have broken out in this town for years . . . the only remotely interesting question the thing provokes is, of course, can it find an audience? If it can, there must be more people around than I thought who will put up with the determinedly second-rate for the sight of Miss Neagle and Miss Hy Hazell chatting about dear old days and dear Jack Buchanan and dear Binkie and dear Jessie Matthews and dear, oh dear, oh dear . . . Miss Neagle goes up and down the staircase; Miss Hazell flings herself into anything in the script or the music that will stay still long enough; Mr Joe Brown is by no means Mr Tommy Steele; and the twin ingénues deploy grins into which, by the end of the proceedings, I yearned to stuff a couple of herrings . . . the choreography, unattributed, appears from internal evidence to be by St Vitus, and the music goes around and around. I comes out here.'

Now one might think that, with such reviews – and Levin's was by no means the worst of them ('brash, charmless, vulgar, obvious and wilfully lacking in wit,' said the first line of the *Daily Telegraph* notice, this from a paper that might still have been thought to stand with Miss Neagle on the conservative-nostalgic ticket alone) – *Charlie Girl* might have closed by the following weekend, especially as Godfrey Winn had already come to its defence in print: 'Isn't it time we had some sort of reliable entertainment guide to protect the average playgoer from the personal judgement of that small, acidulated, self-important group of highbrows who condemn everyone else's taste in theatre as being fit only for the coach trade?'

In fact, the 'average playgoer' was in need of no such protection; whoever they were, the audiences had decided that regardless of critics, maybe regardless even of plot and score and scenery, *Charlie Girl* was what they most wanted to see. It therefore survived at the Adelphi for all of 2,202 performances in a victory run that has been beaten by only six other English musicals. For the record, three of those (*Jesus Christ Superstar, Evita, Cats*) are by Andrew Lloyd Webber, a man who, when *Charlie Girl* first opened, was not quite seventeen; the other three are *Chu-Chin-Chow* (1916), *Salad Days* (1954) and *Oliver!* (1960).

Charlie Girl is the quick two-word answer to anyone who still believes that critics have any real power in the West End, or that musicals have to be good to enjoy a run lasting more than five years. But can anybody now name the men who wrote its music and lyrics? They were in fact David Heneker and John Taylor, neither of whose subsequent careers in the musical theatre has yet matched the amazing success achieved by *Charlie Girl*, which returned (with Cyd Charisse) for a revival in 1986.

Managements unable to front up Anna Neagle as a totem to offset all critical attack had, however, to face the cold reality of 1965, which was that Lionel Bart's *Twang* closed at the end of January having made a net loss of over £80,000. Such a sum had never been spent on, let alone lost by, a London musical before and the news provoked a general run for cover. New musicals were clearly a risk: old musicals were expensive, and in the year when Broadway sent us Barbra Streisand in *Funny Girl*, the best the British could manage was a sudden and inexplicable fascination with industrial unrest among Victorian female matchmakers. No less than two new English musicals (*Strike a Light* at the Piccadilly and *The Matchgirls* at the Globe) dealt more or less adequately with this burning topic, leaving elsewhere nothing but musicals based on escapologists (*Man of Magic*), drag artists (Danny la Rue's *Come Spy With Me*) or old comics (Ron Moody's Grimaldi biography *Joey Joey*). There was also a brisk attempt to get back to Victorian hunting-field nostalgia with *Jorrocks*, but it is doubtful whether any of these would have been eligible for a 'new musical' award anywhere but in a moribund West End.

On the subject of awards, a study of the *Evening Standard* prizegiving lists since 1955 is in itself a history of the British musical in trouble. In the first year a 'best musical' award went to Broadway's *Pajama Game*. In 1956 the category was retitled 'best musical entertainment' and went to the ballet-revue *Cranks*. In 1957 there was no musical award of any kind. In 1958 it went to Broadway's *West Side Story*. In 1959 and 1960 it was, rarely, won by musicals that were English enough to have been created by Joan Littlewood at Stratford East: *Fings Ain't Wot They Used T'Be* and *Make Me an Offer*. But by 1961 the 'best musical' was in fact a revue, *Beyond the Fringe*, and in 1962 there was once again no musical award of any kind. In 1963 it went to another borderline case, the historical anthology *Oh What a Lovely War!*, and in 1964 back to Broadway for *Little Me*. In 1965 there was again no musical award, and for the next four years it went again to Broadway imports: *Funny Girl*, *Sweet Charity*, *Cabaret* and *Promises, Promises*. In 1970 there was again no award of any kind. Thus, in fifteen years, the best musical award of the leading London evening paper had only twice been won by new English musicals; in the next fifteen years it would be won by only another five; such figures make sorry reading in the context of an award specifically designed to honour a British theatre which in all other areas was generally reckoned to be enjoying a golden harvest.

By 1967 *The Boy Friend* was due for a revival, and John Hanson had become the touring king-in-exile for thousands of theatregoers all over the country whose idea of a great musical treat was yet another revival of *The Desert Song*. Understandably dispirited by rapidly rising costs, an increasing ratio of flops to hits and ever more glossy Broadway imports, London managements settled for Harry Secombe in a cod swashbuckler (*The Four Musketeers*), while the first of many attempts to hack a musical out of the life and times of Marie Lloyd was made by Daniel Farson at Stratford East with Avis Bunnage in a role that was later to be attempted, though with not much more success, by Barbara Windsor in the Sherrin/Brahms *Sing a Rude Song*.

The following year brought *Cabaret* from Broadway (not to mention *I Do I Do*, *Man of La Mancha*, *You're a Good Man Charlie Brown*, *Golden Boy*, *Hair* and a revival of *Lady Be Good*), but what mattered about *Cabaret* was that it looked neither imported nor second-hand. In coming to London and setting up a wholly fresh production, Hal Prince began invaluably to make the English think that they could maybe do big musicals after all: his courageous casting of a classical actress with almost no musical background launched Judi Dench as a world-class star, though on a career in musicals which has sadly thus far led only to one other and lesser score (the Mercer/Previn *Good Companions*) and an enforced last-minute withdrawal from *Cats*.

But what mattered about Dench in *Cabaret* was the definition of what the English could do with an American musical: until now, what they had mostly managed was just a rather worse rendering than would be achieved by the average summer-stock or road tour in its native land. Here things were very different: *Cabaret*, though an American score by the great John Kander/Fred Ebb team, was based on an English writer's view of pre-war Berlin, one moreover which had already proved a considerable success in the West End as a straight play – *I Am a Camera* – which had made a star of Dorothy Tutin, the actress whom Dench perhaps most resembles.

Moreover this *Cabaret* was not the same *Cabaret* as the version that ended up on film with Liza Minnelli as its star: where that, as Dench herself has noted, is fundamentally a success story, the stage version was a story of failure. Yet, as Judi Dench's biographer Gerald Jacobs adds, 'most people still think of *Cabaret* as a spectacular movie with a bravura performance by Minnelli. Even for those who admired Judi Dench in the role, points of comparison are easily conceded – Minnelli was the real singer, the better dancer, the star. No contest. But who was the true Sally Bowles?'

And that was what the English could do in musicals: they could play roles better than any all-singing, all-dancing Broadway legend. But to do that they had to have the roles, the directors, the writers; and these were still in very short supply around Shaftesbury Avenue, where the big local hit of the year was yet another critic-defying blockbuster, *Canterbury Tales*. This was an arrangement by Martin Starkie and the composers Richard Hill and John Hawkins of Nevill Coghill's bestselling Chaucer translations, the very same ones that had helped thousands of schoolchildren on their way through English Literature examinations for thirty years.

They proved equally appealing to thousands of theatregoers, who kept the *Tales* at the Phoenix for a five-year run that was to outlast *The Maid of the Mountains*, *Me and My Girl* and *Perchance to Dream* before closing at 2,082 performances, only two short of *The Boy Friend*. 'Bawdy and Boring' was typical of the headlines over several reviews, an opinion apparently not shared by the public.

A year that was elsewhere more notable for its plays with songs (*Forty Years On* and *Close the Coalhouse Door*) ended with an amiably pointless adaptation of Daisy Ashford's *The Young Visiters*, with Alfred Marks in splendid form as the Mr Salteena who was not quite a gentleman; but if, three months after the London opening of the revolution that was *Hair*, you had told an American impresario that the British musical was pinning its Christmas hopes on an entertainment derived from a novella written by a nine-year-old girl in 1890, which had a score by Ian Kellam and Michael Ashton with tunes that many had trouble recalling even during the interval, there might just possibly have been faint surprise.

The following year, 1969, brought *Mame* and *Promises, Promises* from

New York: the West End countered with ritual revivals of *The Merry Widow* and *Lock Up Your Daughters*, following them with a short run of musicals derived from immaculately worthy, if dull, literary works about young girls called Anne: *Anne of Green Gables* and *Ann Veronica* did not even bother with a title change, though for the Dickens singalong of the year they at least shortened *A Tale of Two Cities* to just *Two Cities*. The problem with all of these retreads was well summarized by Michael Billington in *The Guardian*. 'By the end of the evening, one is never clear what it was about the source that first made anyone think it could be turned into a musical.'

By now, however, conversion fever was so rife along Shaftesbury Avenue that desperate managements were even trying to turn Noël Coward plays into musicals, blithely overlooking the fact that if he had wanted them, or thought them suitable, as musicals he himself would have written them as such in the first place. Undaunted, John Taylor now took two of the nine short plays that had made up Coward's *Tonight at 8.30* (several of them had of course been musicals anyway) and turned them into what proved to be catastrophic double-bill at the Palace called *Mr and Mrs*.

By the summer of 1969, six musicals of that year had jointly flopped to the tune of almost half a million pounds. Five of the six were adaptations: *Mr and Mrs*, the two *Anns*, *The Young Visiters*, and *Two Cities*. That left *Belle*, a wild-west life of Belle Starr which had signally failed to draw the town to Betty Grable in person. Shows that were still thriving included *Charlie Girl*, *Fiddler on the Roof* and *Canterbury Tales*, while *Mame* and *Your Own Thing* were new enough for an open verdict: in fact the first worked in London and the second didn't.

But six orchestral productions losing nearly half a million pounds in less than six months at 1960s values did not exactly add up to a climate in which the British musical might yet again be reborn, and the decade ended in some despair with *Phil the Fluter*, an Irish whimsy which was clearly meant to be son of *Charlie Girl* since it was presented by the same management and staged by the same director. In place of the gracious, ageless Anna Neagle there was the gracious, ageless Evelyn Laye; instead of television comedian Derek Nimmo there was television comedian Stanley Baxter; and instead of amiable pop star Gerry Marsden there was amiable pop star Mark Wynter. The result of the mixture as before was yet another reminder that at that point there was really no such thing as a reputable British stage musical.

Opposite. Sarah Badel and John Clements in *Robert and Elizabeth* (1964) by Ronald Millar and Ron Grainer; this musical, based on *The Barretts of Wimpole Street*, ran for two years at the Lyric.

Scenes from 1960s musicals based on classic texts: (*above, left*) Alfred Marks as Mr Salteena in *The Young Visiters* (1968) at the Piccadilly Theatre; (*right*) Kenneth Warren and Jessie Evans as the Miller and the Wife of Bath in *Canterbury Tales* (1968) at the Phoenix Theatre; (*above, right*) Teddy Green as Sam Weller and Harry Secombe in the title role of *Pickwick* (1963) at the Saville Theatre; and (*opposite*) Edward Woodward as Sydney Carlton in *Two Cities* (1969) at the Palace Theatre.

Left. Anthony Newley in *Stop the World, I Want to Get Off* (1961), a revue-like musical jointly created by Leslie Bricusse and Newley himself, which had a run of 500 performances at the Queen's Theatre.

Opposite. Toni Palmer as Elsie in a scene from Lionel Bart's evocation of life in wartime London, *Blitz!* (1962) at the Adelphi; this was the most ambitious English musical attempted since *Cavalcade* thirty years earlier.

Below. Rachel Roberts in the title role of *Maggie May* (1964), at the Adelphi; this Liverpool folk opera was the last of the big Lionel Bart shows.

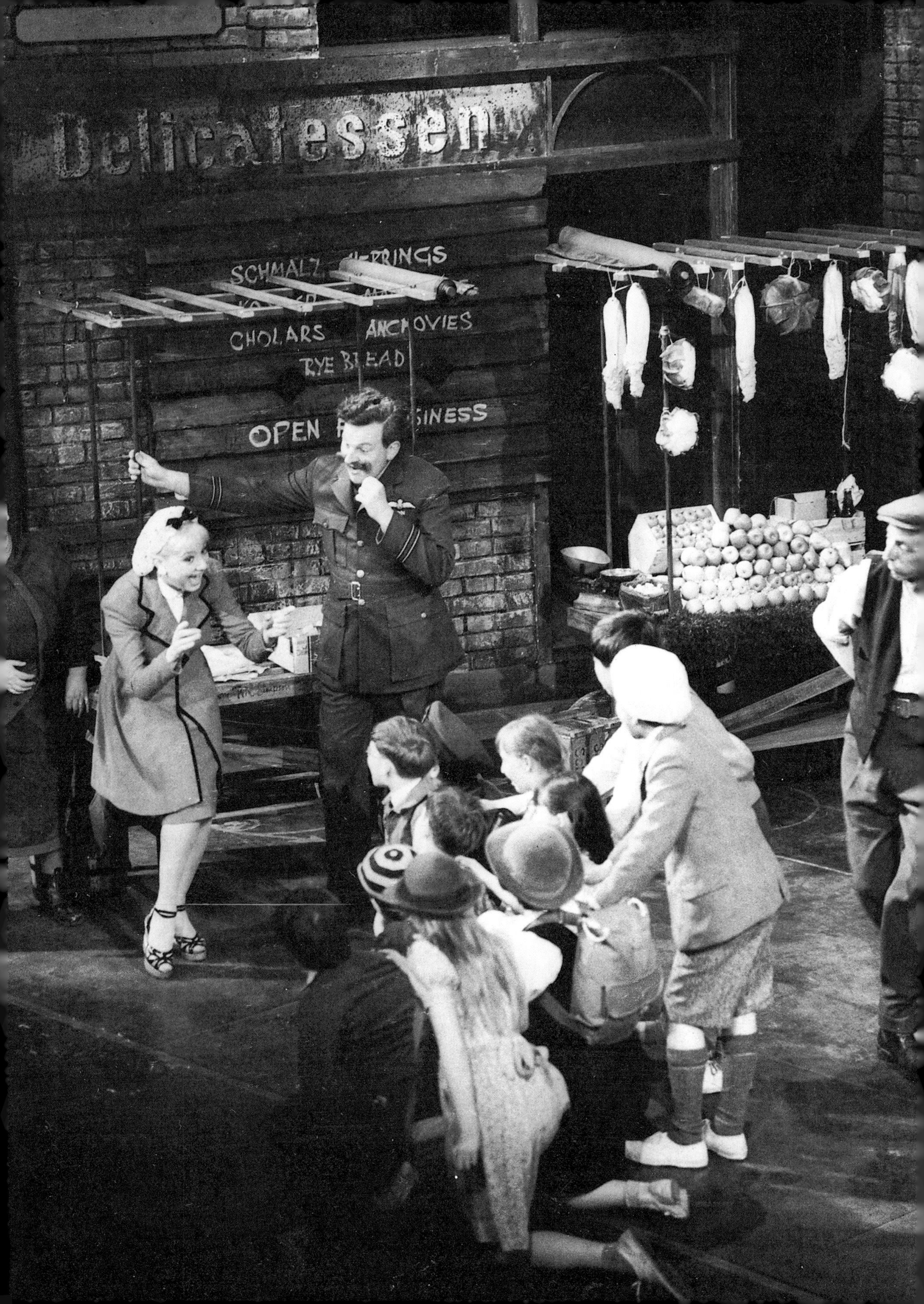
Delicatessen
SCHMALZ
ANCHOVIES
RYE BREAD
OPEN

The Seventies

Stand back Buenos Aires,
Because you oughta know what'cha gonna get in me,
Just a little touch of star quality.

Tim Rice and Andrew Lloyd Webber, *Evita*, 1978

TO GET FROM *Phil the Fluter* to *Evita* in less than a decade was perhaps an achievement roughly comparable to getting from the Stone Age to the Restoration in a single weekend: it was not, however, mere coincidence that the miracle should have happened in a decade when several non-theatrical factors ranging from English triumphs in the international record market to the coming of cheap transatlantic air travel suddenly opened up a West End world that had been geographically and economically cloistered for far too long.

The decade opened, however, with a period piece entitled *Mandrake* which disappeared with all deserved speed from the Criterion (as did this critic at the interval) and then yet another attempt at the home-grown folk opera. *Erb*, of which Trevor Peacock was composer, lyricist and star, set a very serious story about the rise of trade unionism on the railways within the context of a rousing Victorian music hall, and the result was another *Half a Sixpence*, but without the here-a-grin-there-a-high-kick-everywhere-a-twinkle charm of Tommy Steele.

Meanwhile, back in Old Vienna, the Drury Lane nostalgia trip of 1970 was *The Great Waltz*, a rapid run-through of what appeared to be Johann Strauss's hundred best tunes, linked by a plot that was at best unobtrusive. As usual, the most interesting music show in town wasn't a musical at all, but a revue – Kenneth Tynan's *Oh Calcutta* – this one memorable for its nude sketches which kept the audiences flocking in for several years to come; those who preferred their entertainments clothed were left with an admirable Hampstead revival of *Tonight at 8.30* and a potent and brave rock-musical version of *Othello* called *Catch My Soul*, a multi-styled, raucous, frenzied and power-packed show which deserved twice the life-span of *Hair* and in fact achieved about a quarter of it.

International managements were, however, now beginning to notice the one great advantage of the London musical: the cost of staging it was

Opposite. Elaine Paige starring as Eva Peron in *Evita* (1978) at the Prince Edward Theatre (see pp. 178–9).

173

only about one fifth of the investment needed to put on a Broadway equivalent, and at a time when it was already proving prohibitively expensive to try out shows in Boston or Philadelphia, maybe London might just do for a try-out? Thus it was that in 1971 the West End was treated to *Ambassador*, an appallingly underwritten and hopelessly wooden musical which becalmed its audience for nearly three hours in a sea of sickly sentiment before staging a last-minute recovery just before the final curtain fell. Based on the novel by Henry James, not a writer hitherto associated with hit musicals unless of course one counts *The Turn of the Screw*, it starred Howard Keel at his most statuesque and Danielle Darrieux at her most French, making all other accents around her sound not so much mid-Atlantic as mid-Thames. Beyond showing its audience where a budget of nearly £100,000 had gone (mostly on a series of increasingly lavish sets built against a background decor oddly reminiscent of the then new Victoria Line on the London Underground) and trying itself out for New York, *Ambassador* seemed to have no distinct aim of any kind. The acting was only seldom less than embarrassing, the chorus was motivated by a kind of benign inefficiency, and the songs were deeply unmemorable. One longed for Mr Keel to burst into a rousing chorus from *Oklahoma!* or for Miss Darrieux to give up her token attempts at dancing, but in the end what one longed for most was just to be allowed out of the theatre.

The treat of 1971 was undoubtedly *Godspell*, which opened at the Roundhouse before transferring to the West End with a quite remarkable early cast featuring Jeremy Irons, David Essex and Julie Covington and Marti Webb, the last three of whom were to remain at the heart of the British musical through the 1980s while the first went off to the more rarified world of *Brideshead* and the Royal Shakespeare Company. Rarity of the year was a Sandy Wilson musical entitled *His Monkey Wife* – a work concerned with a chimpanzee who marries a schoolmaster and stars in a Cochran revue.

The next year brought Sondheim's great high-rise marital musical *Company* and the Brecht/Weill *Threepenny Opera* to the West End: London countered with the usual revival of *The Maid of the Mountains* and a musical version of *Tom Brown's Schooldays*. As long ago as 1895 Max Beerbohm had pointed out that anything too silly to be said on stage could always be sung there, and he presumably was not only thinking of Gilbert and Sullivan; the succession (some would say direct descent) from opera through comic opera and operetta to the Gaiety and then Broadway musicals had opened up London to an invasion that showed no sign of abating. Of fourteen musicals playing in London in May 1972 seven were American and one was German. Of the non-imported affairs, Emile Littler's revival of *The Maid of the Mountains* brought back to the Palace a show which, audiences were nervously assured by the programme note, had been 'a triumph of first magnitude' when first seen in 1917. Seen on stage more than half a century later, it emerged as one more sad example of the fact that people will accept anything in wartime so long as it makes them suffer. Into the thinnest of plots by Frederick Lonsdale, whose memory was in no way served by its disinterment, Mr Littler saw fit to insert additional numbers by Rudolf Friml, and the resultant orchestral mishmash was vaguely reminiscent of a Palm Court recital into which some members of a local amateur dramatic society had inadvertently wandered.

Still, as an evening of theatrical ghoulishness this *Maid of the Mountains* had its moments: to see the bandit chieftain earnestly staring at the balding head of the conductor in the pit and trying to make believe it was the road through the valley was truly to have earned one's spurs as a theatregoer, and for collectors of Unforgettable Moments in British Theatre there was a finale in which a lady was carried across the stage dressed entirely in fishnetting.

Meanwhile at Drury Lane, Joe Layton was staging a musical *Gone With the Wind* which offered spectacle-crazed audiences the Burning of Atlanta, as performed by dozens of extras and at least one horse. Giving value for money seemed to be the aim here: lavish set changes, thirty songs by Harold Rome, children carefully trained to be as objectionable as Deanna Durbin, and an air of solid, if misplaced, confidence in the material. Why did they do *Gone With the Wind*? Because, like Everest, it was there: purpose and heart were all that the show lacked, but in their place were glamorous dancers and the belief that if you sing loud, dance hard, act big and build scenery high, even success is possible. Tomorrow another two performances, and next year another four hundred.

On home territory, Joan and Jack Maitland's musical adaptation of *Tom Brown's Schooldays* was presumably staged in the belief that all the thousands of theatregoers who had thrilled to the sight of innumerable small boys dressed in the period costumes of *Oliver!* would like to renew the experience. In the event they wisely chose not to do so.

As most of my twenties were spent writing the first biography of Noël Coward, it was not, I suppose, surprising that I should have found such huge delight in *Cowardy Custard*, a musical devoted to Sir Noël which opened at the Mermaid a few months before his death in March 1973. This was not another nostalgia night at Puddle Dock: a young company, few of whom could have been anywhere but in their prams during Coward's heyday, approached the massive compendium of his work with cool efficiency rather than star-struck reverence, and the result was a lightning tour of Masterworks from *Forbidden Fruit* (1916) to *The Girl Who Came to Supper* (1963), pausing along the way for brief extracts from his plays, poems and autobiographies.

What emerged was a dazzlingly swift, sure, crisp, elegant evening which admirably recaptured, summarized and revived Coward's 'talent to amuse'. The classics were all there – 'Room with a View', 'Stately Homes', 'Mrs Worthington', 'Poor Little Rich Girl' – as well as many less familiar Coward numbers, some never performed before in England, others written and long forgotten before anyone thought of ransacking the trunk of his remarkable output.

Cowardy Custard was one of the great company shows of all time, thanks to a troupe which, under Wendy Toye's direction, was led by John Moffatt, Patricia Routledge, Jonathan Cecil, Una Stubbs and Derek Waring, and the measure of its triumph was that in the end one was left not with the memory of a single number, not even the throat-catching 'Secret Heart', nor of a single witticism, but instead of a kaleidoscopic overview of an extraordinary, brittle, carefully nurtured talent for assembling and reassembling the English language into songs and speeches that are the touchstones and keynotes of a generation and a way of life now long gone, but luckily not entirely lost.

But if 1972 was the year of this great farewell to the man who had been at the centre of the London stage musical for thirty years, it was also the year that introduced the public to the composer who would prove his only real successor in terms of often simultaneous West End and Broadway success: Andrew Lloyd Webber. The *Jesus Christ Superstar* he had written with Tim Rice (after their initial *Joseph and the Amazing Technicolor Dreamcoat* which soon followed *Superstar* into the West End) was the first of the great prepackaged blockbusters. Though written in London following the acclaim for *Joseph* which had come from Derek Jewell of the *Sunday Times* after seeing a school performance, *Superstar* in fact had made its debut on long-playing record and then Broadway, only reaching the West End after it had become well established elsewhere. It opened at the Palace (now, suitably enough, Lloyd Webber's own theatre) on 9 August 1972 and stayed there for a decade, to become the longest running musical in the history of the British theatre, a record the same team's *Evita* (1978) had been chasing until it closed in February 1986 after a run of nearly eight years, leaving Lloyd Webber's own *Cats* (1981) now the most likely challenger for that particular title.

In essence *Jesus Christ Superstar* was by *Godspell* out of *Hair*: in terms of taste, it was as unimpeachable as vanilla ice cream and every bit as bland, but judged on its own level as a pop opera designed to reassure the

Opposite. Michael Crawford starring as Charlie Gordon in *Flowers for Algernon* (1979), written by David Rogers and Charles Strouse and based on the book *Charlie and Algernon* by Daniel Keyes.

Overleaf. Elaine Paige as Eva and Joss Ackland as Peron in the original cast of *Evita* at the Prince Edward Theatre in 1978.

middle-aged without actively alienating the young, it had to be reckoned a rousing success. The show's thesis was simple enough: JCS, at the height of his influence and fame, loses the faith of Judas who begins to suspect that the man has grown more important than the message and that things were generally better a while back, or as he succinctly puts it:

> *I remember when this whole thing began,*
> *No talk of God then, we called you man.*

The fact that 'this whole thing' appears to be nothing short of Christianity was not dwelt on for long, and, having equated Christ with a pop idol nearing a fall from the charts, Rice and Lloyd Webber were happy enough to follow it through. The apostles thus became a claque of ambitious fan-club secretaries, Mary appeared to be a semi-reformed groupie, and amid some lavishly designed settings of space-age kitsch Christ moved wearily toward martyrdom, mildly regretting the loss of his earlier enthusiasm for the Messiah business. Again, Rice's lyrics were commendably concise:

> *Then I was inspired*
> *Now I'm old and tired.*

For the first half of *Superstar*, it looked as though the authors might have been on to something: suppose Judas was right after all, suppose Christ had become an hysterical egomaniac best put away, what then? Not a lot, alas; beneath the trendy perspex sets that housed the musical, invention had about run dry, so that the second half had to be content with reblackening the character of Judas, cleaning Christ up for the finale, and making sure the villains were pursued across the stage with what appeared to be electric hotplates as the instruments of divine wrath.

Herod, camp as a row of tents and the show's only real stopper ('Prove to me that you're no fool/Walk across my swimming pool.'), was given the best song, so at last the devil really did have all the good tunes. It is my contention that *Superstar* did no more harm to Christianity as we know it than *Abelard and Héloïse* or the invention of the television Epilogue. But the immense success of a show like this did suggest that it was now possible to cobble together technically brilliant and editorially trite musical hits possessing all the soul of a Boeing 707 and much the same sense of style and interior decoration, and that was more alarming.

Sadly the triumph of the all-new transatlantic long-playing mega-hit virtually obliterated one of the last attempts at a really strong home-

Opposite. Poster for the Tim Rice/Andrew Lloyd Webber blockbuster *Jesus Christ Superstar* (1978).

grown musical of the old school: *Popkiss*, opening at the Globe a few weeks after the arrival of *Superstar*, was a lyrical and nostalgic adaptation of Ben Travers' classic farce, *Rookery Nook*. The pace was perhaps a little slow, but the score by Michael Ashton, John Addison and David Heneker was a wonderfully accurate evocation of the slow-piano Thirties when all songs were sung over bannisters by men with myopic stares to girls with dreamy eyes. John Standing did a passable Jack Hulbert to the Jack Buchanan of Daniel Massey, and the score, now alas long-lost, had all the gentle charm of the Savoy Orpheans. Enjoyment of the show was in direct proportion to the audience's longing for hazy, lazy verses that could be sung in the bath by the congenitally tone-deaf, of whom there were sadly not quite enough to keep it going: but if the whole show could have been sepia-tinted, badly dubbed and shown on television as a classic of the early 1930s, it would have been received with justified rapture.

Victorian nostalgia was again well taken care of by Julian Slade's *Trelawny* (based on Pinero), which introduced Gemma Craven and allowed audiences a last glimpse of Max Adrian in what proved to be the composer's best score by far since *Salad Days*, and also by *I and Albert* which, though it had a score by the Americans Charles Strouse and Lee Adams (simultaneously represented in London by the Lauren Bacall variation on *All About Eve* known as *Applause*) was in all other respects a deeply English affair picking its way elegantly through the sixty glorious years of Victoriana, alighting on those events which could most easily be illustrated in song and dance. John Schlesinger's eye for detail led him towards stage pictures that were as evocative as Victorian beer mugs, and Polly James as the young and old Queen was partnered by a nicely dour Albert from Sven-Bertil Taube and a virtuoso Melbourne/Disraeli double from Lewis Fiander, while Aubrey Woods (who had written the *Trelawny* musical with Slade) turned up as both Palmerston and Gladstone.

But Victoriana now had to give way to the Rice/Lloyd Webber Bible belting: hard on the heels of *Superstar* came the London premiere, in October 1972, of *Joseph and the Amazing Technicolor Dreamcoat*, an altogether shorter (60 minutes) and jokier affair with a score surprisingly reminiscent of Julian Slade's two-piano tinkling, while the lyrics suggested undergradaute parodies of Coward ('All these things you saw in your pyjamas/Are a long-range forecast for your farmers'). When *Joseph* was extended to a full-length evening at the Albery, it also acquired what must be the only Tex Ritter parody ever heard in the West End, and was none the worse for that.

Meanwhile, back at the less inventive end of Shaftesbury Avenue, the Anthony Newley-Leslie Bricusse *Good Old Bad Old Days* was the third rewrite of a show they had first conceived as *Stop the World, I Want to*

Get Off and then improved as *Roar of the Greasepaint, Smell of the Crowd*.
We were still in that sickly-sweet convention of home truths and homilies where Good and Evil were now reduced to cosy God and Devil substitutes with names like Gramps and Bubba. Mr Newley's philosophy of life, which would have fitted comfortably into the space normally reserved for the motto in a Christmas cracker, was again allowed to ramble over a two-hour pantomime. Where London could happily have taken to Newley alone in cabaret, as a writer he was coy, as an actor at best adequate and as a director much less than that: hence the result was a fair old shambles. It couldn't be said that *The Good Old Bad Old Days* actually went to pieces, since it started in pieces and remained that way for most of the evening; indeed, in retrospect the ending, with its bloodstained Kennedy portraits, still qualifies as the bad-taste memory of the decade.

The musical of 1973 was undoubtedly *The Rocky Horror Show*, a high-camp celebration of bad horror movies which managed, uniquely in the annals of the West End musical, to teach New York a trick or two: it is unlikely that *Little Shop of Horrors* would have opened there nearly a decade later, had it not been for the lead of Richard O'Brien's loving parody ('There's a light/Over at the Frankensteins tonight'), complete with a hero who turns out to be not only Transylvanian but also trans-sexual, thereby contriving to give a whole new meaning to the making of men.

The musical moment of the year came at the end of the London premiere of Styne and Sondheim's *Gypsy*, when Angela Lansbury, having allowed her children the limelight for just too long, suddenly decided to show what she could do: 'Hold your hats and Hallelujah, Mama's gonna show it to you', and unforgettably she then did. In an old and ugly red dress, a middle-aged and undeniably chubby lady made you believe for the length of that one song that she was the loveliest, sexiest, and most successful star of them all – and that, gentle reader, is what the musical theatre is all about.

What it was mercifully not all about was a revival at Drury Lane of *No No Nanette*; disinterred half a century after its first Broadway and London appearances and marked by an air of period gloom with a curious absence of any coherent direction, this was for the audience rather like being locked in some nightmarish rehearsal hall and having to witness a series of random strangers coming in and failing auditions. Elsewhere, however, American musical imports of past and present (*Two Gentlemen of Verona, Grease, West Side Story, The King and I* and *Pippin*) were still flooding into town, while the British musical attempted a pathetic life of Charles Cochran and a lacklustre piece (based on Arnold Bennett) called *The Card*, which had the sole and locally dubious virtue of setting Jim Dale on a path to Broadway stardom.

The middle Seventies brought to Drury Lane one big-band show which did have the courage to take on Broadway: *Billy*, based on the Waterhouse/Hall book and film about a latter-day North Country Walter Mitty character, now had the kind of staircase you expected only to find in *Hello Dolly!* and a score by John Barry and Don Black which allowed Michael Crawford in the title role to lay justifiable claim (in Jim Dale's absence in America) to being the British musical's sole successor to Tommy Steele. But Crawford was and remains the best actor of that grouping, and his Billy Liar suggested (in numbers like 'Some Of Us Belong To The Stars') that in a thriving musical theatre such as Broadway's, or in Hollywood – where he went only once, to film *Dolly* with the disappointingly miscast Barbra Streisand – he could easily have become the English Ray Bolger.

Billy ran for well over a year at Drury Lane, and was certainly the best pre-*Evita* score of the decade, not that such praise meant much in a still barren time where the only real challengers were the Mercer/Previn *Good Companions* (which, despite strong performances from Judi Dench and John Mills, was crippled by a kind of transatlantic uncertainty about the concert-party theme of Priestley's novel) and an amiable Beatles lookalike concert called *John, Paul, George, Ringo and Bert*.

This introduced several theatrical talents which were to be among the most important of the next decade, not least that of Antony Sher as Ringo Starr. But musically what mattered about it was a book by Willy Russell, who went on to write *Blood Brothers*, and the casting of Barbara Dickson as an on-stage pianist who sang the Lennon-McCartney numbers in a voice of Liverpool slate: the hard-edged, Brechtian singer and the infinitely more glossy Elaine Paige were to go on to the recording of *Chess* in 1985 as the only female star singers of their generation created by the British musical and capable of acting in them.

Like the *Rocky Horror Show* in the previous year, the Beatles musical went on to win an *Evening Standard* award, and they were the first two home-grown musicals to have achieved that distinction in the fifteen years since *Fings* had won in 1960. The next local winner was to be *Songbook* at the very end of a decade in which the judges had managed to overlook even the existence of Rice and Lloyd Webber. The latter was anyway now in some trouble with *Jeeves*, a peculiarly disastrous attempt to bring to the West End stage a musical arrangement of the P. G. Wodehouse classics, principally *The Code of the Woosters*. The team involved here was a hugely distinguished one (book and lyrics by Alan Ayckbourn, music by Lloyd Webber, direction by Eric Thompson), but nothing in their previous experience seems to have saved them from a series of cardinal errors, the first of which was the casting of David Hemmings as Bertie Wooster. Mr Hemmings had established a line in endearing musical villains with his Mordred in *Camelot*, but to a part

Posters for two of the new musicals of 1974: *Billy* and *The Good Companions*.

requiring ideally Ian Carmichael, or, failing him, Richard Briers, he was woefully unsuited, resorting all too often to the kind of performance which equates charm with twinkling teeth.

Playing his ineffable butler Jeeves, Michael Aldridge had an equally impossible task; as a title character his was almost certainly the most underwritten since Harvey, and he was moreover denied even one solo song, a denial roughly equivalent to building a film around Esther Williams and then shooting it on dry land. Faced with the task of making three coherent hours out of complex Wodehouse plots, a task the great man had managed himself in many better Jerome Kern musicals fifty years earlier, Alan Ayckbourn resorted to a prolonged flashback in which Bingo Little, Gussie Fink-Nottle, Honoria Glossop and all were shuttled on and off stage in a muddled and aimless fashion. The result was a disaster of *Titanic* proportions, from which Tim Rice (who abandoned the lyrics at an early stage) could count himself lucky to have escaped; and yet, as in one or two other cases of long-playing records issued after a show has closed, the score now stands up rather better than that of some of the composer's actual hits.

Elsewhere, not a lot in 1975 unless one counts the import of an American tribute to Sir Noël (*Oh Coward*), Hermione Gingold and Jean

185

Simmons and Maria Aitken in a breathtakingly glamorous London staging of Sondheim's *Little Night Music*, and a *Black Mikado*. This last had Michael Denison as Pooh-Bah presiding with the perfect air of a colonial administrator caught up in native independence celebrations of which he deeply disapproved, and even when he joined in the dancing, it was with an air of superb inadequacy. At a time when the white English stage musical seemed to be in its death throes with *Jeeves*, the success enjoyed by *Black Mikado* and the recent musical based on *Othello* called *Catch My Soul* (both directed by Braham Murray) began to indicate, albeit briefly, that black might well be beautiful for the London theatre of the time.

At the Ambassadors, *Happy as a Sandbag* was subtitled 'all the fun of the 1940s' and if those years had not in fact been that much fun, then audiences could take some comfort in the fact that neither was the show; designed by Ken Lee to be a kind of '*Oh What a Lovely World War II*', it ended up as a ragged concert party which totally failed to do more than sing something simple. By now the great nostalgia shows like Alan Bennett's *Forty Years On* and Joan Littlewood's original *Lovely War* had found a way of putting songs into some kind of social, political and even historical context, a feature that was sorely missing here. But the central problem with the West End musical was still that London lacked the kind of stars Broadway was still just about capable of producing: not only was there no English Ethel Merman, there wasn't even a Gwen Verdon. If Shirley MacLaine had been starting out in the London rather than the New York of the mid-1950s, she'd have ended up in a line of Television Toppers, and even twenty years later when it became clear that there were talents around like those displayed by Una Stubbs, a rarity who could sing and dance and act all at once, she found herself playing in long-running situation comedies on television until the chance of a *Damn Yankees* or even a *Pajama Game* had passed.

Then there was a musical *Nicholas Nickleby* by Sherrin and Brahms, which had nothing wrong with it that a good choreographer, some expensive recasting and one or two hit songs couldn't have fixed, and a Gilbert and Sullivan anthology called *Tarantara! Tarantara!* which established that in this field even a century ago it was a better idea to be a producer than a creator. When he died, Gilbert left £100,000. Sullivan left £50,000. And D'Oyly Carte – £200,000.

There is, however, a special kind of awfulness which afflicts big musicals in trouble, and the affliction was most evident in 1975 at Her Majesty's. From the moment the curtain rose on *Thomas and the King*, to reveal three buxom ladies with frozen smiles trying to entice King Henry II into bed, one was aware that all was not going to be well with Edward Anhalt's new musical. Mind you, the idea itself was not reassuring: T. S. Eliot's *Murder in the Cathedral* and Anouilh's *Becket* might be thought to have said all that was dramatically necessary about the monarch and the turbulent priest and, moreover, to have said it in the most poetic and elegant of ways. Undeterred, Mr Anhalt now reconverted his *Becket* screenplay into a musical which mercifully nobody except me dubbed '*A Little Knight Music*'. An investment of £150,000 and the considerable talents of the designer Tim Goodchild were lavished on a show which featured stained-glass windows, leaping priests, movable archways and incense.

For much of the evening the audience was marooned in the wrong bit of *Camelot*, where all the inhabitants looked as though they should have been on ice-skates and nothing was said which couldn't have been inscribed on the back of a souvenir Canterbury ashtray. The star of this bizarre epic was Richard Johnson as Henry II, giving the kind of tight-lipped performance which suggested he really hadn't meant to be there at all. Standing at the side of the stage, as well he might while the leaping monks and buxom wenches and hissing bishops pranced around him, he managed to indicate that his mind was on higher things, such as the very back of the dress circle. All in all, a collector's piece for those who wanted to see what £100,000 looked like when poured into a structure resembling not so much Canterbury Cathedral as the foyer of the Canterbury Hilton.

As if to reassure British audiences that it too was capable of major misjudgments, Broadway then sent over Rock Hudson in *I Do I Do* and a rare revival of *Irene*, a venture which was not helped by a programme note announcing that at the time of its original outing in 1919 this dubious score had 'spread like a rash across America'.

On the home front, Nola York and Michael Richmond came up with an enchanting small-scale echo of Slade and Wilson in *The Lady or the Tiger*: not as big as *Billy* nor as lyrically orchestral as Sondheim's *Little Night Music*, nor as thoughtful as the same composer's *Company*, *Lady or the Tiger* managed instead – like *Salad Days* and *Valmouth* and *The Boy Friend* before it – to represent the two-piano virtues of the English musical at its non-Broadway best, though by 1976 that was no guarantee of profitability. Nor was *Liza of Lambeth*, a dour musical derived from the first of Maugham's novels and cast in that tradition of cockney-mournful flops like *The Matchgirls* and *Ann Veronica* and *The Card*, all of which had recently tried without success to repeat the winning formula of *Half a Sixpence*.

A vastly more intriguing flop was the Melvyn Bragg/Alan Blaikley/Ken Howard *Mardi Gras*, out of Jerome Kern by way of *Ipi Tombi*: this had everything that *Show Boat* had except that it resolutely refused to float, and at the end of its three hours (by which time water was flooding in through the hold and several of the cast had gone overboard) one was still wondering why. The musical had been put together with some care by thoughtful men who (though they might never have been closer to New Orleans than a cinema travelogue) had evidently seen every B movie that could possibly relate to their theme, so that the dialogue fairly pulsated with great bad lines: 'the male population of this town', announced the heroine, 'have bored through me like the Mississippi hitting the Gulf.'

Bragg's book was a literate and loving imaginary look at the last summer of relative innocence before New Orleans and the rest of America got into World War I, although the second half had its spine broken by a series of top-heavily choreographed voodoo spectaculars of the kind which used to be performed by ladies with daggers in their dentures in front of a dropcloth on the ends of seaside piers.

Mardi Gras had all the right things but in all the wrong places, as if assembled by some mad Frankenstein determined to insert arms into eye sockets: show-stopping numbers arrived long after the show had stopped, and only the revolving stage seemed to have been rightly connected to its power supply. They'd nursed it, they'd rehearsed it, and the blues resolutely refused to be born; yet in there somewhere was an indication that Bragg would go on, with a very different composer, to one of the best musicals of the 1980s.

Elsewhere, this was still a time of musical anthologies: *Betjemania* was a loving tribute to the poems of Sir John, and *Side by Side by Sondheim* was a panorama of the Broadway musical 1955–75 which yet managed to be a curiously and ineffably and totally English achievement. Nobody in America at that time had thought of putting all the songs of Stephen Sondheim into a concert, and this one came out of David Kernan's idea and a Mermaid tradition of composer evenings established by *Cole* and *Cowardy Custard*. What made it doubly remarkable was that – unlike Porter or Coward – Sondheim was at the time of this tribute to him neither seventy nor dead; then somewhere in his middle forties, he had already written nearly all the great numbers of the post-war Broadway musical.

From *West Side Story* through *Gypsy* and *Anyone Can Whistle* to *Follies* and *Pacific Overtures*, Sondheim was here explored, annotated and celebrated until the theatre rang with the cheers of an English audience waking up to the reality of the greatest lyric poet in contemporary world theatre. A company of four (Millicent Martin, Julia McKenzie, David Kernan and Ned Sherrin) moved the show on first into the West End and then to Broadway in what must be considered the most triumphant carriage of coals to Newcastle ever achieved in transatlantic theatre, with the possible exception of the Broadway removal of *My Fair Lady* to Drury Lane, only yards from its Covent Garden setting.

With *A Chorus Line* playing at Drury Lane as a pointed reminder that Broadway had now moved from a generation of big song-pluggers like Merman and Channing to a generation of gypsy chorus dancers, and that in that area too the British hadn't a hope in hell of challenging them, given the current state of London modern dance, the West End fell back on terminal nostalgia (Anna Neagle and Barry Sinclair in a musical of J. M. Barrie's *What Every Woman Knows*), small-scale jokiness (an Agatha Christie parody called *Something's Afoot*) or regional knees-up brassiness (*Leaping Ginger*). Ritual disasters included a Nilsson-Schmilsson eccentricity called *The Point*, as well as *Fire Angel* which was a *Merchant of Venice* singalong apparently staged to show why it was the Americans rather than the English who had managed *West Side Story*.

But then there was *Spokesong*: a Stewart Parker/Jimmy Kennedy musical about the invention of bicycle tyres, an unlikely subject for the stage made all the more improbable by Parker's belief (right, as it turned out) that from the small back room of a cycle repair shop in Belfast he could tell the story of Irish troubles across a century. The metaphor worked wonderfully, and *Spokesong* was yet another reminder of what the English, or at any rate Anglo-Irish, musical could still do to establish a quirky identity far removed from that of Broadway.

The other musical triumph of this time, indeed almost the only one of the 1970s to end up also on film, was Peter Nichols' *Privates on Parade*: more of a play with music, perhaps, but one which had a Denis King score allowing Denis Quilley to do high-camp impersonations of Coward, Dietrich and Carmen Miranda while leading a troop concert party around the Far East in 1948. Nichols and King were here to develop (and later extend to their pantomime *Poppy*) an intriguing technique whereby old-established English musical traditions, in this case revue, could be turned inside out for a much darker study of the immorality of British overseas adventures.

If 1978 saw the arrival of two catastrophic Leslie Bricusse musicals (*Kings and Clowns* and *Travelling Music Show*), a bizarre Italian folk opera (*Beyond the Rainbow*) apparently choreographed by a marine gym instructor on a bad morning, and a brave but doomed attempt by Jule Styne and Don Black to turn Jack Rosenthal's great television comedy *Barmitzvah Boy* into a musical (which they avoided calling *Hello Solly* but still failed to stretch to the wide open stage of Her Majesty's), it is perhaps not surprising that the loudest noise to be heard was the cheering which greeted the opening of *Evita*, a work that brought sighs of critical and managerial relief.

A musical which had been the subject of the best-orchestrated publicity build-up since *My Fair Lady* and which already had £800,000 in the Prince Edward Theatre box-office before opening night on 21 June needed critics like it needed a musicians' strike. What mattered about *Evita* was not that it was perfect, which it wasn't, but that for the first time in the eighteen years since *Oliver!* London could actually boast a

Poster for *Barmitzvah Boy* and the cover of the souvenir programme for *Evita*, two 1978 shows which met with contrasting fortunes at the box-office.

musical which could be exported across the Atlantic with a feeling of pride instead of the usual deep embarrassment.

True, it was only home-grown in relation to music and lyrics and design and casting; the director and choreographer were both Broadway men (Hal Prince and Larry Fuller), and to them had fallen the task of converting the original Tim Rice/Andrew Lloyd Webber bestselling records into a stage show. This they did by cutting some of the original numbers (most notably 'The Lady's Got Potential', which was politically the strongest of the songs), reducing David Essex as the Che narrator to a rather anonymous anchorman lacking the background he was given on the original recording, and putting in some marvellous choreographic jokes about the inefficiency of the Argentinian army.

The result was a tumultuously good first half, followed by a certain sense of anti-climax: a brilliant opening showed an open-air screening of precisely the kind of appalling B movie that Eva herself had once appeared in, this being interrupted by the news that Saint Evita was, alas, dead. After the pageant of the funeral, the action moved back to the beginning of her career; picked up first by a seedy nightclub singer and then by the still seedier Peron, Eva went from showbiz to political strength until, by the end of the first half, she was appearing as the full Lana Turner, every Argentinian's dream of what a leader should be.

Elaine Paige, tiny yet very powerful in the title role, and Joss Ackland as her thug husband (Che apart, they were the only two developed characters in the whole show) both managed Rice's cynical lyrics superbly: 'Showbusiness has kept us all alive/Since 17 October 1945' and 'They need to adore me/So Christian Dior me' are the kind of lines that Porter or Coward would have envied. By the interval it seemed that nothing could go wrong, yet by then it was really all over: Eva had come to power, and all that remained was her rainbow tour of Europe, followed by her lingering death at 33. Denied another lavish funeral like the one already seen up front, the audience had only Che to bring the blackout with the news that Eva's embalmed body then disappeared for seventeen years; despite brilliant use of newsreel footage, the lack of any political base for the show was a problem. The objection to Eva as Superstar was that she was a nasty Fascist lady who deserved star treatment about as much as Lucrezia Borgia. On the original project album, Rice's lyrics suggest that he was well aware of this; on stage, however, helped by the inevitable glow from the footlights, the show came across as a remarkably uncritical treatment of its subject.

Not even that, though, could alter the fact that *Evita* was far and away the best thing to have happened, both musically and industrially, to the West End big-band show since World War II; it might well have been, in Stephen Pile's memorable analysis, 'a history lesson telling in clear terms how a frightful old trout went from whoredom and cabaret singing to be the first lady of her dreadful country', but it was also a £400,000 musical that grossed some £20 million from 2,900 performances (six hundred short of *Jesus Christ Superstar*), only closing in February 1986 in order to make way for Tim Rice's latest score, the ABBA-oriented *Chess*. What also mattered about *Evita* was that, for the first time, an English musical had been marketed as if it were American: film rights were sold for a million dollars (though the film itself has yet to be made), Broadway and worldwide tours were soon negotiated, and there was no way of doubting, as Elaine Paige stood on that stage balcony singing 'Don't Cry For Me Argentina', that the West End musical had at last woken up and grown up. This, after fifty years of dodging the issue, was to be the bid for the big international blockbuster, and it worked: the night of a thousand nights became just that, and more.

The 1970s therefore ended in a rare mood of musical optimism: as if inspired by *Evita*'s triumph, no less than ten musicals came into London in 1979, and only one of these – *Troubadour* – was a total disaster. Of the other nine, six were London premieres, at least two of which took it on themselves to parody the showbiz forms they were also celebrating. Dick Vosburgh's *Day in Hollywood, Night in the Ukraine* was a patchy, intermittently very funny, waspish memory trip for movie addicts ('when Zukor laughed, dust fell from his mouth'); it was full of good mogul jokes ('the trouble with *The Good Earth*, said Mayer, is that Chinese movies don't stay with you: an hour later you want another'), cobbled together with songs of the period and Audrey Hepburn/Sammy Davis impersonations, all leading into a second-half musical tribute to the Marx Brothers which, for the audience, was like being hit over the head with bound volumes of old movie magazines.

Meanwhile, Monty Norman and Julian More managed to invent a mythical songwriter called Moony Shapiro and devote their new *Songbook* to his collected works, a wonderfully neat device which then allowed them to parody the entire twentieth-century history of popular songwriting: 'Say Moony,' a friend calls, welcoming the penniless orphan arriving in New York off the boat from Ireland, 'I'd like you to meet the other kids: George and his little brother Ira, Jerome, Oscar, Richard . . .'.

Both these small gems made the journey to New York, though with rather less success than they'd enjoyed in a city where satire still doesn't have to close on Saturday night. Meanwhile, the King's Head pub theatre in Islington also came up with two small-scale delights, a musical life of Frank Harris and a tribute to Hoagy Carmichael, while two big Broadway scores (*Chicago* and *Guys and Dolls*) were given London productions, the first of them being certainly the equal of the New York original and the second showing how a low-budget pub space (the Half Moon) could often succeed in getting closer to the reality of a score than could a huge chorus line.

This rich year also yielded the Charles Strouse *Flowers for Algernon*, based on the movie *Charly* which was itself an infinitely touching and immaculately crafted plea for the taking of risks in caring for the mentally retarded: not perhaps the most obvious of subjects for a musical, but made by Michael Crawford into precisely what the stage play *A Day in the Death of Joe Egg* would have been like if Nichols had ever conceived that as a musical – an example of just how far the borderline of the form can be advanced if it is done with talent and tact.

And amid the revivals of *My Fair Lady* and *Oklahoma!*, *The King and I* and *Hello Dolly* (the two last with Yul Brynner and Carol Channing, their original Broadway stars), there was also room for Pam Gems' brilliant use of the Edith Piaf songs in a feminist life of the French street singer, and for one memorable disaster. This was *Troubadour*, at the Cambridge, presented by a Japanese consortium and arguably that nation's greatest mistake since Pearl Harbor: a musical of breathtaking awfulness, it was set in 1190, give or take a decade, at the time of the Crusades. *Camelot*, said Noël Coward once, was like *Parsifal* without the jokes; *Troubadour* was like *Camelot* without the plot.

Joan Elliott as Columbia, Shaughan Seymour as the transexual Transylvanian scientist Frank'N'Furter, and Joanna Lloyd as Magenta in Richard O'Brien's cult musical *The Rocky Horror Show* (1973) at the King's Road Theatre, the show's first large venue after it transferred from the 150-seat Royal Court Theatre Upstairs.

Left. Julia McKenzie, David Kernan and Millicent Martin, the stars of *Side by Side by Sondheim* (1976), the Mermaid Theatre's tribute to one of the most prolific songwriters of the second half of the century.

Right. Judi Dench, co-star (with John Mills) of *The Good Companions* (1974) at Her Majesty's.

Below. Anita Tucker as Katisha and Derek Griffiths as Ko-Ko in *The Black Mikado* (1975) at the Cambridge Theatre.

A trio of musicals from Andrew Lloyd Webber: (*above*) Gary Bond as Joseph (led by Potiphar's wife) in *Joseph and the Amazing Technicolor Dreamcoat* (1973) at the Albery Theatre; (*right*) Paul Nicholas as Christ at the Last Supper in *Jesus Christ Superstar* (1972) at the Palace Theatre; and (*below*) David Hemmings, as Bertie Wooster, with Gabrielle Drake in *Jeeves* (1975) at Her Majesty's.

The Eighties

THE 1980S OPENED in a haze of nostalgia and small-scale tribute shows: best of the latter was Robin Ray's Tom Lehrer singalong *Tomfoolery*, while the memory-lane audiences were given a new David Heneker musical about silent movies (*Biograph Girl*) as well as a Sian Phillips/Dennis Lawson revival of *Pal Joey* which for sheer acid brilliance challenged even the Broadway original. There was also the infinitely softer-centred Neil Simon/Hamlisch/Sager musical about songwriters (*They're Playing Our Song*) in from New York to reinforce a curious feeling of showbiz incest: hit scores now seemed to be (here as in *Chorus Line* and elsewhere) about either the writers or the singers or the dancers or the actors of hit scores, an everlasting circle from which few now escaped. Cleo Laine did get as far as her husband's musical about somebody who didn't write musicals (unless of course one counted *Gigi*), but John Dankworth's *Colette* was a disappointing score, coming as it did from the composer of such Nottingham triumphs as *Boots With Strawberry Jam*, which had managed a singing Bernard Shaw and a singing Mrs Patrick Campbell a decade or so earlier.

Stewart Parker continued a quirky but ever-intriguing line of Irish musicals with *Catchpenny Twist*, which had a local pop group caught up in the Ulster bombings, but the musical achievement of the year (honoured by almost all critical awards, though a decidedly short box-office queue) was the Drury Lane production of *Sweeney Todd*, which managed to improve on its Broadway original at least in the title casting of Denis Quilley. Here now was a remarkable shift in the power-base of the musical: not only could Sondheim often be done better in London than on his native territory, but the Hal Prince *Evita* was vastly better staged in the West End than subsequently with the same director on Broadway. At a time when the Great White Way had gone over almost exclusively to dancers and technical gimmickry, Shaftesbury Avenue had suddenly acquired a virtual monopoly of the dramatic actors who

Opposite. Elaine Paige as Grizabella in Andrew Lloyd Webber's *Cats* (1981), directed by Trevor Nunn at the New London Theatre.

could handle the complexities of an operatic score. If one wanted to see the best musicals of the 1980s at their best, one invariably had to come to London, and of no other decade had that ever been true.

Not that there weren't still a few disasters around: 'It's a crazy business,' said the producer of *The Umbrellas of Cherbourg*, announcing its closure after nine performances to a loss of £140,000, 'we were slaughtered by the critics.' Quite apart from the fact that this was a corpse long before it hit the stage, the craziness of the business might have had a certain amount to do with the misguided belief that it was possible to take an old French film, remove its sole asset (Catherine Deneuve) and cobble the leftovers into a stage musical. Whoever could imagine that an old film could possibly be turned into a hit musical? The producers of *On the Twentieth Century*, perhaps; they were alive and well and living at Her Majesty's, just a few hundred yards away from the Phoenix where the *Umbrellas* had so recently been taken down. As the man said, it's a crazy business, but one in which the British were now teaching the Americans the few remaining tricks: not only were Broadway shows better staged in London, but shows were being built there around the music of such American composers as Sondheim, Lehrer and now Leiber and Stoller (in Ned Sherrin's superb *Only in America* anthology) in a way that nobody on their own native territory had ever even tried. As a result, London almost overnight became the capital city of musicals, both old and new, minuscule and massive, native and foreign. It was a transformation which, five years after it began, has still not been fully understood, and it has been essentially the work of two men: Andrew Lloyd Webber, who beyond writing his own scores has encouraged and presented those of others and converted the Palace Theatre into a likely centre for the British musical, and Cameron Mackintosh who, after starting out as a stagehand on *Oliver!*, has formed a London management as devoted to musicals new and old as the RSC is to Shakespeare.

Broadway hit back in 1981 with *Barnum*, *Best Little Whorehouse*, *Pirates of Penzance*, *Woman of the Year* and *I'm Getting My Act Together*, but not one of these looked any worse in the West End than it had on Broadway, and some indeed looked considerably better. Admittedly, home-grown productions had at this point shrunk to a new low, only two in this year demanding any kind of attention. One was *The Mitford Girls*, a Ned Sherrin/Caryl Brahms attempt to turn the celebrated sisters into a sextet of literary Tiller Girls: this did, however, have the benefit of a Peter Greenwell score seamlessly stitched with lyrical new period numbers and genuine old period numbers, and from it one emerged as though having spent several hours being beaten about the head with collected volumes of *The Tatler* for 1920–1940, dazed and nostalgic but not a lot the wiser.

The idea of *The Mitford Girls* suggested that its writers had already rejected such possibilities as '*Side by Side by Sitwells*' and '*Song by Song by Beverley Nichols*': it derived from widespread, if largely incomprehensible, English fascination with the lives of a family forever backing into the wrong limelight. There was the sister who fell for Hitler, the one who invented U and non-U, the one who went to America, the one who married Mosley, the one who became Mistress of Chatsworth and the one who everyone always forgets and is in fact called Pamela. The trouble is that if that was all one knew about them before going into the theatre, it was also all one knew about them on the way out. In a two-and-a-half hour show, there simply wasn't time to cram in six lives plus an enchanting pastiche score, and though it was perfectly acceptable to have a torch singer in a lot of period satin crooning 'I'll fall in love with his funny face', it became somehow less acceptable when you realized that the funny face in fact belonged to the leader of the British Union of Fascists in the 1930s. A helter-skelter social history cobbled together from half-opened family scrapbooks left a lasting impression only of six upmarket chorus girls training for the 1930s equivalent of a Eurovision Song Contest, and whatever else the Mitford 'gels' were, they surely weren't that.

However, 1981 was also the year of *Cats*, a vivid and marvellous gesture of transatlantic defiance: for years we had been told by Broadway that even if Britain now had the actors and the singers for big musicals, the dancers and the choreographers were still lacking. *Cats* was where that theory ended, too. As Gillian Lynne's cat-dancers poured through the auditorium, stroking the napes of unsuspecting necks and arching their backs for the next showstopper, it became clear that neither Lloyd Webber nor his director Trevor Nunn (who also wrote the lyrics for the one number that is not by T. S. Eliot) had attempted more than a celebration of Eliot's original verses linked to the notion of Grizabella as a dramatic force; yet within those limitations and on John Napier's junk-heap setting was created a world total and unique, a world in which Gus the Theatre Cat could recall lost years at the Lyceum, Macavity could be not there and Mr Mistoffoles could bring back old Deuteronomy from behind a magic scarf. Number after number tore the place apart: Wayne Sleep doing the 'Jellicle Ball', Paul Nicholas as the rock-star Rum Tum Tugger, Elaine Paige doing 'Memory' and Ken Wells as Skimbleshanks formed the starriest all-dancing, all-singing team in town, but in the end *Cats* was a triumph for its composer and its director and maybe above all for its choreographer. It showed that, for the first time, Britain could now muster thirty show dancers as talented, versatile and energetic as any team ever fielded on Broadway or in Hollywood. Hits didn't come any more smash than this one, and – as they still say on the London and New York posters – 'now and forever'.

Within the year, a stunning National Theatre revival of *Guys and Dolls* by Richard Eyre established that *Cats* had not been a one-off miracle: the English could indeed now dance as well as any Broadway gypsies if they so wished, and when they had stopped dancing they could, unlike many of their transatlantic counterparts, also take care of the acting and the singing. Although imports were now down to an all-time low (*Little Shop of Horrors* and the *Camelot* revival, both in productions that bore less resemblance than usual to the Broadway originals), London was now creating its very own brand of American musicals. *Destry Rides Again* turned up in an English premiere at the Warehouse, while Dick Vosburgh and Tony Macaulay took the Ben Hecht and Charles MacArthur press comedy *The Front Page* and turned it into a smashing, lilting, big-brass, sentimental singalong succession of fifteen great new numbers. The result, *Windy City*, was as perfect a representation of its Chicago times as any Cagney movie; Walter Kerr had once called the original play 'a machine for surprising and delighting audiences regularly, logically, insanely and accountably', and what the Vosburgh/Macaulay team did was to strip that machine down and reassemble it in perfect working musical order.

An oddly successful Lloyd Webber attempt to cobble two television pieces (*Tell Me on a Sunday*, written with Don Black, and *Variations*) into a *Song and Dance* evening at the Palace, a lacklustre Chichester staging of the Leslie Bricusse movie musical *Goodbye Mr Chips*, and a brave attempt at Stratford East to do the Old Mother Riley story as a music-hall musical (*On Your Way Riley*) rounded off 1982, but 1983 brought another dozen new musicals into London plus a lyrical and long-running revival of *Mr Cinders* as a tribute to the now octogenarian Vivian Ellis.

True, that dozen did contain a few disasters: *Bugsy Malone* was an appallingly inept attempt to put a movie on the stage, while *Marilyn* was a Monroe doctrine of remarkable inadequacy, apparently cobbled together from the pages of old movie magazines. *Nightingale* served to introduce Sarah Brightman (who then became Mrs Lloyd Webber), but it did not achieve a lot else, while *Singin' in the Rain* was a waterlogged staging of the Metromusical saved only by Palladium busloads of Tommy Steele fans. That left *Blondel*, a Minstrel show of dubious merit, by Tim Rice and Stephen Oliver, a glutinous Peanuts musical called *Snoopy*, and an agony-column disaster called *Dear Anyone*.

On the credit side there was a rousing Shavian boxing musical by Benny Green called *Bashville*, two Royal Shakespeare Company musicals (the real pantomime *Swan Down Gloves* and the satire-pantomime *Poppy*) and *Blood Brothers*, which last I would rate alongside *Les Misérables* and *The Hired Man* as one of the three great 'book' musicals of the decade to date. Willy Russell's Liverpudlian folk opera concerned twins who grow up on opposite sides of the social tracks unaware of their true kinship until the truth is revealed when one inadvertently kills the other. Like Sondheim's *Sweeney Todd*, this was an angry musical about blood and death and social corruption; Russell here wrote and composed a marvellously tough, grainy, black show which suggested that the musical could still be used as a contemporary theatrical form of considerable power. Dominating it, and singing most of its best songs, was the Barbara Dickson who had started with Russell in his Beatles musical, and beyond her acid brilliance what made this three-and-sixpenny opera work was Russell's ability to write for a hit-squad cast capable of slamming the rest of the score across the footlights. No other musical has yet attempted to tackle the subject of urban blight in Britain in the Thatcher era, and any that does will have a hard act to follow.

Certainly it was not going to be challenged by *Jean Seberg*, a memorably awful National Theatre attempt to do a Hollywood musical as terrible as *Marilyn* and at that all too successful; 1984 did, however, bring *The Hired Man*, Howard Goodall's marvellous setting of Melvyn Bragg's novel about mining and farming life around the Lake District in the early years of the century. As in *Cavalcade*, which it often resembled, there was the idea here of telling one family's domestic story against a huge background of World War I, pit disasters and the birth of trade unionism. Avoiding the ever-present dangers of ending up looking like a period Hovis commercial down cobbled streets, *The Hired Man* triumphed, as did *Blood Brothers*, because it took its inspiration not from the usual Broadway sources but instead from a quite different and very local tradition, in this case the choral work of Elgar.

The songs in *The Hired Man* were not just a series of welcome interruptions; music ran under dialogue, through scenes, across decades. It was there down the mines, and on the land, and at the wrestling matches and farmers' hiring fairs that gave the show its title – music which rose up and through the narrative line, binding the whole together and giving it an extraordinarily vivid sense of time and place.

It was Andrew Lloyd Webber who presented *The Hired Man* in London, and for that all credit to him: it was hard, however, to be as enthusiastic about his own next musical. In order to have some idea of the nature of *Starlight Express*, one needs to imagine what it must be like to be locked up for more than two hours in a roller-skating rink with a lot of acrobatic dancers while they prepare for a disco. Working here with the lyricist Richard Stilgoe and some backstage engineers of considerable technical brilliance, Lloyd Webber seems to have abandoned any idea of a book or a coherent thought and settled instead for a million-pound Disneyesque extravaganza which has a lot to do with video screens and roller-skates but almost nothing to do with the theatre, let alone trains, and despite the involvement again of Trevor Nunn as director, the overall impression of *Starlight* is one of being invited by an eccentric

Logo for the Andrew Lloyd Webber/Richard Stilgoe musical *Starlight Express* (1984) at the Apollo, Victoria.

millionaire to watch him play with some extremely ingenious and expensive, but ultimately pointless, mechanical toys.

Since then there has been an over-inflated revival of *The Boy Friend* at the Old Vic, a more sensible reduction of *Gigi* from its wide-screen origins to a chamber musical of precisely the kind that Colette might have witnessed while she was writing the original story, and a disastrous Laurel and Hardy biography called *Blockheads*.

London audiences have also been treated to *Figaro*, a reworking of Mozart's opera as a 1960s chamber piece, and a tour of J. B. Priestley's *Lost Empires* with a Denis King score vastly superior to many others (and some of his) that have been heard there lately; there has also been a David Essex musical derived from *Mutiny on the Bounty* but starring only a ship-set of breathtaking ingenuity which it would have been better to put on show at Disneyland without cast or score.

The late autumn of 1985 had also witnessed an outburst of

necrophiliac pop, in the form of stage biographies of Elvis Presley and John Lennon and Judy Garland, but it also saw a rare and marvellous revival at the Old Vic of Blitzstein's *The Cradle Will Rock* from the American 1930s, directed and introduced by its original producer, John Houseman, and starring Patti LuPone, the original Broadway Evita, who moved straight from the Vic to the Barbican and to a Trevor Nunn/John Caird staging of *Les Misérables*. Once in every five years or so, given average theatregoing luck, a musical soars out, providing a feast for the eyes as well as the ears, and this show is one such: a great blazing pageant of life and death at the barricades of political and social revolution in Victor Hugo's nineteenth-century France.

But apart from Victor victorious, what matters about *Les Misérables* is that, like Britten's *Peter Grimes* and Sondheim's *Sweeney Todd* (and for that matter Verdi's *Rigoletto*), it sets out to redefine the limits of music theatre. Like them it is through-sung, and like them it tackles universal themes of social and domestic happiness in terms of individual despair. When the show first opened in a Parisian sports arena in 1980, its score by Alain Boulbil and Claude-Michel Schonberg already seemed to consist of all the great marching songs that Edith Piaf never got around to singing. There is an energy and an operatic intensity here which exists in the work of no British composer, past or present: the sense of a nation's history being channelled through trumpets and drums and violins and guitars and 'cellos.

These songs, ranging from the joyous 'Master of the House' to the

Hewison's cartoon for *Punch* showing Dora Bryan, Cyd Charisse, Paul Nicholas and Lisa Hull in Harold Fielding's 1986 revival of *Charlie Girl*, a popular success in 1965 despite being panned by the critics.

haunting 'Empty Chairs at Empty Tables', have lyrics that have now been filtered through the translations of two former London drama critics, Herbert Kretzmer (author of most of Aznavour's English hits, as well as a couple of 1960s London musicals) and James Fenton (who did the *Rigoletto* translation for Jonathan Miller's superb Mafia production at the Coliseum); these are songs of love and war, death and restoration, together with duets and chorus numbers of dazzling inventiveness.

For this is not the French equivalent of *Oliver!*, nor yet the musical *Nicholas Nickleby*, though it owes a certain debt to both: rather is it a brilliantly guided tour of the 1,200 page eternity of Victor Hugo's text, and indeed there's no way that in three orchestral hours one could ask for more than that. The now-traditional RSC walk-down to the footlights is here, as is a chase through Parisian sewers (in the manner of *The Third Man*) and an autumnal ending worthy of *Cyrano de Bergerac*. There are even a few lovable orphans faintly reminiscent of *Annie*, and the result is a fragmentary, episodic evocation of other shows and other countries. For no musical exists in a vacuum: just as John Napier's rich and rare set is made up of old treasures – chairs, tables, cartwheels, water barrels – so the whole production reflects what Nunn and his co-director have learnt from *Nickleby* and *Cats* and their Shakespeare-based musicals.

But *Les Misérables* does more than just draw on its own theatrical and political origins: like the best of Bernstein and Sondheim, it also pushes the boundaries of music theatre forward, so that it exists in the most dangerous area of the footlights. Like *West Side Story*, this is not a show about glamour or success: and yet, as its score surges through the theatre, one is made aware again and again of how triumphantly it works somewhere at the boundaries of not only Hugo but also Dickens and Brecht.

Les Misérables is everything the musical theatre ought to be doing: it relies on no scenic or choreographic gimmicks, no repetitive phrasing, no simplistic homilies. It is not even a star show, though the first London production at the Barbican and the Palace did contain superlative central performances from Patti LuPone and Colm Wilkinson and Roger Allam and Alun Armstrong, drawn equally from the worlds of rock opera and classical Shakespeare.

The history of the British subsidized theatre's attempts to do musicals has not been a very happy one; but with *Les Misérables*, for the first time, the artistic and technical resources of the RSC came together with the financial management of Cameron Mackintosh, and if the late 1980s yield up a better musical than this one then that will be an added bonus.

Opposite. Life on the barricades, as enacted in *Les Misérables*, the highly successful musical adaptation of Victor Hugo's novel published in 1862; after playing to capacity audiences at the Barbican in 1985, the show transferred to the much larger Palace Theatre, where this scene was photographed.

Two of the best entirely British musicals of the 1980s were imbued with a strong social awareness: (*left*) Barbara Dickson in Willy Russell's Liverpudlian folk opera *Blood Brothers* (1983) at the Lyric Theatre, and (*below*) the cast of *The Hired Man* (1984) at the Astoria Theatre.

Opposite
The period flavour of *Mutiny!* (1985) was splendidly captured in William Dudley's remarkable ship set that took over the entire stage (*above*); however, neither the set nor the presence of rock star David Essex and Frank Finlay made up for a weak score.

Another *tour de force* of stage design was a feature of the Tim Rice/ABBA musical *Chess* at the Prince Edward Theatre (1986); the opening ballet sequence is shown (*below*).

Curtain Calls

FROM WHAT WE HAVE THUS FAR heard of the 1980s, two dominant themes would seem to be emerging in the development of the British musical. First, and perhaps most noticeable, is the belief that if ticket prices are to continue climbing through the £15 barrier, then potential audiences seeking a night away from home entertainment will want ever greater spectacle in return for their investment. In 1984, *Starlight Express* set a new record as the most expensive musical ever staged in Britain, costing in the region of £2,500,000, and two years later *Chess* can be counted in the same financial league. With that kind of money at stake, a successful record plus a Broadway deal, and if possible a film option as well, are needed months if not years before a first night: when it first went into rehearsal, *Chess* had already been available on tape and disc for almost two years; similarly, Andrew Lloyd Webber's *Phantom of the Opera* was being heavily promoted via television and disc around Christmas 1985, almost a year before its triumphant staging in October 1986.

In these conditions, familiarity is all; but when Lloyd Webber went public, investors knew that in acquiring shares they were buying into the future success of a man whose *Cats* – playing in London and New York – was taking the equivalent of £600,000 a week in America alone. His newly floated company was reckoned to be worth around £35 million, and at a time when, ironically, Broadway is out of step, out of tune and out of pocket (with major new musical production at an all-time low), it is to these Lloyd Webber events that jealous transatlantic eyes are now turning.

But alongside a post-*Starlight* belief that future musicals may have to be roller-discos or boxing matches or stock-car races as well, if they are to attract sufficient crowds to recoup what has become a massive investment, there goes a quite different belief in what might be called the 'roots' musical. Admittedly, the best of these, Howard Goodall's *The Hired Man*, lost Lloyd Webber money at the box-office, but it came as a reminder that there remained the countryside music of a nation which can still take the Last Night of the Proms to its heart. If one divides 1980s musicals into *Starlight* and *Hired Man* categories, then clearly the

Rice/ABBA *Chess* and the Cliff Richard *Time* will come down on the side of *Starlight* spectacle; but on the other side of the fence there are the Willy Russell musicals, dark though they may be, and faint signs that there are other composers out there wishing to write specifically small-scale English scores or romantic throwbacks to a past era, as for example in *Phantom of the Opera*. A healthy West End would be one in which the loud and the soft, the big and the small, could co-exist: but the running costs of a musical now (Cameron Mackintosh estimates that of *Cats* at just under £70,000 a week) make it increasingly unlikely that lyrical two-piano nostalgia jobs have much of a future away from the pubs and clubs of the Fringe.

In the summer of 1984, no less than twenty-two musicals new and old were playing in Greater London, at roughly one in every two theatres; by the winter of 1985/6 that figure had remained constant, though with (reassuringly) a slight rise in the number of non-Broadway and non-vintage shows. New local musicals in 1986 included two based on the lives of great composers (Julian Mitchell's *After Aida* and Robin Ray's *Café Puccini*), as well as a World War II score from Howard Goodall (*Girlfriends*) which had its world premiere at the Oldham Coliseum, providing yet further proof of a new-found regional interest in big-band shows. Indeed, had it been left to the West End, British audiences would not have seen a Sondheim show since *Sweeney Todd* in 1983. Elsewhere, however in 1985/86 the Manchester Library Company staged both *Follies* and *Pacific Overtures*, Chichester revived *A Funny Thing Happened on the Way to the Forum* and the Everyman in Cheltenham gave a British premiere to *Anyone Can Whistle* fully twenty years after it was first seen on Broadway, while Watford managed a wonderful *Wonderful Town*.

In London the National Theatre came up with a *Threepenny Opera* which opened with a funeral parade brilliantly choreographed by the true star of their *Guys and Dolls* (the dance director David Toguri), but then ran rapidly downhill as no other members of Peter Wood's company seemed able to decide whether they were engaged in celebrating a classic musical or savagely satirizing capitalist corruption. The cause of the small-scale musical was much advanced, however, by Mel Smith's *The Gambler*, which opened by offering its audience the chance to win back the price of their tickets on the toss of a coin before proceeding to prove that we are all gamblers at heart. A brisk little show (set roughly halfway between *Guys and Dolls* and the infinitely darker dramatic world of John Godber's *Bouncers*), it moved from Sandown Park racecourse through dog tracks to a casino where the stakes were raised from money to blood, and Mel Smith's chubby eccentricity kept it away from the borderlines of a thriller or a moral tract. It proved to be a running parody of punters and crooks and jockeys and bartenders, as well as men with so much space between their ears that they could double as ice buckets, and contained some strong and very funny insights into the gambling life: if Damon Runyon had ever written a semi-improvisational show for a small British stage, it would have been this one.

'Greetings,' said the disembodied head of Laurence Oliver, emerging uneasily from an extraterrestrial egg suspended high above the stage of the Dominion Theatre at the start of the Cliff Richard rock musical *Time*: 'I am Akash. All your questions will be answered.' Unfortunately, they were not. Mine would include: how come the greatest actor of the twentieth century was entering his eightieth year, involved, if only in facsimile, in what might well prove to be one of the worst musicals of that century (and I have not forgotten either *Troubadour* or *Thomas and the King*, nor, come to that, Mel Brooks' legendary *Springtime for Hitler*)?

What *Time* had, in lieu of an idea or a score or a script or a cast, was a designer: the star of *Time* was the only true star to have emerged from the British musical in the 1980s, John Napier (of *Cats* and *Starlight* and *Les Misérables*) who turned the Dominion into a planetarium where, under the constant blaze of laser lights, twenty tons of scenery would nightly rise to the rafters like a spaceship. This was not a set: it was a feat of mechanical engineering which rendered all humans (and certainly those involved here) totally unnecessary except on the nights when it broke down. After more than twenty years, Tynan's *Blitz!* nightmare had indeed come true.

Olivier's nostrils had a weird habit of moving off the screen in different directions, and during his longer speeches he appeared to be reading some celestial Autocue machine with an understandable mixture of irritation and amazement that he should have been asked to get his Shakespearean lips round such platitudinous garbage as 'To know me you must truly know yourself' and 'Go forth with love'.

The temptation to go forth with hate into the night after about twenty minutes of blinding laser-lighting and a deafening rock score that seemed to have been fed through a synthesizer at the wrong speed was considerable, but that Napier set did command attention, if only in the hope that it would finally rise up and demolish all its occupants before setting off across the auditorium in search of the show's creator, Dave Clark.

But *Time* came, after *Mutiny!* and *Starlight*, as ominous proof that some audiences really do want their musicals to resemble a mindless *son et lumière* staged in a theme park; if, following Olivier's lead, actors are allowed to send in their performances by effigy or replica, then surely

Opposite. Poster for *The Hired Man* (1984).

Overleaf. The original cast of *Starlight Express* at the Apollo, Victoria in 1984:
Frances Ruffelle (Dinah), Chrissy Wickham (Ashley), Stephanie Lawrence (Pearl)
and Ray Shell (Rusty) on the roller-skating rink designed by John Napier.

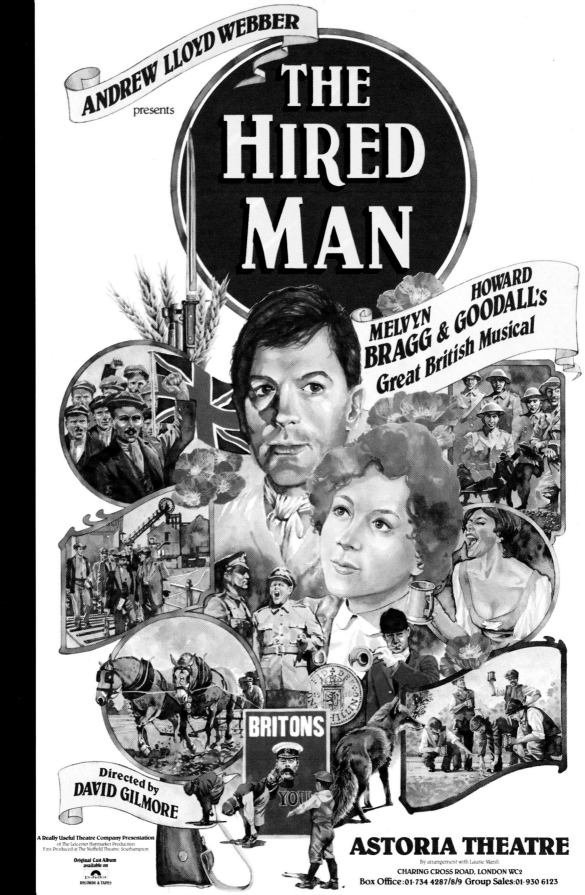

that same privilege should now be afforded to theatregoers who could then also stay home at night and avoid a severe risk of brainrot.

True, the storyline of the Tim Rice/ABBA *Chess* was not exactly detailed either, but what mattered about his vastly better show was that Trevor Nunn, taking over the production from Broadway's Michael Bennett only eight weeks before the opening night, had hauled the concept album into a remarkably coherent dramatic shape. From its opening parody of *White Horse Inn* right through to a long Chorale conclusion, this was a staging of considerable intelligence and invention played out on a brilliantly engineered chessboard which could tilt and light up and travel in all directions but was, mercifully, never given solo star billing. Around it were ranged banks of video screens to give the audience everything from newsreels of the Hungarian Revolution of 1956 (the heroine lost her father there) through to newsflashes of the latest Soviet or American scores in the all-important tournament, but even here Nunn managed to distance his actors from the technology so that they remained in control of the stage throughout. He also managed to bring Elaine Paige far from her earlier role as a rather frozen Eva Peron, so that (now playing the secretary to the bully-brat American champion, at least until she falls in love with his Soviet opponent) she gave a performance of dramatic as well as musical stature, one that does indeed give us the promise of a musical leading lady for the future.

The ABBA score still seemed to owe more than a little to a decade of Eurovision song contests, but Tim Rice's lyrics came as further proof that he is the most wittily stylish rhymer since Noël Coward, while the production as a whole managed to use the chess metaphor with considerable variation and looks a more than likely prospect for Broadway in 1987 – another show that can be exported with confidence rather than the old despair.

Indeed, with stocks of unrevived Broadway blockbusters now sharply depleted, and precious few new ones coming along at a time when the New York theatre has not had a major musical hit in the three years since *Cage Aux Folles* first opened there, the British musical has once again begun to seem an attractive option, though there is always the danger that the British theatre may soon be approaching a Broadway-like crisis of its own. Faced with a choice between, say, *The Hired Man* and a starry revival of *Oliver!*, most regional managements at least would probably settle for the latter, and in doing so they would be wrong, for if new

Opposite. Two 1980s revivals. (*Above*) The tennis party in Vivian Ellis' *Mr Cinders*; this 1929 show, when revived in 1983, transferred from the King's Head Theatre Club to the Fortune and played there for over 500 performances. (*Below*) Noël Gay's 1937 hit *Me and My Girl* was brought to the Adelphi in 1985 by Gay's son Richard Armitage; here, Robert Lindsay (who also triumphed in the show on Broadway) and Emma Thompson are seen on stage.

shows do not become established in their own time, where are the revivals to come from twenty years hence?

There is still, though, the feeling that a hit musical is anyway un-British: until the 1980s the only ones that ever travelled well were total period pieces – Coward's *Bitter Sweet*, Wilson's *The Boy Friend*, Bart's *Oliver!*, all set in a well-defined and deeply European past, a realm which few American composers apart from Lerner and Loewe ever had the expertise or the desire to invade. The one or two exceptions to this rule, the Bricusse/Newley *Stop the World* or the Monnot/More *Irma la Douce*, were also set in never-never lands (the Paris of *Irma* has been visited by no tourist or resident) that did not threaten the usual Broadway stage territory.

But above and beyond the sheer musical and technical expertise in the making of big-band shows (of which Broadway had a virtual monopoly from 1920 to 1980), there was another great advantage enjoyed by the American as distinct from the British musical: American musicals were the ones that got filmed and recorded in the land where films and records had most of the power and most of the audiences. No British composer before Lloyd Webber ever had scores that travelled the world on disc or film as rapidly as those of the American contemporaries. To this day, the songs of Ivor Novello, Vivian Ellis, Noël Gay and Julian Slade are largely unknown outside Britain, as indeed are their hit shows: when the revival of *Me and My Girl* reached Broadway in August 1986, Noël Gay was making his debut there some thirty years after his death.

It was partly in the hope of cracking that geographic problem that Rice and Lloyd Webber took to issuing their shows on disc months, sometimes years, before they got them into rehearsal. But the dominance of the American musical in London is still considerable and pervasive, even in a time of *Cats* and *Phantom* and *Les Misérables*: of the sixteen musicals playing in London during the summer of 1985, seven were established Broadway hits (*Little Shop of Horrors*, *Pump Boys and Dinettes*, *42nd Street*, *West Side Story*, *On Your Toes*, *Guys and Dolls* and *Barnum*) while a further three were new stage versions of old Hollywood hits (*Gigi*, *Seven Brides for Seven Brothers* and *Singin' in the Rain*). Of seven remaining non-American shows, three (*Cats*, *Evita* and *Starlight*) were Lloyd Webber's, one was an updated Mozart opera (*Figaro*) and one a nostalgic revival of *Me and My Girl*. That left only one brand-new fully British score in town, and what was it? The David Essex *Mutiny!*

Easy talk of a rebirth of the British musical therefore needs to be heavily qualified: given the cost of over £2 million for a show like *Starlight*, the number of British composers who can command immediate backing of this order can be counted on one finger, and the irony is that, with Broadway apparently in a state of near-terminal collapse, in a year when they couldn't even find a leading musical player to whom to give a

Tony award, and the West End supposedly benefiting from a boom caused by large numbers of American tourists attracted by the favourable exchange rate of the dollar against the pound, there were still more new scores to be heard in New York than in London. However, the sharp decline in the number of American tourists visiting London in the summer of 1986, caused by fears of terrorist activity as well as by a much less favourable exchange rate, may yet bring about another shift in the balance of international theatrical power, but one that is as yet unpredictable.

In other ways, however, the transatlantic balance is suddenly starting to change: two Lloyd Webber shows (*Evita* and *Cats*) now seem likely to make it into the top twenty listings of Broadway long runs, while in the autumn of 1985 Cameron Mackintosh, still operating out of a West End office, had three musicals playing on Broadway, three in London and three more in Australia. No other British composer ever had a show in that Broadway top twenty, not even Coward, and Webber moreover was the first ever to have three musicals playing simultaneously in London and New York. Equally, no London manager since Charlot in the 1920s has ever had three shows simultaneously in production on Broadway.

But if Coward, arguably the most versatile and pro-American of all twentieth-century British stage composers, could in a generally triumphant career spanning more than fifty years achieve only two hit musicals on Broadway, and thirty years apart at that, we should perhaps cease to wonder what happened to all those who came after him. Nor does it diminish the genius of Lloyd Webber to point out that his success has been achieved at precisely the moment when the international record industry had awoken to London in the wake of the Beatles, and when Hollywood had totally ceased to be part of the musical equation. For Coward and his contemporaries, Broadway and the West End were five days apart by boat, and a song would take maybe a year to make the crossing. Nowadays, a score can be recorded in London, staged in New York and promoted on television everywhere – all within a matter of weeks; and just as the coming of cheap air travel resulted in London and New York audiences starting to look and sound much the same, so suddenly did their shows.

But despite the changes and the many advances in the general state of the British stage musical over the last decade, there remains one central difference between the perception of the song-and-dance show in the West End and the way it is perceived on Broadway, and it is one which explains and conditions most of the other differences. When the New York theatre was going through the trauma of its lacklustre 1984/85 season, one producer there told *Variety* that 'a couple of big musicals could turn this whole thing around'. What he knew, of course, was that a big musical hit somehow changes the whole face and feeling of

Broadway: cab drivers, hotel porters, head waiters all look happier after a really good first night with an orchestra in the pit. That simply doesn't happen in London, where there is no way that a bad season can be 'turned around' by a musical. The British simply don't regard musicals as being at the centre of their theatregoing lives: indeed when a classical director like Trevor Nunn of the RSC goes off to direct *Cats* – which venture will probably turn out to have been the greatest theatrical success of his entire working life and certainly the most profitable – he is still somehow vaguely regarded as having been slumming.

There is still a deep and curious reluctance to admit around London that a great musical can also be the greatest form of theatre; leading British actors once regarded as at least semi-classical in London (Rex Harrison, Richard Burton, Richard Harris) have always had to go to Broadway to do their first singing, while the great stage ladies have always been classical dames – from Edith Evans to Peggy Ashcroft – rather than the great bandshow troupers of the Merman-Martin line. Indeed, if Angela Lansbury had stayed in the country of her birth and parentage, her chances of ending up on the musical stage would have been considerably more remote.

Even now, a decade on from the first arrival of *Evita* on disc, those among the greatest British actresses who can also sing (such as Vanessa Redgrave) almost never do, while the only great classical actor to have sung the lead in a West End musical has been Paul Scofield in *Expresso Bongo*, and that was nearly thirty years ago.

The musical is still regarded in Britain as a risk, intellectually as well as theatrically: for a while after *Cabaret* it looked as though Judi Dench might have been able to break through some of those artificial barriers, in the way that as a director Trevor Nunn now has, but when she had to withdraw from his production of *Cats* any such hopes went with her.

So if this is, as I still firmly believe, a time to celebrate a new-found confidence in the British musical theatre, it is also a time to recognize how far it still has to go: were it not for Rice and Lloyd Webber (neither of them infallible, as *Blondel* and *Jeeves* indicated), it would be hard to talk of a native revival at all.

Musicals enjoy a boom in a period of economic recession: what was true for the Hollywood 1930s of Busby Berkeley has been proved true again by all the old singalongs that have thrived in London and New York in the early 1980s. An audience that has trouble finding the money for its tickets is also keen to see how that money is being spent, and musicals with huge sets and lavish costumes fulfil an economic and escapist need. They also pose no real challenge: in the case of a revival, where one can actually go in humming familiar songs, the public can also be reasonably sure of what they are is buying in advance at the box-office.

Members of the cast of *Time* (1985) on stage at the Dominion Theatre: behind Cliff Richard are Dawn Hope, Jodie Wilson and Maria Ventura.

It would be a brave theatrical prophet who could see in all of this any precise outline of future developments in the musical theatre, and I have never believed in the theory of the drama critic as racing tipster: as some audiences put on their tap shoes and shuffle off to Buffalo to plug into a past that was only ever theirs on cinema screens, and as other audiences demand ringside seats at a space-age event like *Starlight Express*, there is still a third type of audience seeking out small-scale new shows that have something to say about the way people live in the present.

Perhaps in reaction to the sheer gloss of Broadway nostalgia, recent new musicals – from *Sweeney Todd* to *Blood Brothers* – have been living on the razor's edge, which is also where *Les Misérables* will be found; these are the shows which patently do not believe in the purely escapist theory of musical theatre, and in them may well lie the survival of the form as anything but trite. It might be better to end up with a slit throat from *Sweeney* than a broken neck caused by looking too far back over one's shoulder at Rodgers and Hart. On the other hand, I might now, in 1986, be willing to take bets on an Ivor Novello Festival being staged at Drury Lane before the decade is out: in musicals, as Sondheim once noted, anyone can whistle.

Index

Page numbers in italics refer to illustrations

MANAGING
DIRECTOR :

GAIETY

To-Day at 2, and To-Night and Eve

THE O

By JAMES

Lyrics by ADRIAN ROSS and PERCY GREENBANK

Additional Number

Lady Violet Anstruther	(Principal Pupil at the
Caroline Vokins	... (of a Matr
Zelie Rumbert	... (an Adv
Thisbe	(Private Secretary
Countess Anstruther ...	... (Violet
Josephine Zaccary ...	(Pupil Teacher at the
The Hon. Guy Scrymgeour	(Mr. Cheste
Dr. Ronald Fausset ...	(a Country
Mr. Aubrey Chesterton ...	... (Minister
Comte Raoul de Cassignat ...	(of the Qu
Zaccary	(a Professional
M. Frontenbras ...	(Comte Raoul
M. Merignac ...	Sec
Registrar	... ...
Master of Ceremonies ...	...
M Deauville	(French Min
Meakin	(Gardener at Ho

Debutantes—Misses KITTY MASON DORIS BERES
ETHEL OLIVER,
Visitors and Pupils—Misses MARGUERITE GRAY,

Stage Director ... ...

Orchestra under the dire

ACT I. Scene ... The Counte
ACT II. Scene 1 ... ...
Scene 2 ... ...
Scene 3 ... ...

Scenery by Mr. HAWES CRAVEN.

All the elaborate Costumes desig
Dresses executed by Miss FISHER, Messrs. B. J. SIMMONS & Co., M
Madame VERNON, MORRIS ANGEL & SON, J A. HARRISON CO., L
Gentlemen's Hats by HENRY HEATH, (Ltd.)   Wigs by CLARKSON
Electric Effects by G. POYNTON APP

Stage Manager ... Mr. A. E. DODSON

BOX OFFICE (Mr. A. P. OXLEY

The Bars in this Theatre are under the direct cont
selected and guarante

Extracts from the Rules
(1.) The name of the actual and responsible Manager of the Theatr
(2.) The public can leave the Theatre at the end of the performance
(3.) Where there is a fire proof screen to the proscenium opening, i
in proper working order.
(4.) Smoking is not permitted in the Auditorium.
(5.) All gangways, passages and staircases must be kept free rom c